About Island Press

sland Press is the only nonprofit organization in the United States whose principal purpose is the publication of books on environmental issues and natural resource management. We provide solutions-oriented information to professionals, public officials, business and community leaders, and concerned citizens who are shaping responses to environmental problems.

In 2000, Island Press celebrates its sixteenth anniversary as the leading provider of timely and practical books that take a multidisciplinary approach to critical environmental concerns. Our growing list of titles reflects our commitment to bringing the best of an expanding body of literature to the environmental community throughout North America and the world.

Support for Island Press is provided by The Jenifer Altman Foundation, The Bullitt Foundation, The Mary Flagler Cary Charitable Trust, The Nathan Cummings Foundation, The Geraldine R. Dodge Foundation, The Charles Engelhard Foundation, The Ford Foundation, The Vira I. Heinz Endowment, The William and Flora Hewlett Foundation, The W. Alton Jones Foundation, The John D. and Catherine T. MacArthur Foundation, The Andrew W. Mellon Foundation, The Charles Stewart Mott Foundation, The Curtis and Edith Munson Foundation, The National Fish and Wildlife Foundation, The National Science Foundation, The New-Land Foundation, The David and Lucile Packard Foundation, The Pew Charitable Trusts, The Rockefeller Brothers Fund, Rockefeller Financial Services, The Surdna Foundation, The Winslow Foundation, and individual donors.

Making Collaboration Work

Making Collaboration Work

Lessons from Innovation in
Natural Resource Management

Julia M. Wondolleck and Steven L. Yaffee

ISLAND PRESS

Washington, D.C. • *Covelo, California*

Library of Congress Cataloging-in-Publication Data

Wondolleck, Julia Maric.
    Making collaboration work : lessons from innovation in natural resource management/Julia M. Wondolleck, Steven L. Yaffee.
        p. cm.
    Includes bibliographical references and index.
    ISBN 1-55963-461-8 (cloth) — ISBN 1-55963-462-6 (paper)
        1. Conservation of natural resources—United States.   2. Natural resources—United States—Management.   I. Yaffee, Steven Lewis. II. Title.
S930.W65 2000
333.7′0973—dc21

                                                    00-008858

Printed on recycled, acid-free paper ∞ ♲

Manufactured in the United States of America
10 9 8 7 6 5 4 3 2

Contents

Preface xi

Part I: The Promise and Challenge of Collaboration in Resource Management 1

1. Building Bridges to a Sustainable Future 3
   Why Is Innovation Occurring? 5
   A New Style of Resource Management 11
   The Uses and Mechanisms of Collaboration 18
   A Guide to Making Collaboration Work 19

2. Why Collaboration? 23
   Building Understanding 24
   Making Wise Decisions and Building Support for Them 30
   Getting Work Done 36
   Developing Agencies, Organizations, and Communities 41

3. The Challenge of Collaboration 47
   The Basic Dilemma 48
   Institutional and Structural Barriers 51
   Barriers Due to Attitudes and Perceptions 58
   Problems with the Process of Collaboration 63
   Overcoming Barriers 66

Part II: Lessons from a Decade of People Working Together 69

4. Building on Common Ground 71
   A Sense of Place or Community 73
   Shared Problems or Fears 76
   Shared Goals or Interests 78
   Compatible Interests 82

5. Creating New Opportunities for Interaction   87

   Working at Outreach through Communication   89

   Establishing New Structures   92

6. Crafting Meaningful, Effective, and Enduring Processes   99

   A Meaningful and Legitimate Process of Interaction   101

   An Effective Process   108

   An Enduring Process   115

7. Focusing on the Problem in New and Different Ways   119

   A Willingness to Try New Approaches   121

   A Holistic Perspective   124

   Problem Focused, Not Bound by Positions or Procedures   127

   Not Bound by Traditional Conceptions of Agency Roles   130

   Learning Together   132

   Bounding the Problem with Credible Information   134

8. Fostering a Sense of Responsibility and Commitment   139

   Transforming "Them" to "Us"   142

   Ownership of the Problem and the Process   146

   Commitment   148

   Fairness   153

9. Partnerships Are People   157

   Shattering Misperceptions and Fostering Understanding   159

   Building and Sustaining Relationships   162

   Motivating Involvement   168

   Cultural and Community Differences   171

10. A Proactive and Entrepreneurial Approach   175

   Dedicated, Energetic Individuals   177

   Proactive, Not Reactive   180

   Taking Advantage of Existing Opportunities   183

   Nothing Succeeds Like Success   186

   Persistence Pays Off   191

11. Getting Help, Giving Help 195

   Resource Mobilizing, Not Resource Constrained 198

   Accessing Expertise and Ideas 200

   Building Public and Political Support 203

   Getting Help by Giving Help 206

Part III: Getting Started 211

12. A Primer for Agencies 213

   Imagining Collaborative Possibilities 214

   Enabling Employees to Be Effective at Collaboration 218

   Encouraging the Development of Collaborative Relationships 222

   Evaluating the Experience with Collaboration 224

   Committing to the Process and Products of Collaboration 225

13. Ensuring Accountability 229

   The Critics' Concerns 230

   The Issue of Accountability 232

   The Traditional Response 234

   The Balance between Control and Flexibility 235

   Promoting Accountable Collaboration 237

14. A Message to Individuals 247

   Summary Advice 249

   A Guide to Getting Started 250

Notes 253

Index 267

About the Authors 279

Preface

This book provides a set of lessons for practitioners and others who want to understand the role of collaboration in resource and environmental management and how to make it work. We draw on roughly ten years of research that has focused on learning how people have worked together successfully to solve common problems, resolve conflicts, and build partnerships in order to move their communities and agencies toward a more sustainable direction.

We offer these insights as a contribution to the important transition now underway in American natural resource management. For a variety of reasons (further discussed in chapter 1), we are in a period of challenges and opportunities that is as significant as the period one hundred years ago when President Theodore Roosevelt, Gifford Pinchot, and others invented a set of principles for management of public resources. We have an opportunity to move toward a more sustainable set of management practices and policies. Collaboration of necessity will be a part of this transformation along with more and better science and different management strategies. To realize this opportunity, we need to learn from experience and find out in very practical terms what works and what does not.

Our collective research in the area of public resource management goes back twenty-five years. For many of those years, we analyzed problems in agency decision making and management. In studies of the U.S. Fish and Wildlife Service's decision making in implementing the Endangered Species Act (ESA),[1] the USDA–Forest Service's implementation of national forest planning,[2] and the Forest Service's response to the spotted owl controversy in the Pacific Northwest,[3] we developed a very good understanding of what goes wrong in natural resource policy and management. That work provides a useful descriptive model of how our public decision-making institutions tend to function. Such studies provide a social critique that has deep roots in the academic world.

What we did not know is how things could go right. We suggested changes in public policies and agency management practices but were unsure whether they would work or not. After fifteen years of study, we knew these truths to be self-evident: that agencies tended to be biased and ineffective, traditional decision-making processes tended to be biased and ineffective, and our societal context was unlikely to bring about a change in either. It was a tiresome and discouraging image given the pressing environmental and social problems that sorely needed attention.

We also were frustrated by adversarial decision-making processes in which everyone became very good at telling one another what was wrong, but few had an interest in finding creative positive solutions. Stories of ineffective government bureaucrats, rapacious developers, and unyielding environmentalists make for interesting copy. They generate fund-raising dollars for interest groups and provide the foundation for political gains. But in a world where environmental problems are not just a stage for political drama, we need to move beyond the state of impasse and cynicism prevalent in the last couple of decades. People face real health and quality-of-life issues, other species continue to decline, and the fate of the world that we share rests on the actions we take as a society. How can we get on with it?

About ten years ago, we shifted our research approach from a focus on failure to an effort to explore success. We started to look for examples of successful management so that lessons could be drawn from them and used as broader prescriptions for resource managers. Our particular interest was in understanding how agencies could build links with groups outside the agency walls. We knew from the nascent science of ecosystem-based management that managers needed to consider larger spatial areas and longer time frames. Since landownership is shared among many public and private parties with varying interests and capabilities, some level of cooperation and collaboration was needed. Agency managers had no choice but to look outward. And our earlier studies indicated that when they had not formed effective links with the world around them, they had gotten into trouble. They needed to build bridges across the boundaries defined by geography, interest, and perceptions.

Our first effort at exploring success was a study undertaken for the USDA–Forest Service's Pacific Northwest Research Station and entitled "Building Bridges across Agency Boundaries: In Search of Excellence in the U.S. Forest Service."[4] When we told people that we were going to catalog examples of things the agency was doing right, their first reaction was "That's going to be a short study." But their next response was "You know, there are a few places where people are doing good things." Based on a survey conducted through the Forest Service's electronic mail system and interviews with representatives of nonagency groups, 230 situations were identified as examples of successful public-private cooperative working arrangements involving Forest Service personnel. From those we identified 35 situations that represented the diversity evident in the 230 situations and that warranted extensive research. Case studies were written and lessons were drawn from the collective experience about the reasons that situations were perceived as successful, factors that facilitated their success, and obstacles that participants faced and the ways that they were overcome. We also asked participants for their advice to others seeking to form collaborative relationships in natural resource management.

A couple of definitional issues immediately presented themselves. What constituted a collaborative relationship? An extensive academic literature on cooperation and interorganizational collaboration provided a starting point. Collaboration scholar Barbara Gray defines collaboration as "(1) the pooling of appreciations and/or tangible resources, e.g., information, money, labor, etc., (2) by two or more stakeholders, (3) to solve a set of problems which neither can solve individually."[5] Cooperation involves individuals or groups moving in concert in a situation in which no party has the power to command the behavior of the others. Most definitions emphasize that such multiparty relationships are voluntary, involve face-to-face interaction and interdependence, and seek specific goals. In our case, these relationships had to cross boundaries defined by organizational affiliations, interests, perceptions, geography, or jurisdiction.

We also wanted to broaden the traditional notion of collaborative relationships in natural resource management to include a diverse set of arrangements. Partnerships in which a nongovernmental group like Ducks Unlimited works on public lands have been in existence for many years, and they are an important type of agency-nonagency link. But many others are also critical (as discussed in chapter 2). We saw multiparty working groups trying to solve common problems or resolve disputes, interagency information networks, and simple relationships such as an agency staff member participating in community-based development discussions as elements of an important set of relationships between agencies and others. Each involves a linkage—a formal or informal relationship or structure—which we sometimes describe as a bridge. Collaborative behavior and processes take advantage of these bridges to enhance resource management.

Another definitional issue was determining what was success. How did we assess whether a collaborative relationship was successful or not? While we could screen out some examples because they did not meet our definition of collaboration, in most cases we relied on the judgment of multiple participants. That is, we defined success largely in terms of the perceptions of the people involved in these efforts. If an effort was viewed as successful by participants from across the spectrum of involved interests, we took their word for it and worked to understand why they perceived it as a success. Most often the first explanation for why a case was deemed successful was simply that people were working together, and that alone represented a tremendous step forward. Fortunately, early evidence from our studies also suggested that such improvements in the process of human interaction were leading to improved ecological and social outcomes.

How long did a relationship or process need to be in place in order to be considered successful? What happens when a success turns sour? In many cases, projects that bridge agency boundaries are short term in nature. They may achieve longer-term benefits but are designed to involve interaction only over a fixed time period. In other cases, successful interaction for a period of time may disintegrate as conditions or people change. We took the perspective that lessons could be learned about the ways groups achieved success from efforts of varying duration. Indeed, even when groups fell apart, important lessons could be secured about how they stayed together and what ultimately weakened them. Hence, the relationships described in some of the cases in the book are no longer in place. Some, such as the Deerlodge National Forest Plan case, fell apart, while others, like the Quincy Library Group, were transformed in dramatic ways. Still others, like the Beartree Challenge, quietly dissipated as participants changed. We include their stories to understand why people viewed the early stages as successful and why the relationships did not continue. Often they provide unique insights.

The issue of change over time framed two follow-up studies to our Building Bridges work. In a second round of work on the Building Bridges cases, entitled Sustaining Success, we went back to the original 35 cases to understand which bridges were still in place and to what extent they were being used for collaborative work.[6] We also studied 20 cases of national forest plan appeals that were resolved through negotiation to understand what happened following settlement.[7] These cases were examined over a period of three to five years to see whether the purported long-term benefits of collaboration were achieved and, if so, under what circumstances.

Since our research had focused so much on situations involving the Forest Service, we broadened our case study work in the second phase of the Building Bridges study to include other federal agencies, state agencies, and private organizations. Two additional studies focused on multiparty negotiation and collaboration in endangered species management. One study, undertaken for the Administrative Conference of the United States, examined 13 cases of negotiation over endangered species protection.[8] Another focused on multiparty negotiation and collaboration in habitat conservation planning conducted under the provisions of the ESA.[9] Several of those cases involved large-scale planning in urban areas, including several in Southern California.

Two additional pieces of research provided lessons that we incorporate in the book. An investigation of 105 sites in which ecosystem management was underway gave us another large-scale data set in which we could examine the kinds of process characteristics that promoted and obstructed progress in achieving an ecosystem-based management approach.[10] In addition, a study of 10 cases of collaborative resource management that focused specifically on the issues raised by critics of collaboration contributed examples and insights.[11]

This book is the culmination of this ten-year period of research. We have a huge data set that describes the experiences of people working across boundaries in a variety of settings, from formal dispute resolution to public-private partnerships. Our data allow us to tell a range of stories about real people working through collaborative interactions. They also provide a foundation for drawing lessons about the determinants of success that appear true across the diverse case experience. Moreover, these lessons have direct implications for policy makers seeking to reinvent natural resource policy, managers attempting to find a management style that works on the ground, nongovernmental groups seeking to influence management direction, and communities trying to find a better, more productive mode of civic interaction.

The stories themselves are useful and important. Indeed, we see these stories as an organizational and social change mechanism. Quite simply, people learn from stories because stories conform to the way humans think.[12] Stories engage us emotionally. They provide "something that one can care about or someone with whom [the reader] can identify." Because of their "interestingness," stories are highly memorable.[13] Anecdotes and metaphors are particularly powerful tools of explanation and persuasion. They allow listeners to use preexisting cognitive frameworks to understand a new situation. We could describe a situation as seventy forty-acre clear-cuts evenly dispersed across a six-square-mile, old-growth management unit, or we could describe it as fragments of old-growth forest in a sea of clear-cuts. Both are accurate, but one uses a preexisting image to help the listener understand a new situation, and it requires much less conscious thought to get to that point.

The stories summarized in this book can be a useful training device for students and mid-career professionals. Indeed, we use longer versions of some of the cases exerpted in the book in short courses. By providing images of success, we hope to provide ideas to those mired in traditional modes of action and empower those who are already seeking new approaches. Humans have a centuries-old history of conveying ideas and norms via storytelling and only a decades-old experience with more rational modes of analysis. Indeed, one study suggested that government officials tend to make decisions more from generalizations based on their own personal experiences and situations than on rational grounds. They rely on stories more than objective, analytic, decision-making processes.[14]

This book goes well beyond telling stories, however. Its core is a set of lessons drawn from the multiple stories. We relay eight themes that in our view are critical to successful collaboration. We do not view the book as a step-by-step, "how to" manual. Due to the diversity of collaborations and settings, we are not sure such a manual is possible. Rather, practitioners need to develop collaborative efforts within a framework of understanding. The core mission of this book is to provide such a framework.

The book's lessons should be applicable to a wide range of issue areas. While many of the cases involve natural resource professionals, we believe the lessons about collaboration hold true in a variety of public policy realms, including public health, social services, and environmental protection, among others. Indeed, when we share insights with scholars involved in other policy areas, we are struck by the similarities of the lessons they are drawing from case studies involving public-private partnerships and interorganizational dynamics of a variety of kinds, including those in the private sector. The underlying principles and challenges are the same: How can we foster the human interactions necessary in the face of complex but shared issues of concern, in times of declining budgets and dispersed expertise? The lessons in this book can help.

These lessons are described in practical terms. Key insights from the academic literature are summarized in a few places, but most academic references have been confined to footnotes. In places, we refer to the Building Bridges, Ecosystem Management, and Habitat Conservation Planning studies and invite readers to use them as reference works. But we have chosen not to bog down the presentation with a lot of citations referring to original sources.

Beyond stories and lessons, we describe a set of implications for agencies and individuals seeking to build bridges in the course of their other management activities. By analyzing the reasons for success and describing the barriers faced by participants and how they were overcome, we hope to assist those charged with mobilizing change in the agencies. It seems likely that collaborative approaches will be part of their future. For example, recently released draft regulations for national forest planning mandate a collaborative approach.[15] Nongovernmental organizations pursuing ecoregional planning include collaborative, multiparty work as an important cornerstone.[16]

We do not embrace collaboration as an end in itself. Our objective is that progress be made on environmental problems, not that people "feel good." As we say repeatedly in this book, collaboration is not a panacea. It does not fit all circumstances. Often, it is not an easier or less costly process than more traditional administrative or judicial decision-making approaches. We need to scrutinize its outcomes and how they relate to law and broad public interest. Nevertheless, we believe that in many circumstances collaboration can enhance people's understanding, narrow the range of disagreements, build concurrence about necessary direction, and produce on-the-ground environmental improvements.

This book was a collaborative effort. We have drawn on the ideas, insights, and hard work of many others, including academic colleagues and many,

many practitioners actively engaged in collaborative processes. We want to thank the hundreds of people who agreed to often lengthy interviews, many of whom were revisited over several years. In almost all cases, we have been impressed by the dedication of the people who affect natural resource management from a variety of public and private settings. Their interest in better on-the-ground management is unmistakable, and often remarkable, given the high levels of anxiety and stress associated with resource management in recent years.

We want to thank the agencies and groups that have supported our research over the years. First and foremost, Roger Clark and the USDA–Forest Service's Pacific Northwest Research Station provided the core funding for the Building Bridges work. We greatly appreciate their support, as well as that provided by the USDA Cooperative State Research Service's McIntire-Stennis research program, the Administrative Conference of the United States, The Wilderness Society, the National Wildlife Federation, and the School of Natural Resources and Environment at the University of Michigan. We have been fortunate to work in a unique natural resources school that values the contributions of both social and natural scientists and provides a great platform for scholarship and learning. We have also benefited from a long-standing relationship with Island Press and in particular want to thank Barbara Dean and Barbara Youngblood for their support and assistance throughout this project.

We have been blessed by a fantastic set of graduate students over the years, many of whom worked on the cases that have contributed to our research. We want to thank Christy Halvorson, Elise Jones, Steve Lippman, Linda Manning, Robyn Roberts, and Jennifer Thomas-Larmer for their hard work and insights on the Building Bridges studies. We also want to acknowledge the contributions of a large set of graduate research assistants who participated in our other studies of collaboration in natural resource management: Peter Aengst, Jeremy Anderson, Jodi Asarch, David Bidwell, Todd Bryan, Jay Chamberlin, Alan Clark, Christine Coughlin, Irene Frentz, Chris Grunewald, Paul Hardy, Merrick Hoben, Laurel Horne, Raney Lamey, Susan Loucks, Sussanne Maleki, Dirk Manskopf, Ali Phillips, Shannon Quesada, Clare Ryan, Harlin Savage, Rachel Selk, Margot Smit, Barbara Thorpe, Emily Tibbott, Beth Wheatley, and Elizabeth Worzalla. Many of these former students are actively working to improve the environment through collaborative, cross-landscape efforts across the United States. We take great pride in their accomplishments and thank them for their commitment and dedication.

Finally, we want to thank our families and children for their understanding and support. Our daughters, Anna and Katie, advised us several years ago not to write another book and have had to endure the effects of our not taking their advice. We thank them for graciously accommodating a limited dinner menu, fewer trips to the mall, and many dinner conversations about "work." Through their behavior, they have taught us a great deal about collaboration and the barriers to achieving it. Their smiles and the hopes they embody for the future make us appreciate on a day-to-day basis the critical need to find ways to more effectively envision and move toward a sustainable future. Perhaps by focusing a little more on success than failure, we can get on with it.

Part 1

The Promise and Challenge of Collaboration in Resource Management

Chapter 1

Building Bridges
to a Sustainable Future

A new style of environmental problem solving and management is under development in the United States. Government agencies, communities, and private groups are building bridges between one another that enable them to deal with common problems, work through conflicts, and develop forward-thinking strategies for regional protection and development. From management partnerships and interagency cooperation to educational outreach and collaborative problem solving, this new style of management is developing organically in many places in response to shared problems and the simple need to move forward. In other places, agency initiatives have helped to create opportunities for meaningful involvement that were not possible in the past.

Consider the case of the Kiowa National Grasslands of New Mexico, where a collaboration between the USDA Forest Service, the Natural Resource Conservation Service (NRCS), and local ranchers has greatly improved the quality of the area's rangeland. In 1991, Forest Service District Ranger Alton Bryant and Mike Delano of NRCS broke with convention and decided to cooperate in assisting ranchers who worked both private land and public land under permit. Under the jointly administered program, rather than having different management schemes for public and private lands and a mix of advice from Forest Service and NRCS staff, a rancher sits down with representatives of both agencies to develop a long-range plan for the affected area. According to Delano, by managing all of a rancher's land as a "single operating unit," the needs of wildlife, cattle, and environmental restoration can be addressed.

One of the first ranchers to try out this idea on her parcel was local rancher and civic leader Ellen Grove. In her words, she is "sold on it." On her approximately fifteen hundred acres of private and permitted land from the Kiowa Grasslands, Grove fenced in sixteen individual paddocks and installed a new water storage and transport system to service each of those paddocks, all at a substantial cost to herself. She rotates her cattle through the series of paddocks as the vegetation begins to show stress and does not return them to a paddock until the vegetation in it has completely recovered. Other improvements include live snow-fence plantings, wildlife habitat, and wetlands creation. Although initially hesitant to break with ranching techniques that her family had always used, Grove was pleasantly surprised by improvements in the land and cattle.

Improvements in environmental quality were staggering. After three years, Grove had more diverse vegetation. Some native grasses thought to have been locally extinct have reappeared on previously degraded parcels, and cottonwoods and willow seedlings are sprouting in the riparian area. Wildlife habitat has improved so that over fifty species of birds were recently recorded where previously there were only a handful. According to District Ranger Bryant, the "crowning jewel" of Grove's efforts has been the dramatic improvement in the riparian area. An old creek bed that had been dry since the 1950s has once again been running with water and providing wildlife habitat, a powerful symbol of environmental restoration.

Not surprisingly, with the environmental improvements came health improvements for the cattle. Both conception and birth rates have improved in most cases, with weaning weights higher as well. In addition to improved quality of health, ranchers have actually increased the carrying capacity of their parcels. For example, when Ellen Grove began the program, she was running 47 cattle. At the end of the third year, she was running 115 cattle and hopes to consistently support 80 head with continued environmental improvement.

There are literally hundreds of such success stories throughout the United States. Some efforts, such as the Applegate Partnership in Oregon, the Chicago Wilderness project in Illinois, and the Malpai Borderlands in New Mexico, have received considerable public attention, while others are striving quietly to make a difference. Such efforts in some places are called public-private partnerships or alternative dispute resolution approaches. Elsewhere they are described under the labels of ecosystem management, collaborative stewardship, community-based environmental protection, civic environmentalism, and sustainable development. Whatever terms are used to describe them, they are generally place-based, cooperative, multiparty, and grounded in high-quality information. Of necessity, they involve building relationships between individuals and groups who have been isolated or alienated from each other.

And by all accounts, they are the pioneers in a new style of natural resource management in this country.

Collaborative resource management has its roots in age-old notions of neighborhood and community, but it is not a purely interest-driven approach that can allow natural resources or certain interests to be exploited. It recognizes the need to ground decision making and management in good science but understands that technical factors are only one of many important considerations in making wise public choices. The new style of management helps to build a sense of shared ownership and responsibility for natural resources by moderating a top-down style of government agencies that has tended to disempower landowners and local interest groups. But it also recognizes that government as a partner can provide unique resources, incentives, and opportunities important to collective efforts.

On the one hand, such an approach to the management of communities and resources is revolutionary and responds directly to the problems inherent in industrial era management that has emphasized narrow objectives, top-down control, tight boundaries, and extensive rules and formal structures to institutionalize public policies. On the other hand, a style of management that emphasizes people getting together to cooperatively solve shared problems seems almost like common sense. Yet most observers of the protracted conflicts over natural resource management in recent years agree that common sense is not so common.

The virtues of collaboration, cooperation, creativity, and communication are extolled daily on children's television, yet the more dominant image of adult behavior conveyed through the media is one of conflict and competition at all levels—personal, political, and societal. Indeed, many of the big ideas of our times—evolution, free-market capitalism, and pluralism—derive their vitality from competition. We preach cooperation yet practice competition. Both have their place in resource management, and both draw from wellsprings of human behavior. But we need to learn how to manage the tension between them in ways that sustain and restore the quality of the natural environment and enhance the quality of people's lives.

Why Is Innovation Occurring?

Collaborative efforts are proliferating for many reasons. Some efforts are a direct response to problems caused by past public policies and management practices. Others reflect the current organizational and social context of management. Still others spring from new ideas and energies. Together they have provided an impetus for the growth of collaborative initiatives.

The Costs of Impasse

Some efforts have developed in response to the problems evident in resource management in recent decades. One of the laudable goals of the past three decades of resource policy has been to expand the participation of various groups in the development and implementation of management strategies. Through review processes established by laws like the National Environmental Policy Act (NEPA) and the National Forest Management Act (NFMA), opportunities to challenge agency decisions granted through citizen suit provisions, and agency outreach programs, a greater diversity of interests has become involved in decision making. These opportunities occurred at a time when the public's interest in natural resources was diversifying, and the values held in land and water expanded considerably. Changes in political culture in the United States reinforced this diversification process, as interest groups that were focused on narrow issues replaced political parties as the dominant mechanism for political involvement, and the power to determine outcomes spread across those groups.

The result of this valuable process of diversification has been a remarkable fragmentation of interests, as many legitimate interests battled each other to a standstill.[1] Traditional "boundary-spanning" forces (such as political parties, government decision-making processes, and religious and civic organizations) have been ineffective at bridging the number and kinds of interests at play today in natural resource management. As land has been developed and water appropriated, increasing resource scarcity has made it difficult for decision makers to craft win-win solutions, that is, decisions that give something to everyone. Decisions that are viewed as win-lose (in which any gains one group gets imply losses to another) promote virulent conflict as groups compete for a fixed set of possibilities.

Multiple fragmented interests, balanced political power, and the decline of integrative forces have produced impasses at the policy and ground levels. As a result, conflict persists as issues move through many different avenues for intervening in decision making. Issues like management of the old-growth forests of the Pacific Northwest bounce from administrative to legislative to judicial arenas and involve decision making by numerous local, state, and federal agencies.[2] Decisions made rarely hold, and decision making looks like a game of hot potato.

Natural resource management has been in a state of impasse at many levels over the past decade. Battles over owls in the Northwest, woodpeckers in the Southeast, and gnatcatchers in Southern California and fights over forest and range management plans and rural development strategies throughout the country have raged unabated through numerous communities, courtrooms, and media. To some, the only cost associated with these battles is delay, and delay can be a benefit to one side or the other.

But there are also very real costs associated with these impasses. Huge amounts of energy and human resources—whole careers of agency and interest group staff members—have been spent on one issue or another without a clear sense of resolution. The hostility levels in communities have risen, undermining the fabric of civility that allows individuals to live with one another. Uncertainty increases as decisions are overturned, which makes it difficult for individuals and firms to plan their future. People do kick their dogs and beat their spouses when faced with persistent stressful situations. Over time, life in impasse deadens one's sense of possibilities and capacity for creative problem solving. People burn out.

Some innovative collaborative partnerships and conflict management approaches have sprung up to overcome this state of paralysis. In essence, collaborative processes become ad hoc boundary-spanning mechanisms that foster an integration of disparate interests, values, and bodies of information while promoting trust and building relationships. In the Applegate watershed, years of adversarial conflict had produced impasse. According to Bureau of Land Management (BLM) range manager John Lloyd, "We got to the point where we just had to sit down and start talking."

Pervasive Mistrust and a Declining Sense of Responsibility

One cost of the current mode of decision making has been a declining sense of trust in government and in each other, and a reduced sense of responsibility for common property resources. These declines are not limited to the natural resources realm; rather, they are an outgrowth of broader public attitudes. For example, the public's faith in government has been dropping steadily for several decades.[3] Public alienation is near an all-time high. More than six in ten American adults feel a sense of powerlessness and disenchantment with the institutions that influence much of their lives.[4] Indeed, less than half of the public expresses a significant level of confidence in many U.S. institutions, including the Supreme Court, banks, public schools, television, organized labor, and big business.

A decline in participation in civic affairs has paralleled these trends. This decline can be seen at an aggregate level through indicators such as the number of Americans who vote.[5] It can also be seen in communities that traditionally have run on the engine of citizen involvement. For example, an essay written by Harvard University professor Robert Putnam entitled "Bowling Alone: America's Declining Social Capital" uses the decline of neighborhood bowling leagues as a metaphor for the atrophy of citizen participation in local civic groups. In Putnam's view, "The quality of public life and the performance of social institutions . . . are powerfully influenced by norms and networks of civic engagement." Involvement in civic life builds understanding, relationships, and trust that enable disputes and disagreements to be dealt with. It can build shared values, a perception of common problems, and a sense of individual responsibility for shared resources and can moderate extreme behavior. However, according to Putnam, "There is striking evidence . . . that the vibrancy of American civil society has notably declined over the past several decades."[6]

There are many reasons for the decline in involvement in civic affairs by citizens. Changed social dynamics at home and in the workplace, altered preferences on how to spend leisure time, development of housing and urban forms that promote isolation and minimize neighbor-to-neighbor interaction, and the rise of telecommunications systems that diminish the need for community-level information sharing and relationships—all have had an effect. Ironically, the solutions to past problems have reinforced a trend toward disengagement. Since the end of World War II, we have seen a process of institutional empowerment as big business, big government, and organized interest groups evolved to move society forward.

As institutions took on more, individuals took on less and became disempowered and isolated from the collective choices that affected them but that others made. In the 1940s and 1950s, individuals looked to big business to take care of them. In the 1960s and 1970s, big government was thought to be the answer, and organized interest groups were viewed as an easy and effective mechanism for "being involved." In the 1980s and 1990s, when those institutions failed to achieve their perceived promise, the public blamed them for its collective problems.[7]

Analysts from all sides of the political spectrum highlight the need to foster civic involvement and a heightened sense of individual responsibility. In his first column of 1995, columnist David Broder noted, "Unless more Americans start working with each other on shared civic enterprises and learning to trust each other, the formal government of this nation will probably lurch from one credibility crisis to the next."[8] In his first column of 1996, Broder noted that little had changed and that "the restoration of social trust, civic institutions and civil debate [were] the sine qua non of a healthy society."[9] In describing the creation of the Upper Klamath Basin Working Group, a multiparty citizen-led effort focusing on ecological restoration and economic stability issues in southern Oregon, former Senator Mark Hatfield (R-OR) stated, "This new approach relies on what has become a Republican theme of restoring decision-making power into the hands of people at the local level. Not surprisingly, if people are given a mission and some parameters within which it can be accomplished, they will find a way to make things work. Especially if they are given the opportunity to develop the structure of the solutions and the power to prioritize them."[10]

Collaboration in resource management can help provide fertile ground for the development of a heightened sense of citizen involvement and responsibility, and it can help rebuild a sense of trust in government institutions and each other. Indeed, involvement in the kind of public-private arrangements that are underway can yield benefits well beyond those seen in the traditional voluntary and civic associations perceived by Alexis de Tocqueville as the source of America's social cohesion in the 1830s. America is a much more diverse place than it was two hundred years ago. Since we value that diversity, we have to foster mechanisms that deal creatively with the differences inherent in a diverse society. Many communities are turning to collaborative processes to increase the opportunities for citizen involvement and provide forums in which diverse values can be discussed. Over time, they can help to rebuild the trust and civility needed to move forward. As environmentalist and Applegate Partnership participant Jack Shipley notes, "It was desperation and gridlock that brought us together, but it is trust and respect that keep us going."

No Other Way to Get Things Done

Many of these innovations have occurred because the participants simply had no other way to move forward and they felt a strong need to do so. For example, those involved in collaborative management of the Elkhorn Mountains in Montana stress that this type of cooperation will have to occur more in the future. Going it alone "is not even an option," says Forest Service District Ranger George Weldon. About cooperation he says, "It's just necessary. We have to cooperate to do our jobs properly." BLM Manager Merle Good agrees that this is "the wave of the future." "We have fewer dollars and fewer people in our agencies now, and it's not going to get any better," he says. Nancy Upham, Forest Service facilitator of the Coalition for Unified Recreation in the Eastern Sierra, notes, "With downsizing comes recognition that we've got to pool our resources, not duplicate efforts, and share whatever we can."

By all accounts, resources available to public management agencies became more constrained in the 1980s and early 1990s. Hostile political executives cut budgets of agencies like the U.S. Fish and Wildlife Service (FWS) in the 1980s, and declining timber sales generated less revenue and political support for agencies like the Forest Service and the BLM.[11] Efforts to reduce the federal budget deficit focused on the few places where the budget was discretionary, and that included domestic programs such as environmental protection and natural resource management. In many places, reductions in force, early retirements, and limited new hires have left units understaffed and overworked, even as they are asked by policy makers to do more. For many, creative resource-sharing partnerships have become the only way to get tasks such as habitat restoration and public education accomplished.

Even without these kinds of resource constraints, in many places there has been an evolving realization that reliance on one sector of society is unlikely to produce satisfactory outcomes. Reliance on big business led to overexploita-tion of resources and humans. Reliance on big government resulted in top-down, bureaucratic programs that were often insensitive to public concerns. Reliance on private landowners exercising absolute property rights neglects important transboundary concerns, including the protection of biological diversity. Progress will come only from taking advantage of the unique capa-bilities of each of these elements of society through the creative interplay of a network of groups and agencies.

Entrepreneurs at Work

Some of these innovative collaborative efforts have also resulted from the activities of entrepreneurial individuals who push forward, sometimes at great odds. Opportunities always walk hand in hand with problems, as the need to solve a problem creates the possibility of significant change. Some people in these cases realized the benefits that were possible from a different mode of action and went beyond the call of duty to make it happen. They worked hard, found ways around red tape and organizational turf, pushed others for-ward, and catalyzed creative activities on the ground. While it is a cliché in a world that thrives on clichés, people can and do make a difference. In many innovative cases of collaboration, ordinary people helped foster creative part-nerships that have made a difference in communities and landscapes through-out the country.

Ironically, shrinking confidence in institutions such as government has helped to foster this entrepreneurial behavior. Declining faith in the ability of elected and appointed leaders to articulate necessary direction has mobilized the leadership abilities of individuals throughout government and the public. In government agencies, a weakened sense of top-down internal control has promoted this change, as has a generational change in staffing, as the post-NEPA generation rose to middle-management positions and challenged traditional approaches favored by organizational leaders. A sense of hopeless-ness on the part of top agency leaders created a window of opportunity for individuals with creative ideas. Nothing was working, so why not try some-thing new?

We would be remiss not to note the importance of public-sector programs in helping to initiate and maintain many of these innovative efforts. The For-est Service's cost-share partnership program; the U.S. Environmental Protec-tion Agency's Community-Based Environmental Protection program;[12] EPA's National Estuary and Remedial Action Planning programs;[13] the FWS's Habi-tat Conservation Planning program;[14] and the Oregon Watershed Enhance-ment program;[15] among others all provided critical resources and impetus for creative collaborative initiatives. Statutes such as the Endangered Species Act

(ESA), the Clean Water Act, and the NFMA provided incentives for people who traditionally would not even talk to one another to work together. And overall administrative policies, such as President George Bush's "thousand points of light" and the reinventing government effort of the Clinton administration, helped foster a mood of creative partnership and innovation. By all accounts, these initiatives have seeded many successful activities on the ground and have paid off their initial investments severalfold.

A New Style of Resource Management

These on-the-ground innovations are partly an outgrowth of a new style of resource management that is in evolution from the approach that dominated the first hundred years of conservation activities.[16] At the turn of the century, the Progressive Conservationists articulated a set of principles for resource management that has provided operating guidelines for the past hundred years.[17] Responding to unfettered overexploitation of natural resources in the second half of the 1800s, individuals such as Gifford Pinchot, the first chief of the Forest Service, pointed to the need to manage public resources in a way that would yield "the greatest good, to the largest number, for the longest time."[18] The best way to achieve that objective was through technical analysis that emphasized maximizing use subject to long-term sustainability constraints. Technical experts divorced from the corrupting influences of the politics of the times could best determine the public's interest. Both underuse and overuse were seen as wasteful. At the time, it was an important and necessary change for the better, and that paradigm of management became the heart and soul of agencies like the Forest Service.

For the first half of the twentieth century, that approach worked well. Demands on public resources were low, and, while scandals occasionally erupted, government agencies performed a largely custodial role in their oversight of the public lands.[19] After World War II, the situation changed. An expanding industrial economy stimulated new demands on public resources. The mobility provided by automobiles and interstate highways brought many citizens face to face with the spectacular resources in the federal lands portfolio. The industrial era had also produced a way to manage organizations that emphasized top-down control, production, and measuring objectives by narrow criteria, and the public resource agencies adopted those approaches as they sought to deal with the rising demands facing them.

It was hard not to get swept up in the common pursuit of growth, fueled by what appeared to be almost unlimited resources. For the Forest Service, for example, industrial-sized production of wood fiber rose to the head of the line as an objective for public lands. This objective was good economics and good politics. By providing a clear measure of success, "getting the cut out," it also fit an organizational style that emphasized allegiance to the agency. Promotion from within, strong formal and informal mechanisms for socializing new hires into the culture of the agency, and penalties for nonconformance produced a fairly homogeneous organization.[20] While the Forest Service provides the classic model of the resource management agency of the 1950s and 1960s, by all accounts, many state departments of natural resources and other federal agencies emulated its example. They built fairly mechanistic, dominant-purpose agencies that were effective at producing harvestable timber and shootable deer but were bound to run into problems as public values shifted.

That shift occurred in a big way in the 1960s and 1970s. An increasingly urban population increasingly valued wilderness and nonconsumptive recreation. Public lands became a recreational playground and an escape from urban life as countless Americans headed for public parks, forests, and seashores with children and campers in tow. At the same time, an evolving understanding of the downside of industrial life fed concerns about toxic chemicals and pollution. Books such as Rachel Carson's *Silent Spring* and catastrophes such as the Santa Barbara oil spill made visible through the miracle of television helped to popularize pollution as a public concern. Simultaneously, suburban sprawl led to a concern about the loss of open space and natural areas, as countless Oak Meadows and River Pines subdivisions were named for the ecosystems they replaced.

All of these concerns came together in the 1970s. The first Earth Day, held in April 1970, signified the birth of a national environmental movement; numerous environmental laws were passed, interest groups were formed, and politicians jumped on the environmental bandwagon. While the energy crises of the 1970s slowed down the momentum, they did not change the evolution in public values and the concomitant institutionalization of those values in law and politics as groups such as the Natural Resources Defense Council and The Wilderness Society developed the resources and influence to pursue their concerns.

Changing attitudes toward government fed by the Watergate scandal, the Vietnam War, and the Reagan administration's antigovernment rhetoric and actions pushed along the public's dissatisfaction with natural resource management. Not only were emerging values in natural systems not being adequately provided for through public policy, but the agencies in charge were not to be trusted. The industrial era management model failed the agencies in trying to adjust to the changing interests and attitudes of the public, and their efforts to respond appeared heavy-handed and at times disingenuous. Agency leaders and the elected officials they served preached accommodation to the changing public values at the same time commodity levels produced from public resources rose to record levels.

Agencies did respond in more than token ways to the changing value base of natural resource management in the country, but they were stymied by their traditions and styles. Public involvement became a rallying call for agencies in the 1970s. Many created elaborate public involvement mechanisms, but most were created in the image of the technocratic model that was well entrenched in agency traditions: "Tell us your concerns, and we will figure out a solution." This linear model of public involvement was better than no involvement at all but was rarely satisfying to those who participated. Further, it raised expectations that agencies were then unable or unwilling to satisfy. For many agency officials, greater involvement with the public raised questions about their role as the implementers of public law. It directly conflicted with a long-standing view that "we know best." Agency leaders feared a loss of control and a weakening of their influence as outside groups (including other agencies) became involved in their decision-making processes. Ironically, by not finding ways to incorporate real public involvement in decision making and implementation of management strategies, the same agency officials lost the control they had worked so hard to maintain.

The final nail in the agencies' coffin came from the changing science base and the democratization of information that occurred throughout the 1980s and 1990s. Conservation biology and landscape ecology flowered in the 1980s, bringing forth new methods and concepts for resource management. Increasingly, agency management practices were undermined by the evolving science base. Simultaneously, other groups developed the ability to collect and analyze technical information, enabling them to successfully challenge agency decisions on scientific grounds. Control over decision making and direction was wrested from agency leaders by undermining their fundamental source of legitimacy: technical wisdom.

The result of this evolution of resource management ideas and institutions has been the impasses described above. Agency legitimacy was undermined, and politicians and interest groups who traditionally had dominated resource and environmental policy found their influence ebbing. Interest groups of a variety of sizes and shapes fought their way to a standstill, and the public, already suspicious of "the government," became even more frustrated.

Some agencies, like the Forest Service, tried to respond by redefining their role as a neutral balancing point between diverse interests viewed as clients. But the limited slack in the natural resource base and their approach resulted in everyone being angry at everyone else. One Forest Service employee commented, "If everyone is angry with us, we must be doing something right." But anger and frustration are not helpful, and the fact that several Forest Service offices have been bombed in recent years and land management personnel have been warned to stay out of areas in public ownership indicates the potential for violence and tragedy associated with the current state of affairs.

In response, many people have argued that a new style of resource management is needed. Most say that the pendulum promoting the technocratic model of the last century of resource management needs to swing back toward a more democratic model. This is not to argue that science is not an important part of wise resource management in the twenty-first century. Indeed, scientific requirements for management far exceed those of previous models. But a new approach must acknowledge to a greater extent the human dimensions of management choices and the uncertainties and complexities in potential decisions, and build understanding, support, and ownership of collective choices.

An evolving consensus in the natural resource management literature points to sustainability as a primary objective. The recent U.S. Department of Agriculture Committee of Scientists charged with evaluating the scientific basis for the management of national forests and grasslands noted, "As a collective vision, sustainability means meeting the needs of the present generation without compromising the ability of future generations to meet their needs. As an approach to decision making, it calls for integrating the management of biological and ecological systems with their social and economic context, while acknowledging that management should not compromise the basic functioning of these systems."[21] While the committee suggested that the concept of sustainability dates back to the Pinchot days, it noted, "We have broadened our focus from that of sustaining commodity outputs to that of sustaining ecological processes and a wide variety of goods, services, conditions and values."

Emerging notions of sustainability have important implications for resource management. A number of changes are needed to reinvent management strategies and policies. As detailed below, analysts suggest that resource and environmental management needs to operate on different geographic and temporal scales; deal with complexity, uncertainty, and change; acknowledge and make sense of the community of interests; decentralize decision making; and provide images of success.

Operate on Different Geographic and Temporal Scales

Most of the literature highlights the fragmentation of landownership in the United States and the need to shift to an ecosystem-based approach to resource management. Secretary of the Interior Bruce Babbitt notes that for more than a century, federal land managers have "compartmentaliz[ed] the American landscape," yet "the lands we manage do not fit into neat compartments." "Our new mission, then, is to look beyond the fences," he says.[22] His view of the need to expand beyond artificial administrative boundaries is reinforced by the literature on ecosystem management, which unanimously advocates management at broader geographic and temporal scales.[23] According to University of Arizona researcher Ann Moote and cowriters, who summarized much of this literature in 1994, "Ecosystem management must work over larger spatial and longer temporal scales than has been the norm in resource management. It requires management across ecological, political, generational, and ownership boundaries."[24]

A broader geographic perspective has also been compelled by the increasing realization that nonfederal and private lands must contribute to conservation objectives. For example, biologists estimate that nearly 90 percent of the more than twelve hundred listed endangered and threatened species occur on nonfederal lands, and half occur exclusively on nonfederal lands.[25] More than half, including nearly two hundred animal species, have at least 81 percent of their habitat on nonfederal lands.[26] In order to achieve recovery, it seems clear that federal agencies will need to cooperate with other public and private landowners. Securing the assistance of private landowners is even more important when trying to create habitat corridors and open space in urban areas, or trying to clean up development-generated sedimentation or agricultural runoff into streams.

Deal with Complexity, Uncertainty, and Change

A number of analysts argue that management needs to incorporate an expanding base of information about ecosystems and human societies. In *Creating a Forestry for the 21st Century: The Science of Ecosystem Management*, University of Washington researchers Kathy Kohm and Professor Jerry Franklin identify four overarching themes involved in the practice of ecosystem management, two of which deal with the need for better information. They argue that the single most salient theme of the contributions to their book is the need to appreciate the complexity of ecological and organizational systems: "Appreciating the complexity of systems and managing for wholeness rather than for the efficiency of individual components place forestry in the context of a much broader movement toward systems thinking."[27] They also highlight the importance of developing a rich body of site-specific knowledge since management is heavily context specific.

However, these and other writers recognize that our knowledge is incomplete and that information, values, and goals change over time. University of Florida ecologist C.S. Holling suggests, "Ecosystems and the societies with which they are linked involve unknowability and unpredictability. Therefore sustainable development is also inherently unknowable and unpredictable. . . . Evolving systems require policies and actions that not only satisfy social objectives but also achieve continually modified understanding of the evolving conditions and provide flexibility for adapting to surprises."[28] His prescription is a process of "adaptive environmental management and policy design,"[29] which involves setting a course of action based on a set of hypotheses, monitoring what happens, and reevaluating the direction based on what one learns. Williams College professor Kai Lee suggests that adaptive management can serve as a "compass," helping us to find appropriate direction, while conflict bounded by negotiation can provide a "gyroscope" that can keep us balanced as we move in the appropriate direction.[30]

Acknowledge and Make Sense of the Community of Interests

Others argue that public resource managers need to acknowledge the expanded set of public values and interests in natural resources and the environment and actively involve representatives of those interests in decision making and implementation. Former Forest Service deputy chief Jeff Sirmon and coauthors have argued the need to "create and nurture communities of interests, combined with a flexible and comprehensive approach to public involvement called open decision making."[31] They rely on the work of Harvard psychiatrist Ronald Heifetz, who argues that a community of interests exhibits a different leadership style, in which responsibility for problem solving falls on the group, and members of the group must struggle with "their orientation, values, and potential tradeoffs."[32]

Timothy Duane of the University of California at Berkeley suggests that three types of communities be involved in ecosystem-based resource management: "(1) communities of place, which are tied to physical space through geography; (2) communities of identity, which are tied to each other through social characteristics but may transcend place; and (3) communities of interest," whose commonalties lie in the benefits they receive from a resource or the costs they impose on it.[33] In his view, the participation of all these communities is "not merely a luxury in ecosystem management—it is necessary for its success." Participation provides a foundation for the development of what Robert Putnam has called "social capital"[34]—trust, norms, and networks of relationships—and leads to better and more resilient decisions. Many others have argued that effective participation can be achieved only by involving multiple interests in collaborative decision-making processes.[35]

Decentralize Decision Making

An extensive literature on environmental regulation argues that reliance on top-down, command-and-control regulation has resulted in inflexible and inefficient policies at the ground level and needs to yield to a more decentralized decision-making approach.[36] Political scientist DeWitt John links this argument most closely to the need for collaborative initiatives at the local level. He argues that top-down regulation worked well for controlling point-source pollution and preservation of individual species but fails when attempting to deal with the current generation of environmental problems: nonpoint-source pollution, pollution prevention, and management of ecosystems. His solution is "civic environmentalism," which is "a more collaborative, integrative approach to environmental policy than traditional regulation"[37] and "is an ad hoc process of custom designing answers to complex environmental problems in a specific location. It is profoundly different from the processes by which our government usually does its work."[38] The place-based approach of civic environmentalism, developed by the U.S. Environmental Protection Agency (EPA) as Community-Based Environmental Protection,[39] relies on a more extensive information base grounded in the specific context of a site and typically uses a broader set of policy instruments (technical assistance, public education, subsidies, incentives, etc.) to accomplish ends.

Decentralized, consensual decision making is also promoted by individuals concerned with managing organizations in an information age. In *Reinventing Government*, David Osborne and Ted Gaebler note, "Fifty years ago centralized institutions were indispensable. Information technologies were primitive, communication between different locations was slow, and the public work force was relatively uneducated. . . . But today information is virtually limitless, communication between remote locations is instantaneous, many public employees are well educated, and conditions change with blinding speed. There is no time for information to go up the chain of command and decisions to come down."[40]

Their prescription for the changing management condition is to decentralize authority and responsibility. According to Osborne and Gaebler, "Entrepreneurial leaders instinctively reach for the decentralized approach. They move many decisions to the 'periphery,' . . . into the hands of customers, communities, and nongovernmental organizations. They push others 'down below,' by flattening their hierarchies and giving authority to their employees."[41] The result is the creation of organizations that are more flexible and innovative, with better employee morale and productivity. Most deploy employees in problem-oriented teams and reduce their insulation from the "real world."

Provide Images of Success

We would add to these themes the need to provide positive imagery that suggests ways that agency officials and citizens can bring about new management approaches. Most models of innovation in organizations identify factors such as perceived crisis and strong leadership as important elements influencing change. It is our belief that most of the resource management agencies have been in crisis mode for quite some time and that a new crop of leaders is taking office. They are motivated to change but lack a clear set of images of what could be. Stories of successful action can provide ideas for those faced with a crisis; they can similarly motivate on-the-ground experimentation more proactively. Indeed, the use of images of action is more likely to be motivating to ground-level staff, to whom policy prescriptions may seem vague and unconnected to reality. Having a collection of images and ideas in their heads may be more compelling than any set of equations or prescriptions.

The Uses and Mechanisms of Collaboration

Collaboration has a role to play in responding to each of the thematic changes discussed above. It can help create the networks of relationships that relate administrative or political boundaries to those defined by problem or ecosystem. It can assist in the development of rich pools of knowledge that draw from diverse sources and provide a framework for interdisciplinary learning and problem solving. Building bridges between public and private parties can generate a diversity of ideas and approaches, so that decision makers have a menu of responses available to deal with changing conditions, problems, and values. It can also help administrative agencies stay in touch with changing public values and knowledge. Collaborative processes can help agencies and interests understand each other, while providing a decision-making framework that involves groups in a way that builds support and ownership. They also can help provide structures through which post-decision monitoring and evaluation can take place. Images of successful collaboration can help motivate agency staff and citizens alike. In the best of worlds, it also can help create a dialogue about shared values and problems and assist in rebuilding a sense of individual responsibility for collective problems.

Collaboration is not the goal of resource management, but it can be a helpful stepping stone to more effective management. More specifically, we see four major uses of collaborative processes in resource and environmental management:

- building understanding by fostering exchange of information and ideas among agencies, organizations, and the public and providing a mechanism for resolving uncertainty;

- providing a mechanism for effective decision making through processes that focus on common problems and build support for decisions;

- generating a means of getting necessary work done by coordinating cross-boundary activities, fostering joint management activities, and mobilizing an expanded set of resources; and

- developing the capacity of agencies, organizations, and communities to deal with the challenges of the future.

Since there are numerous reasons to establish relationships, not surprisingly there are many forms that collaboration can take. Some approaches are temporary and informal, while others are long-standing and institutionalized. Some involve traditional elements of agency behavior, while others are new. Although we have categorized collaborative arrangements into twenty types elsewhere,[42] we chose not to do so here for the simple reason that most efforts at interorganizational partnerships involve multiple activities. A management partnership, such as occurs when Trout Unlimited restores fisheries habitat on national forest land, often involves public education and interagency coordination as well. While chapter 5 discusses some of the structures that have allowed collaboration to flourish, it is important to view collaboration as a mind-set that can be accomplished in a variety of ways. Rather than a stand-alone task that agencies call public involvement or outreach, collaboration is part of the way that many resource management activities should be carried out.

A Guide to *Making Collaboration Work*

This book explores collaboration as a key element of a new style of resource management and environmental problem solving. It has two primary objectives: to tell the story of numerous collaborative efforts across the country, and to make sense of the current experience. We seek to provide images of success that others can emulate and an understanding of the ways that individuals involved in these efforts achieved success. What exactly did they do in order to be effective?

The book provides a framework that others can use in building partnerships, resolving conflicts, and solving problems collaboratively. Our objective is to further legitimize interagency and multiparty efforts within the realm of natural resource and environmental management, and to make efforts at building bridges more effective. We rely on the voices of real people by describing as many of their stories as possible. These are people like Maria Durazo-Means, a district forester in Alaska's Tongass National Forest, who accepted the challenge of her supervisor to implement nontraditional approaches to tapping the resources and ideas of a diverse and geographically dispersed set of communities interested in recreational activities in the forest. As she puts it, "In the past, recreation project planning has been a bit like the job of the lonely Maytag repairman. A lone person or two trying to think of new ways to serve that big public out there. This plan represents our effort to break loose from our Maytag mode."

We include the story of nongovernmental individuals as well: people like Jack Shipley and Jim Neal, one an avid environmentalist, the other the owner of a forestry management company, who were often at odds but shared a frustration with the continued polarization of resource management issues in their valley. Together, they decided to chart a "different approach to managing the half-million-acre Applegate watershed." Their goal, and the goal of the many agency and nonagency individuals who joined them, was, according to Shipley, "to work toward solutions, leave partisanship at home, [and] put ecosystem health in front of private agendas."

These are people who cannot afford the luxury of believing in collaboration as an abstract, God-and-motherhood notion in which the story ends with all parties walking hand in hand into the sunset. Rather, they understand the hard work involved in making partnerships function. Their goals were to improve the on-the-ground situation, not to achieve some imagined state of bliss. FWS refuge manager Steve Thompson notes the significance of the name of the Cameron County Agricultural Coexistence Committee in South Texas: "The farmers came up with that title, and I think it's pretty interesting, because coexistence is really what it's about. It's not saying that we are all going to love each other. We're just going to find a way to work together and come to some common ground."

We tell these stories and present their lessons in three segments. The rest of part I provides an overview of the diverse set of collaborative activities underway in the United States and illustrates the challenges inherent in them. Chapter 2 expands on our introduction by describing the multiple uses of collaboration in natural resource and environmental management and illustrates them with short examples. Chapter 3 reviews the obstacles facing individuals and organizations seeking to develop cross-boundary partnerships and provides a foundation for understanding the ways that people overcome these problems.

Part II explains what people have done to be successful. In our view, eight key factors explain the success of the roughly two hundred collaborative initiatives we studied. Chapters 4 through 11 explore these factors and illustrate them with examples from the case studies. Successful collaborative efforts:

- build on common ground established by a sense of place or community, mutual goals or fears, or a shared vision (chapter 4);

- create new opportunities for interaction among diverse groups (chapter 5);

- employ meaningful, effective, and enduring collaborative processes (chapter 6);

- focus on the problem in a new and different way by fostering a more open, flexible, and holistic mind-set (chapter 7);

- foster a sense of responsibility, ownership, and commitment (chapter 8);

- recognize that partnerships are made up of people not institutions (chapter 9);

- move forward through proactive and entrepreneurial behavior (chapter 10); and

- mobilize support and resources from numerous sources (chapter 11).

Part III steps back from the case material to provide a guide to agencies, groups, and individuals seeking to promote collaborative activities. Chapter 12 provides a set of specific steps for agency leaders seeking to foster the use of partnerships and collaborative processes. Chapter 13 describes ways to ground collaborative efforts involving public resources in mechanisms that ensure accountability and effective performance. Chapter 14 concludes with a short message to individuals considering collaborative processes.

Based on the experience contained in these case examples, we are unabashedly optimistic about the potential for good to come from expanded collaborative efforts. Such relationships are not a panacea. Critics highlight concerns about accountability, the connection of collaborative efforts to law, and the demands these efforts place on public and private groups, and we discuss those issues. But the bottom line is this: The dispersed and finite nature of existing human and financial resources, both public and private, the complexity of the problems that we face, and the sheer diversity in our society mean that there really is no choice. Creative ways to bridge multiple capabilities and concerns will be a necessary part of American life in the twenty-first century. They offer an exciting way to foster the traditional values of shared responsibility and democratic involvement while dealing with complex issues in a highly diverse society.

Chapter 2

Why Collaboration?

What are the objectives of collaboration in resource management? Why should agency staff complicate their lives by reaching out to groups outside their agencies? Why should members of a community spend time in meetings interacting with people with whom they have been in conflict? The worst answers to these questions lie in the set of reasons often given by agency staff for engaging in public involvement or collaboration: "The law requires it," "It is politically correct," "A democracy requires public involvement," "Agency leaders have mandated it," or even "The public will agree with our plans if we tell them what we intend to do."

The best answer to these questions is simple: Collaboration can lead to better decisions that are more likely to be implemented and, at the same time, better prepare agencies and communities for future challenges. Building bridges between agencies, organizations, and individuals in environmental management is not an end in itself. Rather, it is a means to several ends: building understanding, building support, and building capacity. By developing interpersonal and interorganizational linkages, managers can be better informed and make choices about future direction that are more likely to solve the problems at hand. Programs are more likely to be implemented successfully if they are supported and owned by affected groups. In addition, collaborative decision making and on-the-ground partnerships can enhance the capacity of agencies and communities to deal with problems in the future.

Without collaboration, managers are put in an impossible situation. They need to make decisions that rely on an increasingly large base of information, but they do not control all the necessary information. They want to make the "right choice" but increasingly find that there is no clear technical solution. They need to make credible and legitimate decisions but do not understand how to balance the range of values the public assigns to natural resources, particularly in a time of constrained resources. They need political leaders and the public to support their decisions but are unlikely to obtain support without active and meaningful involvement by stakeholders in decision making. Managers also need resources to achieve on-the-ground management but increasingly are constrained by limited staffing, funding, and expertise. They need their agencies to grow as public values and knowledge change yet often are caught in bureaucratic and personal efforts to hold on to past modes of action.

Collaboration can help managers deal with these needs. It is not a magic bullet that can transform public-sector resource management, but, along with necessary scientific, policy, and organizational innovations, it can help. This chapter describes the multiple objectives of collaborative resource management and illustrates them with short descriptions of a variety of innovative partnerships underway during the 1990s.

Building Understanding

While at one time public agencies and individual landowners controlled much of the information needed to manage their lands, today information is ubiquitous. Relevant information is collected and stored in many places, and it can move rapidly across great distances. Internet-based geographic information files containing data obtained from satellite imagery may be more useful than the timber stand maps contained in thousands of Forest Service file drawers. Compilations of data relevant to issues such as old-growth protection and endangered species management may be best provided by nongovernmental organizations such as The Nature Conservancy (TNC) or The National Audubon Society. No longer is the Forest Service or the state department of natural resources the only source of good information.

Nor is the information explosion limited to data sources. Ideas are equally important, and the best ideas about management of resources and communities may come from a diverse set of sources. Tested ideas about how to achieve landscape-scale management may come from nongovernmental groups like TNC or regional planning agencies like the Adirondack Planning Agency or the Pinelands Commission. Ideas about how to employ decision-making tools such as gap analysis may best come from federal agencies like the U.S. Fish and Wildlife Service or state agencies like the Idaho Game and Fish Commission that have experimented with such techniques.[1] The best sources of ideas about economic development in resource-dependent communities may lie in consulting firms specializing in economic revitalization. As agencies seek to revitalize their organizational strategies and norms, learning from firms such as 3M that have built strong, decentralized, entrepreneurial structures may be appropriate.² Such knowledge-sharing arrangements are vitally needed to serve as conduits of data and ideas appropriate to resource management in the twenty-first century.

The explosion of information is not just a result of technological innovation in the area of computing and communications. Rather, groups outside agencies developed parallel expertise so that they could understand and challenge agency decisions as decision making became increasingly technical and complex. While reporting requirements such as environmental impact statements and national forest plans enabled those outside the agencies to better understand agency intent and reasons for making decisions, it also forced interest groups and state agencies to develop the capacity to understand the information in those documents. The democratization of expertise that resulted helped create the sense of impasse described in chapter 1 as agency experts battled interest group experts and often lost the battle. Increasingly, nonagency sources of information on issues like forest management were viewed as more credible than agency sources. While this was a bitter pill for agencies to swallow, the good news is that quality information and expertise now exist in many places outside agency walls. Building knowledge networks is important to access those sources of information.

In addition, changes in the information needed to manage resources mandate information-sharing arrangements. The development of conservation biology, landscape ecology, ecosystem management, and other resource management disciplines has created a rich knowledge base for management, but it requires agencies and other landowners to "do good science" at a deeper level of understanding and detail than has ever been necessary. For example, a concern with larger-scale processes such as fire regimes requires acquiring new information across broader geographic areas, and the enhanced understanding of micro-site processes such as the role of fungi in nutrient cycling requires gathering new kinds of site-level data. More science is needed in management, and partnerships between scientists and managers in a variety of organizations can help.

As agencies respond to a wider array of human interests and values in public resource management, agency staff need to reach out to acquire information about the nature of those values, aspirations, and concerns. There is no reason to believe that agency staff members can understand those concerns on their own, and it is unfair to expect them to do so. Changes in law and regulations require expanded understanding of human values and attitudes; research and common sense suggest that the only way to achieve that understanding is through communication with stakeholders and other individuals.

Just as important, the public also needs an enhanced understanding of the wide range of considerations involved in managing natural resources and communities. As the American population has urbanized, it has become less in touch with natural systems and the infrastructure that supports the lifestyles of its members. Paradoxically, Americans have become more supportive of environmental protection at the same time their demands for the consumption of natural resources have risen. Moderating those demands and promoting conservation of natural resources require closing this loop, so that American consumers and users are more aware of and responsible for the impacts of their actions on public resources.

Building understanding on the part of the public is also critical at the site level. While Americans have always mistrusted government, they have become even less trusting and more cynical in the last three decades. The proliferation of expertise from many sources has made them more confused and even less willing to trust agency experts. While chapter 1 suggested that there are numerous reasons for these changes, their upshot on the ground is that people involved in management and decision making must work at deliberately building the understanding of affected groups of the reasons for making choices and the constraints that they face. Bridges built between a variety of groups can provide vectors through which understanding can be increased.

Information Sharing

Most partnerships seek to promote sharing of existing information among partners via formal or informal arrangements, such as staff members swapping data on a common management issue, computer networks that allow for shared use of a geographic information system, and ongoing monitoring committees. Environmental problems exist partly because people lack the information to act appropriately. Providing information through outreach and exchange can help redress the situation. As the Blackfoot Challenge's Becky Garland, local business owner and former vice president of the Big Blackfoot Chapter of Trout Unlimited, notes, "People were dying for information . . . to do the right thing. They were trying to make their wrongs right."

The Darby Partnership is an informal watershed-based collaborative effort that serves as a mechanism for information sharing among more than thirty agencies and organizations. Located in west-central Ohio, the Big Darby and Little Darby Creek's 580-square-mile watershed is one of the most diverse aquatic systems in the Midwest. The watershed supports eighty-six fish species and more than forty species of mussels, thirty-five of which are rare or endangered. The river system is a designated National Scenic River and was named "one of the last great places in the Western Hemisphere" by TNC. The partnership of agencies, environmental groups, and local governments and organizations acts as a think tank for conservation efforts and promotes "information dissemination" among members, according to Ohio EPA representative Marc Smith. The partnership's activities include efforts to reduce runoff from farms by educating farmers about sediment reduction methods, and education of others in the watershed about issues such as septic tank maintenance, stream bank erosion, household hazardous waste, and the need to protect wooded riparian corridors.

A larger-scale initiative is the Southern Appalachian Man and the Biosphere (SAMAB) cooperative, which spent two years in the mid-1990s pulling together an ecological assessment of this 37-million-acre region that ranges from northern Alabama to West Virginia. The assessment is "a description of conditions that goes beyond state, federal, or private boundaries." The cooperative consists of nine federal agencies, three state agencies, the Tennessee Valley Authority, and the Oak Ridge National Laboratory. It was assisted by university researchers and representatives of nongovernmental organizations. The effort collected ecological, social, and economic data to "facilitate an ecosystem-based approach to management of the natural resources" within the area. According to the preface of the five-volume study, "This cooperation significantly expanded the scope and depth of analysis that might have been achieved by separate initiatives. It also avoided duplicating work that might have been necessary if each agency had acted independently."[3] Project organizers hoped that ultimately the effort would improve decision making by creating a common information source and would forge relationships between agency officials.

As information is exchanged, it becomes part of a shared knowledge base necessary for problem solving that is "owned" by all the members of the collaborative group. For example, the Eel River Delta Sustainable Agriculture Committee, a group of farmers and state agency representatives focused on water-quality issues in that area of Northern California, invited state agency staff to monthly meetings to exchange information. According to Dennis Leonardi, a third-generation dairy farmer in Ferndale, California, and the director of the local chapter of the California Farm Bureau Federation, "We know what this environment is like, which many of the regulators don't. So we were able to share with them how the river works, how the water works, how the creek flows, and the kinds of things that we do. And then they shared what their concerns were, with effluents getting into the creek and degradation of streams, habitat for fish. As that dialogue progresses, what you have is a sort of shared opinion that grows."

Learning from the Public

Some agencies have created mechanisms to solicit information, ideas, and concerns from the public. These public involvement strategies include a variety of traditional techniques such as public hearings and comment periods on draft decisions, as well as numerous less traditional approaches, such as open houses at national forest offices, information tables at supermarkets, surveys, and futuring workshops.

In southeastern Alaska, an innovative public involvement effort led the way in reducing long-term tensions while building a plan for recreation. Spread across three islands in the Sumner Strait and part of the mainland of southeastern Alaska, the Tongass National Forest's Petersburg Ranger District was plagued by controversy over timber planning and "lots of distrust" due partly to the diversity of the region's residents: a logging community; the native village of Kake; a community of environmentalists who are interested in living off the land; and the larger town of Petersburg, which relies primarily on fishing, as well as timber, mining, and tourism. District Ranger Pete Tennis decided to collaboratively develop a five-year recreation plan as a means of building relationships within area communities and paving the way for better interactions in the future.

The centerpiece of the effort was an aggressive and highly visible public involvement campaign used to canvass area communities for their ideas on desired recreation projects. The campaign used the media and a range of informal involvement techniques (further described in chapter 5) to develop a new set of communication channels between the public and the agency. As a result of the process, "People that once would not even talk to the Forest Service were working with and excited about something we were doing together. . . . This was the first time people were talking about the Forest Service in a positive light. . . . The forest supervisor was on a cloud because people would stop him and tell him what a great thing it was," according to District Forester Maria Durazo-Means.

Educating the Public

Other collaborative efforts have been established to increase the public's understanding about the environment, management challenges, or the missions of the agencies. For example, numerous nonprofit groups like the San Gorgonio Volunteer Association in the San Bernardino National Forest run interpretive centers in state and national forests and parks, and the Forest Service maintains partnerships with the private sector including those involving cruise ships, trains, resort lodges, and ski areas. A partnership with Amtrak was begun in the early 1990s that placed Forest Service interpreters on trains in Colorado, Oregon, and Montana in the summer. The interpreters use a public-address system to tell passengers about the history, culture, natural history, and management of the surrounding areas. In a creative and low-cost manner, the program reaches many nontraditional Forest Service customers such as "inner city, foreigners, easterners, ethnic groups, and older Americans," according to Marcella Wells, Forest Service interpreter in Colorado. "Many of the passengers have never seen mountains before. We let them know that much of what they're seeing is public land—their land. It's a real eye-opener."

An innovative partnership in the lower peninsula of Michigan that has been in place for more than twenty years educates the public about the Kirtland's warbler, a federally listed endangered species. The partnership includes the Forest Service, the Michigan Department of Natural Resources (MDNR), FWS, the Michigan Audubon Society, TNC, timber companies, and local communities. The warbler is dependent on eight- to twenty-year-old jack pine forests that can be perpetuated only through management involving timber harvest and prescribed burning, techniques that can be viewed by the public as harmful to the forest and unaesthetic. The government agencies see the partnership as critical to the future of the warbler because all three agencies manage suitable habitat (40 percent by the Forest Service, 55 percent by the MDNR, and 5 percent by the FWS), and public acceptance of these techniques is necessary. While there is no way of knowing how much the education partnership contributes to recovery, the bird's population has doubled from a low of 167 pairs in the early 1970s. According to Forest Service biologist Rex Ennis, the collaborative efforts have resulted in local support, and "without that support, the things we need to do would be a lot harder than they are now."

Managing Uncertainty through Joint Research and Fact-Finding

Besides sharing existing information and involving and educating the public, many collaborative efforts expand understanding by generating new information and dealing with uncertainty through joint research and fact-finding. For example, the Eel River Delta Sustainable Agriculture Committee received funding from state and federal agencies to test water quality throughout the delta in order to acquire more reliable baseline data. Farmers and agency managers carried out field investigations together to determine the level of the floodplain and establish methods for water-quality regulators to evaluate dairy operations. Joint fact-finding not only resolves key areas of uncertainty, it also strengthens personal relationships among participants in a collaborative effort. The Eel River effort's joint fact-finding trips helped build trust among participants.

Some efforts at joint fact-finding have involved formalized negotiations in which those involved in an ongoing controversy collaboratively work through differences in understanding about facts, theory, and methods. Such negotiations can bring together experts from different agencies and groups to examine information and its implications, and attempt to bound the uncertainty surrounding expert judgments about the state of reality and what is likely in the future. An example comes from the EPA rule-making process involving the manufacture of new wood-burning stoves. Faced with the need to regulate air emissions from woodstoves, partly in response to divergent state initiatives, in 1986 the EPA convened a fifteen-person working group representing industry, environmentalists, and state and federal agencies. Considerable uncertainty existed about the effectiveness of different emission-control technologies and the likelihood that firms could retool to meet different standards. The group worked through a process whereby technical issues were identified, discussed, and resolved, either by agreement on a particular number or model or more often by bounding the range of possibilities. Over time, the technical consensus that developed allowed the groups to buy into new rules that were "not criticized after publication and which most parties believe are as scientifically and technically sound as possible . . ."[4]

Making Wise Decisions and Building Support for Them

Collaboration is also necessary as a means of making effective choices about the future of a landscape or community. The nature of the choices in natural resource and environmental management has changed; hence, the way decisions are made needs to change. Traditionally, land managers determined how best to achieve a narrow set of objectives, such as maximizing the volume of timber available for harvest. They controlled most elements of their decisions and the means for implementing them. In addition, they were fairly independent politically, either operating out of the eye of public scrutiny or relying on support from narrow constituencies. In cases where objectives were in conflict, the resource base provided enough slack to give all interests what they wanted.

Today there is a huge and conflicting set of management objectives established by law, supported by public values, and expressed as demands by interest groups. With many legitimate objectives, there is no single right answer to the question of how to manage a landscape. Rather, various directions benefit different interests in divergent ways. That is, management decisions are perceived as value-based choices that determine the answer to the classic political question: Who gets what when? With a fixed land base, expanded demands result in competition among interests of a magnitude unseen in earlier years. While in past years, managers could give everyone much of what they demanded, they are unable to do that today.

At the same time that public interests and objectives in natural resources expanded, the representatives of those interests became more effective at challenging agency decisions. The proliferation of a broad set of interest groups effective at administrative appeals and litigation means that agency decisions rarely endure. An increase in political power held by nontraditional constituent groups, combined with the weakening of traditional agency constituents, has changed the politics underlying public resource management. Management directions once thought inconceivable are now possible.

These changes in the context of decision making have made the job facing resource managers much more challenging, particularly when combined with the need for much more information, described above. Appropriate direction is more difficult to determine; information requirements for effective decision making are huge; public and political support is more important yet harder to secure. The traditional image of the agency manager as the technical expert making benevolent decisions in the public interest has been undermined by public mistrust of government. The result has been the state of impasse and frustration described in chapter 1.

These fundamental shifts in the context of decision making require changes in the processes through which choices are made. Decision-making processes must employ more and better information, balance competing interests, enhance understanding and credibility, and build support for outcomes across a spectrum of political interests. Involving stakeholders in forums designed to share knowledge, expose concerns, build relationships, establish trust, and encourage creative problem solving is more likely to produce this kind of decision making than is a traditional process in which experts retreat to closed rooms to make choices that only they feel are best. In contrast to a technical decision-making approach, collaborative efforts build understanding and support for decisions. Even when the ultimate decisions are the same, people need the opportunity to engage as partners in the decision-making process so that they take ownership of outcomes. This is particularly important since implementation often relies on the support and contributions of involved parties, and their support is more likely if decision making is viewed as credible and legitimate, which an open and inclusive process can foster. Unlike adversarial political and legal processes, collaborative approaches get more information out on the table, help to find creative solutions that can achieve multiple objectives, and build relationships that can facilitate future interactions.

Forming relationships across organizational boundaries is also a means of building support for needed management direction. Whether you view politics as good or bad, the reality is that public resource managers function in a political environment where there is competition for resources and direction. That reality means that agency leaders at least must build concurrence, if not active support, for desired direction. If they do not work to build support for agency direction in the political environment, they will not succeed in sustaining desired courses of action. Political leaders will dictate agency direction, and the resources for carrying out important agency priorities will not be available. While some see such activities as "unprofessional" or "corrupting," it is important to understand the legitimate functions of political linkages as a two-way information channel: informing local, state, and national politicians of management issues and concerns while incorporating the perspectives of elected officials (as representatives of the American public) into the understanding of agency officials.

Collaboration has an important role in recrafting resource management decision making. By fostering a shared focus on common problems, helping to resolve disputes through a process of effective negotiation, and contributing to the development of support by political officials and the public, collaborative decision-making approaches can yield wiser and more enduring decisions.

Solving Common Problems

Many collaborative efforts focus on solving shared problems or a set of different problems that can be addressed best through cooperative action. They may involve one-time meetings to focus on a recent problem or ongoing interactions on a range of issues. Often they reorganize the relationship between agencies and nongovernmental groups by downplaying the "authority" role traditionally maintained by government agencies. Effective collaborative problem-solving efforts work hard at building communities of interest that face shared problems. Many arrangements have linked groups that traditionally saw little purpose in working together. These efforts foster a strong sense that "we are all in it together," and that solutions to community-scale problems require true collaboration.

In southwestern New Mexico, a grassroots coalition of private landowners and ranchers has formed the Malpai Borderlands Group to address a set of threats to the diverse array of vegetative communities within the "mountain islands and desert seas" that characterize this region. A hundred-year history of fire suppression in the region has been a major influence in the loss of native grasslands, and human use and development threaten increased landscape fragmentation. The loss of productive grasslands and ecological diversity concerned both environmentalists and ranchers and led to the formation of the Borderlands Group, whose goal is to "restore and maintain the natural processes that create and protect a healthy, unfragmented landscape to support a diverse, flourishing community of human, plant and animal life." Working closely with federal, state, and local government and universities, the group has developed strategies to promote prescribed burning across public and private ownerships and has developed a voluntary grass-banking program. By donating a permanent conservation easement on their property, ranchers can receive grass for their livestock from other ranches.

Resolving Disputes

Some efforts seek to resolve specific conflicts that have arisen between the stakeholders in an issue. We use the term *dispute resolution* to encompass the more formal use of collaborative problem-solving techniques in resolving a specific conflict. Effective dispute resolution often involves a third-party facilitator or mediator who helps the disputants develop and implement a process to collaboratively explore their differences and find appropriate settlements when possible. Such processes are created as adjuncts to formal administrative decision making, so that agency decisions are facilitated (though not determined) by consensus judgments about appropriate direction.

There are many examples of such processes, including success at the policy level in which new rules derived through formal negotiations between affected parties have been promulgated by the U.S. Environmental Protection Agency.[5] Many site-level disputes have also been handled effectively, including national forest plan appeals settled through formal negotiations.[6] All seek to mold the differences in perspectives and interests held by numerous groups involved in an issue into a process of effective decision making.

Within three months after the final land management plan for the Deerlodge National Forest in Montana was released in late 1987, appeals were filed by coalitions of environmental and timber groups. In response, Forest Planner Ron Hanson, with the support of Forest Supervisor Frank Salomonsen, initiated a negotiation with representatives of the groups. While the groups were pessimistic about the potential for success, they reluctantly agreed to meet and chose representatives of their coalitions. The Forest Service hired a mediator, supported the negotiations by providing maps and other materials, and represented the agency's concerns as a party to the negotiation. Issues for discussion centered on the allowable timber sale quantity, roads, land allocation, and wildlife population and habitat. The group worked through the issues one at a time through a process of written proposals, discussion, and counterproposals. Once people began to understand each other's concerns, areas of agreement were sought. "Surprisingly," according to environmentalist Sean Sheehan, "there were more areas for agreement than expected."

More than a year later, after twenty-five meetings totaling almost two hundred hours, an agreement was signed. Just as important to the participants are the relationships that were fostered by the process. While implementation of portions of the agreement was undermined by weak support by the Forest Service regional office and transfers of personnel, the relationships established through the negotiation process have paid off. For example, when the National Wildlife Federation had a problem with an agency project, NWF attorney Tom France was able to call Ron Hanson, explain his reservations, and settle the problem over the phone. France attributes this improved relationship to the negotiation process. In another instance, conservation and industry groups got together on their own and made a proposal for action on road management and submitted it to the Forest Service.

Building Concurrence and Support

Many collaborative efforts build public and political support for the directions imagined by partnerships. They use the media to promote an initiative and make it more likely to succeed. They also try to influence political leaders by demonstrating broad-based support through coalition formation and linkages with elected officials. While government officials are constrained from "lobbying" or influencing electoral contests, they can inform and educate elected decision makers and the individuals to whom elected officials listen. They do this partly by providing information in a form that is useful to political leaders and by building relationships with key decision makers.

In the Mill Creek Canyon Management Partnership outside Salt Lake City, those involved needed to actively promote public and political support. Mill Creek Canyon is a popular recreation area less than one hour's drive from Salt Lake City. Eighty-one percent of the canyon is national forest land. In the past, high-density recreation use in the canyon resulted in high rates of vandalism and other crimes, extensive damage to picnic and trail areas and the surrounding land, and severe degradation of Mill Creek's water quality. According to the Forest Service, 70 percent of the recreation sites were in "substandard" condition and deteriorating. Recognizing that Salt Lake County also had an interest in providing safe, quality recreation in the canyon, the Forest Service and the county discussed a memorandum of understanding (MOU) that would outline ways in which they could work together to protect the canyon.

Central to proposals for changing the situation was the need for increased funding, and an innovative entrance fee program was proposed. But county commission politics and the efforts of a small faction of citizens opposed to the proposal generated a significant amount of negative public response. "There was a little bit of underlying resistance to the project," says Bruce Henderson, director of park operations for Salt Lake County's Parks and Recreation Division. "Some people saw it as another way for local government to get their tax dollars." Jim White, Salt Lake Ranger District's recreation forester, says that the press exacerbated the problem. "The press picked up on this," White explains. "They tried to whip something up over it." As a result of the atmosphere created by unfavorable press coverage, two of three county commissioners came out in opposition to the plan (one of whom had supported it previously), and without their approval, it could not go forward.

In response, Forest Service District Ranger Michael Sieg started working with the local media about the problems in Mill Creek Canyon and the benefits of a fee program. The strongest opponents of the plan appeared to be the local newspapers and the county commissioners, even though polls showed two-thirds of the public were supportive. White believes that much of the opposition was based on misunderstanding and that Sieg's ability to work with the media essentially solved that problem. "The district ranger was really good at being up-front with the press," White says. Often, Sieg would not wait for the press to call him; *he'd* call with news or comments. "This was a departure from the traditional bureaucratic way of being as closed as possible," White says. "The openness of the district ranger with the press helped sway public sentiment and turned the opinions of the press around. In the end they were portraying us as the good guy." He says, "Forest Service [leaders were] nervous about this candidness at first, but it worked."

White says this openness helped clarify the issues and eventually influenced the election of a new county commission. The two commissioners who had opposed the project were up for reelection in 1990. Sensing an opportunity, their challengers seized the Mill Creek Canyon proposal as a central issue and used it to gain votes. Both challengers won decisively, even though one was considered to have no chance of winning. With the new county commission strongly in favor of a fee program, the MOU was soon signed and the partnership was underway.

In some situations, by providing an opportunity for nongovernmental organizations to be involved in agency decision making, agencies have reinforced their own ability to make tough decisions. For example, in several habitat conservation planning efforts, the involvement of outside stakeholders, particularly scientists from other organizations, has strengthened the negotiating position of FWS. According to FWS biologist Joe Zisa, "Public participation makes all the difference in the world in terms of product, because it puts added pressure on the applicant to do the right thing, and it puts the Service in a position of strength in the negotiations." He adds, "Management would have been less likely to listen to their staff that some of these issues were problems if public comment had not reinforced them."[7] Comments on permit applications by members of the Swamp Squad, a network of more than one hundred volunteers who patrol wetlands in northeastern Illinois to detect violations in wetlands protection laws, also help strengthen the hand of the U.S. Army Corps of Engineers and EPA in pushing for changes. According to Swamp Squad coordinator Dr. Ken Stoffel, "If a lot of people commented, the Army Corps and EPA had a tendency to listen to those comments. . . . It almost seemed like they were asking for comments from the public to help them modify the project and some of its detrimental effects."

Getting Work Done

Natural resource and environmental management requires managers to do more with a static level of resources, and collaborative management is one strategy for coping with this dilemma. As discussed in chapter 1, the nature of the objectives and problems facing managers in the twenty-first century requires greater levels of coordinated action than were necessary in the past. For example, managing along ecosystem rather than administrative or political boundaries requires managers to look beyond their own units and take joint action. Problems like global climate change, the displacement of native species by exotics, and the wide-ranging nature of sensitive species like the Pacific salmon mandate management strategies that are regional in scale.

Even leaving out the need to bridge fragmented landscapes, the job of management has become intrinsically more difficult. Enhanced understanding of the complexity of natural systems, expanded awareness of the human dimensions of management choices, declining slack in the natural resource base, and an expanded set of laws and public values require managers to deal with a range of new considerations. To do that requires them to draw on a variety of types of expertise and capabilities that may not be available within traditional public resource management agencies. Collaborative management can provide a mechanism by which the dispersed capabilities of a diverse society can be brought together and applied to resource problems.

One solution to the need to access new sources of expertise and capabilities would be enhanced public spending on environmental management. But it is unlikely that budgets will keep up with the magnitude of demands. Even in an expanding economy, there appears to be little political will for more spending, and many agencies, like the Forest Service, are actively dealing with reductions in workforces. As a result, their choices are limited: either less gets done, what gets done is done poorly, agency workers get much more productive, or agencies find alternative ways to access needed capabilities and resources. While operating efficiencies need to be pursued, one way to deal with resource constraints lies in forming relationships with groups outside agencies. Indeed, given reductions in force and budget limitations, agencies may simply have no other way to get needed work done.

Such relationships have a number of benefits. Since they involve few fixed costs, they are flexible. Short-term work projects can be initiated, carried out, and terminated without incurring the administrative costs of regular Civil Service workers. They can provide access to expertise and resources not currently available inside agencies. By involving users and individuals affected by resource management, partnership arrangements can create a sense of ownership of public resources that may help to protect public lands. Since cooperative working arrangements require a commitment of time and energy on the part of outside groups, such arrangements also provide a market test for services requested from public lands. It requires users to demonstrate commitment, not just make demands.[8]

Cooperative arrangements also can buffer the losses in institutional memory as agency staff transfer out of an area. For example, an environmentalist in one case we studied suggested that community-level involvement in Forest Service decision making was necessary in order to ensure on-the-ground successes in the face of frequent personnel transfers: "People [in the Forest Service] move through here so quickly. They are always in the planning stages; implementation is minimal. If the community is involved, they will provide the continuity that is necessary."

Coordinating Efforts

One set of collaborative efforts coordinates the existing activities of a range of partners in order to cope with the geographic and functional fragmentation that exists across agencies, organizations, and levels of government. Interagency arrangements emphasizing coordination and cooperation seek to provide more unity of purpose and perspective when agency programs and styles conflict. The Kiowa Grasslands effort in New Mexico described in chapter 1 is a great example of two parallel programs—the Forest Service's range management and the NRCS's extension services—finding a way to provide complementary advice to ranchers.

In the northern portion of the lower peninsula of Michigan, a similar effort has been underway since 1994 to coordinate land management by federal and state agencies. In this region of mixed northern hardwood and oak-pine forests, the Huron-Manistee National Forest extends over one million acres, and three state forests spread over an additional two million. Public and private lands are used extensively for recreation, timber and wildlife management, and oil and gas production. Recognition of the interconnectedness of these lands led to the formation of a joint ecosystem team involving the Forest Service, the Michigan DNR, and the BLM. An important objective of the team was to coordinate management efforts by developing a set of Resource Conservation Guidelines. Developed over a five-year period with public input and the involvement of local organizations, the document provides ecosystem-based guidance for activities by the three agencies and the FWS and the National Park Service. These activities include a revision of the national forest plan, joint planning for oil and gas development, and an update of the Kirtland's warbler recovery plan.

The Anacostia Watershed Restoration Committee (AWRC) is an interagency partnership in a very different setting. Located along the southern edge of Washington, D.C., the Anacostia drains some of the region's most densely populated areas before entering the Chesapeake Bay. Stormwater runoff laden with sediments, toxic substances, and excessive nutrients has degraded water quality and harmed aquatic organisms in the river and its tributaries. The Metropolitan Washington Council of Governments (COG) designated the Anacostia as a priority watershed in 1979, and the nonprofit advocacy group American Rivers designated it as one of the nation's most threatened rivers.

The State of Maryland and the District of Columbia began a bilateral partnership to address sediment runoff and raw sewage discharge but soon "decided that it really made more sense to pull in the people that are actually implementing the projects—which were the local governments," explains Lorraine Herson-Jones, COG's manager for urban watershed planning. An agreement signed with Prince George's and Montgomery counties led to the formation of the AWRC, which was later joined by the U.S. Army Corps of Engineers. The committee's goal is to take a watershed approach to restoration efforts and "coordinate various aspects of the restoration that are happening in each of the individual jurisdictions," according to Herson-Jones. Most of the committee's projects are initiatives of its individual members, rather than the group as a whole, though it has undertaken several joint activities including outreach, conferences, and lobbying to change legislation. While the group's efforts lie primarily in communication and coordination, it has enhanced the sense of identity within the watershed and created a sense of hope that improvements are possible. Under the Corps' oversight, federal agencies that affect water quality in the watershed have developed a joint work plan, and their efforts were named a demonstration project under the Clinton adminstration's program to apply ecosystem management concepts in an urban environment.

Sharing Management Responsibility

Other efforts go beyond coordinating actions to include active joint management by multiple partners. They involve partnerships between landowners who seek a common objective through joint action. For example, the Siuslaw National Forest and TNC jointly manage habitat of the Oregon silverspot butterfly. (This case is described more fully in chapters 7 and 10.) By sharing information and managing across boundaries, the two organizations have improved the status of the butterfly population. In addition, the knowledge accumulated from the Forest Service–TNC partnership has been shared with others that have silverspot populations on their lands. As a result, management plans have been developed for a local National Guard unit, which recently found silverspots at its training site; the Oregon Department of Transportation, which has a road that traverses silverspot habitat; and several private landowners.

In eight midwestern states, the FWS has partnered with local soil and water conservation districts (SWCDs) and the National Fish and Wildlife Foundation (NFWF) to increase wetlands restoration efforts on private lands. In this partnership, the National Association of Conservation Districts and the local SWCDs contact local landowners and raise a portion of the funds needed for restoration work. The NFWF matches the funding, and the FWS administers the program and provides technical advice. In its first year of operation, thirty-two SWCDs in seven states participated in thirty-eight projects and restored some 2,063 acres.[9]

Mobilizing Resources

Many partnerships provide mechanisms for groups to combine resources for mutual benefit. The Kirtland's warbler partnership in Michigan links the resources of several organizations to enhance habitat management and public understanding. The three involved agencies—the Forest Service, the MDNR, and the FWS—arranged with the Michigan Audubon Society to jointly fund a public information pamphlet on the Kirtland's warbler. The professionally produced pamphlet includes information on the bird's habitat needs and management, the recovery plan, and how the public can help with recovery efforts. Audubon paid printing costs for the cover art, and the MDNR paid for other printing costs. All four groups assisted in the development of the pamphlet and helped distribute it. Audubon contributes funds to pay a naturalist who leads visitors on hikes through the habitat and paid for the construction of fifty interpretive signs posted in the bird's habitat. Audubon also arranges for a biological survey of the status of the warbler, using funds provided by the Forest Service under a cooperative agreement.

In the Mill Creek Canyon partnership between the Forest Service and Salt Lake County, the revenue-generating capabilities of the county government were used to generate a funding base for restoration efforts. An innovative funding arrangement allowed local citizens' money to be spent on a national forest in a way that directly benefits both them and the resource. While everyone wanted to improve the situation, 81 percent of the canyon was national forest land, and the Forest Service did not have funding to do the necessary rehabilitation. The agency wanted to institute an entrance fee to the canyon but was stymied by government procedures that did not allow a national forest to keep the entrance fees it charges (instead, the funds revert to the U.S. Treasury).

In response, a memorandum of understanding was created with the Salt Lake County Parks and Recreation Division whereby the county agreed to administer the fee and then donate the money to the forest in the form of matching funds for a Challenge Cost-Share grant. The fee was set at $2 per car or $20 for a season pass, and an entrance station was built at the mouth of the canyon. In 1991 and 1992, the county donated $208,000 to the Forest Service for rehabilitation work after keeping $100,000 in collected fees for start-up and administration costs. As a result of those contributed funds, the Forest Service received an additional $352,000 from Congress in Challenge Cost-Share money.

By all accounts, the partnership has been successful in many ways. The Forest Service constructed new user facilities, restored the streambank, and paid for the daily presence of a ranger, who gives guided walks and interpretive talks. The county sheriff reported that vandalism and other forms of disorderly conduct in the canyon dropped 42 percent after the effort began. Also, the partnership spawned contributions from volunteers, who helped with cleanup and trail construction.

Partnerships that involve volunteers provide another example of the ways that collaborative arrangements can generate new resources for management. Partnerships involving volunteers range from the use of groups as alternative service providers in public facilities to the more unusual Swamp Squad, which monitors wetlands development activity in the greater Chicago metropolitan area. As reported in the *Chicago Tribune,* "Through the Swamp Squad's efforts, several large wetlands that might now be parking lots and shopping malls still exist . . . helping to control flooding and purifying groundwater."[10] Owners of illegally filled wetlands have paid thousands of dollars in fines and have been required to repair the wetlands they have damaged. One enforcement officer at EPA called the Swamp Squad "a great help" and commented, "We couldn't ask for anything better." Indeed, the EPA awarded the group a $50,000, three-year grant to support its wetlands protection efforts. According to EPA official Dale Bryson, "The Swamp Squad will be the EPA's eyes and ears in the community."

In areas where public lands are adjacent to dense population centers, collaborative arrangements that use volunteers have access to the talents and energies of a tremendous pool of young adults, retirees, and other citizens. For example, located just north of the densely populated Los Angeles basin, the San Gorgonio Ranger District of the San Bernardino National Forest has expanded the resources it has available for recreation and public education through a cooperative arrangement with the 120-member San Gorgonio Volunteer Association (SGVA).

Since they wear a Forest Service uniform with a volunteer badge, the SGVA volunteers represent the agency to many visitors. The volunteers staff the district's Barton Flats Visitor Center, which had been closed during the budget cuts of the early 1990s, and conduct more than one hundred interpretive programs, which together reached thirteen thousand forest visitors in 1992. The group offers campfire programs in the campground and programs at the twenty-six children's camps within forest boundaries. Some thirty thousand children, primarily from inner-city areas in Southern California, pass through those camps each summer. The SGVA also has worked on trail maintenance and rebuilt the visitor center, and it periodically helps pay for district projects, such as interpretive exhibits and repair of the water system at the visitor center, using the proceeds of sales at the visitor center.

For its part, the Forest Service has invested time and energy into cultivating and training the volunteers. Three Forest Service employees attend the SGVA board's monthly meetings. They also train the volunteers for all activities they will perform for the forest. Nevertheless, the value of the labor and good will generated by the relationship pays back the agency many times over. According to the district ranger, "It goes without saying that without the association's involvement, these . . . contacts would not have been made."

Developing Agencies, Organizations, and Communities

Finally, collaboration provides an opportunity for transforming the agencies and organizations that manage natural resources and environmental quality and the communities that interact with them. Partnerships between agencies, organizations, and community groups can provide vehicles for sharing expertise and ideas as public agencies reinvent themselves for the management challenges of the next century and communities diversify their economic bases and social values.

Agencies need to develop the capacity to deal with the resource management challenges described in chapter 1, and collaboration can help. One of the reasons that public resource management agencies got into so much trouble in the 1970s and 1980s was that their expertise and values base became outdated. As these organizations recreate themselves, they need to go beyond simply acquiring more information. They need to update the skills of their current workforce by accessing a host of educational resources, including those in universities and other agencies. New natural science, expanded social science, and evolving ideas of organizational management and decision making suggest the need for current employees to utilize short courses, certificate programs, and the like. Short-term rotations to other organizations' work sites can expose an agency's employees to a range of perspectives and skills. Training conducted collaboratively also has the side benefit of building contacts and understanding across organizational lines.

Organizational capacity goes beyond expertise to include a diversity of attitudes and perspectives. America has always been a diverse society that is home to many cultures and values, and its demographics suggest a future that is even more diverse. Yet public resource management agencies have relied on a workforce that is fairly homogenous. Agencies like the Forest Service took pride in an extensive yet subtle network for socializing employees into the culture of the organization,[11] which suppressed some of the individual differences more reflective of the world outside the agency. To manage resources in the public interest, agencies must expand their value base in order to understand the range of public groups: their concerns and how to reach them. To do this requires interaction with people of different values and cultures, which by definition means building bridges with the world outside agency walls.

Beyond enhancing the perspectives of current employees, building bridges across agency boundaries can help recruit new employees with enhanced skills and diverse perspectives. For example, recruiting women and members of minority groups requires understanding and access not currently present in many public resource management agencies. Identifying and motivating urban Americans to seek employment in natural resource management calls for new marketing and recruiting strategies. Using outside organizations as selection, training, and "feeder" mechanisms may be one of the most effective ways to build cultural and knowledge diversity in agency workforces.

The relationships between agencies and communities can also assist in the ongoing process of community development. Agency staff may be some of the most highly educated individuals in an area, with substantial knowledge of science, planning, and economic development. Contributing these skills to a region can help communities change and can generate new role models for children, particularly in areas at the margins of tradition. For example, seeing women and racial minorities in professional and organizational leadership roles may be empowering and eye-opening for children in many small rural communities. Publicly owned resources also can provide the base for a variety of socially desirable activities. Hosting school field trips, employing prison work groups in CCC-like encampments, serving as a base for national community service work groups, and providing test sites for college researchers are all ways to share the great wealth of publicly held resources with individuals and groups around their borders. Forming linkages to do this provides a vector for organizational and individual learning both inside and outside public agencies. It is one tool among many other important strategies for helping a complex society understand and adapt to change.

Finally, collaborative relationships form the basis for an important public service at a societal level. To a country concerned about science education and knowledge of life skills such as conflict management, the process of public resource management provides an ideal training ground. Abundant public lands in a nation that is almost half publicly owned and managed provide a host of opportunities for the public to observe natural processes in action and participate in experiments in managing those processes. They also provide marvelous opportunities for discussing the societal implications of various decisions, and to experiment with various decision-making processes. Even more significant, involving the public more fully in the management of common property resources has important value-forming functions: helping to shape the values perceived in natural resources, reinforcing the need for democratic institutions to make choices about collective goods, and fostering a sense of responsibility. Building bridges that inform and involve many different types of groups can assist in this knowledge and value-formation process.

Building Staff Capabilities

A number of organizations have established relationships with outside groups in order to enhance the capabilities of their staffs. For example, a partnership initiated in 1993 between Georgia Pacific and the National Wild Turkey Federation (NWTF) provides training for Georgia Pacific's foresters. According to Greg Guest, communications manager for forest resources at Georgia Pacific, the partnership has been quite successful: "The NWTF helps us train our foresters in the appropriate things they can do to enhance or improve the habitat for wild turkeys. For instance, when they are reseeding a logging road, what kind of grasses do turkeys really like? When you're clear-cutting an area, what are the best angles of the clear-cut? Not just a nice square block, but a more jagged-edge plot or an uneven-edge plot is better from a wildlife perspective. Where we can do those things, we are doing them. . . . Where habitat is not going to be suitable for turkeys, if we find turkeys, we try to work with the federation to get them relocated to an area where it is more suitable." Guest also notes a ripple effect in the way that NWTF's ideas are transmitted to other landowners: "Our foresters can in turn pass along some of the same tips to interested landowners they have contact with. So they can sort of parlay that into more habitat being improved for turkeys."

Another partnership was initiated by the Forest Service's Pacific Southwest Region and Research Station in 1989 to encourage students from groups that are historically underrepresented in Forest Service staffing to pursue natural resources careers. Started in response to a court-ordered workforce diversification mandate, Commencement 2000 is intended to produce inner-city graduates for recruitment by the Forest Service. The program emphasizes natural resource career awareness and precareer training in feeder schools from elementary and high schools to the University of California at Berkeley and Merritt Community College in Oakland. It is overseen by a steering committee involving thirteen government, business, and nonprofit partners and coordinated by a full-time Forest Service staff member. A pilot effort was started in 1990 in Oakland, California, targeting African Americans. In 1992, the program expanded to include Native American students. Eventually, the program sought to include Asian American and Hispanic youth, linking urban schools to all eighteen national forests in California.

While its ultimate success in recruiting people of color into Forest Service positions is not yet known, the program has achieved a variety of outcomes. Curricula have been developed, and equipment necessary for training students has been provided. Forest Service personnel instituted a tutoring program to help students with basic reading and math skills. Numerous students have worked in Forest Service summer jobs and have participated in "career shadowing," working and living alongside Forest Service personnel and their families. Robert Smart, a district ranger on the Eldorado National Forest who worked with the career shadowing program, expressed his enthusiasm for the project: "You have a sense you are finally beginning to score, that something can be done about our social problems. . . . We're reaching into groups of folks who have not had an opportunity to learn about the natural environment. Even if they don't choose to work for us, they will be more enlightened citizens."

Developing Communities

Agencies and other natural resource management organizations can also contribute their expertise to the needs of adjacent communities. The Trinity GIS Center in Northern California provides training in sophisticated geographic information systems to residents of resource-dependent communities. Located in Hayfork, a small town of 2,500 people surrounded by the Shasta-Trinity National Forest, the center was established in 1993 by a partnership of seven federal, state, and local agencies and organizations. One of its core missions is to promote community development to help replace lost logging jobs by providing local citizens with training and skills needed for GIS-related jobs. The center has established a partnership with Shasta Community College, and students can take the center's GIS classes for community college credit.

More than one hundred students have completed the center's training program since it began, and the center's current instructors are all local graduates of the program. About half of the program's graduates have been local field staff of agencies such as the Forest Service and the NRCS, and half have come from the local community. A number of the program's graduates have gone to work for the Forest Service, while others work for the center on its various contracts. The center also has developed programs to train high school students and helps run a worker training program that provides people with a six-month position that combines fieldwork with classes in ecology and forest management for college credit.

Other collaborative initiatives have sought to promote community development by supporting specific projects in communities adjacent to public lands. For example, a partnership between the Clifton-Choctaw Tribe and the Kisatchie National Forest in Louisiana has "allowed individuals in the tribe to improve their quality of life in measurable ways," according to District Ranger John Baswell. The five-hundred-person tribe, located on a 4.7-acre reservation, is a nonfederally recognized tribe that suffered adverse economic effects when the local timber industry stopped processing "short wood." When Baswell was put in charge of the Rural Development Program for the Vernon Ranger District, he approached the leaders of the tribe to explore partnership possibilities.

The Tribal Council came up with a proposal to construct a small tree nursery that would grow longleaf pine seedlings and start a pine straw-baling operation. The tribe was awarded a $15,000 Challenge Cost-Share grant to start the endeavor and now has a contract to supply the Forest Service with 100,000 pine seedlings. The Forest Service supplies the tribe with seeds and buys the seedlings at the end of the growing season. The Forest Service assisted the tribe in many ways, including proposal writing, product marketing, silvicultural practices, and networking with communities off the reservation. Anna Neal, tribal coordinator for the projects, remarked that this type of assistance was very useful because "people from my tribe can work hard but don't know much about interacting outside the reservation."

Building this bridge to the local tribe was a small investment of time and resources for the Forest Service yet one that yielded significant returns for the community. According to Forest Service liaison Alan Dorian, "It was just seed money, but it gave the tribe self-reliance and independence." Anna Neal agrees: "For a community of people headed toward self-determination, every small project helps." District Ranger Baswell concludes, "We are not talking about much, but the income has really made a difference in these people's lives. It allowed some of the families to keep their children in school or to keep their lights and fuel on for the winter. . . . This project is particularly important because the Clifton-Choctaw Tribe is not federally recognized and therefore gets no federal assistance—we are really filling a niche here."

By forming collaborative arrangements of a variety of kinds, communities and agencies have been able to build a foundation for more effective resource management. Through enhanced understanding, more effective decision making, expanded means for getting work done, and broader support for needed action, on-the-ground management has improved. Along the way, collaborative arrangements have improved the capacity of agencies and communities to deal with future problems. Collaboration is not an end in itself; it is one strategy for achieving more sound and sustainable resource management.

Chapter 3

The Challenge of Collaboration

If collaboration is so useful, why doesn't it happen more often? Why is it so challenging? By all accounts, efforts to bridge the boundaries between agencies and groups are difficult and take a lot of care and feeding. They require individuals and groups to navigate the rocky shoals of human relationships, deal with problematic attitudes, do things in ways that have not been traditional, and spend limited energy and resources on activities that may or may not produce benefits. Often, agencies, elected officials, interest groups, and the public have not been supportive of those efforts, and individuals have struggled to figure out how to proceed. It is important to understand the difficulties facing the development of such arrangements and the ways that individuals and groups have overcome those difficulties. By developing this understanding, better bridges can be built that are grounded in the hard work and experiences of others.

In this chapter, we summarize the literature on cooperation and collaboration as a starting point in understanding ways to achieve effective collaboration. We begin by outlining the basic dilemma described by social scientists when considering the topic of cooperation or collaboration. In viewing the world as a place where human behavior involves self-interest pursued through competition, they argue there is little reason that rational people will cooperate. Indeed, a range of specific barriers hampers the creation of linkages and the use of collaborative behavior in them, and the bulk of this chapter describes those barriers.

Fortunately, all is not bleak. The chapter concludes by summarizing the reasons that cooperation does take place—in theory and in reality. Much of the rest of the book provides our insights into why cooperation occurs and how it can be accomplished on the ground. While most of this chapter is about obstacles, its message is more upbeat when juxtaposed with the many cases of success. Collaboration takes effort and can be difficult, but obstacles can be overcome. By following the guideposts established by the innovators in our cases, individuals, agencies, and groups can succeed in ways that are empowering, stimulating, and productive for all.

At the outset, we want to note that not all issues are amenable to a collaborative solution, and some interests may not benefit by participating in certain collaborative efforts. Where fundamental value differences exist among the stakeholders and collaboration involves compromising those values, a negotiated approach may not be appropriate.[1] Where an organization wants to establish a precedent or influence policies broader than the situation at hand, going to court or lobbying the legislature might be more effective. Where perceived power imbalances among stakeholders mean that stronger parties see little need to compromise or otherwise involve weaker parties, it may be in neither group's interests to collaborate.[2] Weaker parties in such situations may be better off letting the conflict or problem persist in the hope that growing public awareness of the problem will shift the balance of power.[3] Where groups can do better pursuing their interests in other decision-making realms, they should do so.

But such conditions exist less often than one might think. What appears to be a disagreement over fundamental values often is revealed to be differences over preferences, and room for mutually acceptable agreements is found to exist. At other times, groups can agree to disagree about certain issues while making progress on others. When groups truly understand issues and their interests, they often begin to perceive interdependencies that balance power. So-called weak parties are often needed to support or not challenge decisions and their implementation. Other decision-making arenas may look better in the abstract, but a close examination may indicate that they cannot produce stable decisions and instead generate time- and energy-consuming uncertainty, hostility, and impasse. In many situations, collaboration is a preferred alternative if the barriers to building bridges are not overwhelming.

The Basic Dilemma

A rich literature on cooperation and collaboration describes the inherent dilemmas underlying multiparty cooperative arrangements. Much of this literature divides human interaction into two sets of behaviors: competition and cooperation.[4] It iews competition as the more "rational" behavior when viewed from the perspective of the individual. That is, when considered in the short-term perspective that characterizes most individual decision making, an individual's objectives seemingly can be best pursued through competition:

pursuing advantage, exploiting others, hiding or distorting information, etc. Inherent in this behavior are two dilemmas: the individual's long-term interests are often at odds with behavior that is rational in the short term; and the collective society will not do as well as it could if more cooperative behavior was fostered.

These dilemmas are well established in economic and natural resource management theory. Garrett Hardin described the "tragedy of the commons" in 1968, noting, "Each man is locked into a system that compels him to increase his herd without limit—in a world that is limited. Ruin is the destination toward which all men rush, each pursuing his own best interest in a society that believes in the freedom of the commons."[5] Hardin was not the first to describe this dilemma. For example, Aristotle noted, "What is common to the greatest number has the least care bestowed upon it. Everyone thinks chiefly of his own, hardly at all of the common interest."[6] Indeed, most models of human behavior, including those in economics, evolutionary biology, and much political science, presume self-interest maximization that tends to undermine the potential for cooperative interaction.

Hardin's solution to the dilemma was grim: a strong, centralized authority that could make socially beneficial rules and enforce them. "Mutual coercion, mutually agreed upon" was needed.[7] "If ruin is to be avoided in a crowded world, people must be responsive to a coercive force outside their individual psyches."[8] A competing set of analysts argued that privatizing common property was the only solution. For example, Robert J. Smith argued, "The only way to avoid the tragedy of the commons in natural resources and wildlife is to end the common-property system by creating a system of private property rights."[9] In his view, "by treating a resource as a common property . . . we become locked in its inexorable destruction."

Much of this literature employs the metaphor of the "prisoner's dilemma" to articulate the behavioral dilemma and think about managing it in complex systems of human behavior. The classic prisoner's dilemma involves two accomplices to a crime who are arrested and questioned in separate rooms.[10] Neither can talk to the other, and neither knows what the other is saying to the authorities. There is limited evidence to convict them on the major crime, so without a confession from one or the other prisoner, all the authorities can do is convict the two of them on a lesser charge. Each prisoner is promised that if he helps the authorities and confesses, he will receive a lighter sentence (while his compatriot receives the full punishment). If both confess, the value of their confessions is less, and both will receive a medium-length sentence.

Given this situation, both of the prisoners will do better by confessing than by cooperating with each other. Collectively, though, they will do worse. If they both remain silent, they will be convicted on a lesser charge with a combined amount of jail time that is less than any of the other alternatives. Individually, rational choices promoted by self-interest, mistrust, and lack of communication combine to lead the prisoners not to cooperate with each other, and hence to an individually and collectively suboptimal outcome. That is the prisoner's dilemma, and it has been used in hundreds of scientific papers to describe the dilemma of cooperation in all kinds of human interactions.[11]

Of course, most human interactions deviate from those between the prisoners in the dilemma in several critical ways: individuals usually have the ability to communicate directly with one another and often have the ability to establish the rules of the game together. In addition, most will continue to interact with each other, so that their behavior is conditioned on a presumption of future interaction. Hence, the dilemma that remains is much more subtle: How do we get individuals or groups with potentially conflicting motives to deal with each other, communicate effectively, and begin to trust one another so that areas of mutual interest can be explored?

Contained within this dilemma is a host of everyday challenges in human behavior that require people to set aside stereotypes and misperceptions and evaluate the perspective of others involved in an interaction. Many basic aspects of human behavior oppose cooperative efforts. Individuals evidence a strong need for autonomy and control that can frustrate efforts that appear to challenge both. A similar need to feel competent can threaten activities that require individuals to develop new understanding and learn new behaviors. Ironically, a strong need for love and belonging binds people to relationships that sometimes limit their prospects for change. People act aggressively to protect those relationships from outside challenge and at times get trapped by those relationships. For example, a Forest Service official might feel a need to fulfill the obligations created through a long-standing relationship with timber industry officials or timber staff officers within the agency and, as a result, might resist necessary changes in agency direction.

Biases in human judgment also influence the ability to craft collaborative approaches. For example, psychologist Max Bazerman describes the "myth of the fixed pie" as a fundamental bias of human judgment that tends to limit cooperative behavior. Based on his research, Bazerman argues that individuals "assume that their interests directly conflict with the other party's interests," even when creative win-win solutions are possible.[12] If you believe in a zero-sum world, where the gains to one party are obtained only through costs to another, then the only rational behavior is to compete for the biggest share of the fixed pie you can get. However, rarely are situations in resource management truly zero-sum. Solutions can be found that bridge disparate interests, settlements can be linked to future decisions, and issues on the table can be linked to other issues off the table. Bazerman argues, however, that fundamental biases of individual human cognition limit individuals from trying to find such mutually beneficial solutions. Their biases promote competition and stifle cooperation.

These kinds of biases against cooperative behavior exist at the societal level as well. For example, sociologists argue that cultural norms in the United States emphasize individualism to a much greater extent than those of other countries, and that our focus on individual rights and opportunities leads to neglect of collective responsibilities. Jean Pasquero, a professor at the University of Quebec, observes that in the United States, "the 'pioneering metaphor' of the individualistic entrepreneur is still a major obstacle to collaborative processes."[13] Rosabeth Moss Kanter observes, "North American companies, more than others in the world, take a narrow, opportunistic view of relationships. . . . American companies frequently neglect the political, cultural, organizational, and human aspects of the partnership."[14] A study of U.S.-Japanese joint ventures found that Japanese firms seemed more willing to invest in collaborative efforts and that American firms' focus on the short-term bottom line often precluded them from recognizing the long-term benefits of collaboration.[15]

Institutional and Structural Barriers

In practice, there are many obstacles to effective collaboration. Problems result from the institutional structure within which collaboration takes place, the ways that individuals and groups think about collaboration and each other, and the manner in which collaborative processes have been managed. These obstacles affect the willingness and capacity of people in all sectors to participate in collaborative activities. Some are easy to deal with, while others are intrinsically difficult. All combine to make collaboration challenging, but not impossible when individuals work hard at overcoming the obstacles.

Lack of Opportunity or Incentives

In many places, few opportunities for collaboration exist, and the incentives perceived by the stakeholders push them away from working together. For example, most policy processes are pulled forward by the engine of adversarial conflict. Most legislative and judicial decision making fosters win-lose outcomes, and the best strategies are the most competitive ones. Judicial processes are explicitly adversarial; groups are cast as opponents who need to make the strongest case for their own interests, and only one will win. It is in no one's interest to think of outcomes that split the difference or produce creative, win-win decisions. While legislative behavior traditionally has had a strong element of reciprocal cooperative behavior fostered through mutually beneficial compromise, activities increasingly have become adversarial as interest groups have defined the agenda, campaign financing has come to dominate the concern of legislators, and media visibility has promoted extreme partisan behavior.

As described in chapter 1, administrative decision making has taken the form of a top-down paternalistic process in which agencies listen to public concerns and generate decisions based on their sense of science and public interest. That model of decision making leaves little room for collaboration. The incentives it creates push groups to accentuate their differences rather than searching for common ground. It provides few opportunities for exploring common interests or creative solutions. For example, Dale Blahna and Susan Yonts-Shepard identified "the complex, technical planning process" adopted by the Forest Service and other public agencies as a significant barrier to meaningful public involvement.[16] During the forest planning process, they say, "Most forests met the minimum legal requirements for public involvement by using the least confrontational methods possible. The input during most of the planning process was by written or one-way communication, and interactive public involvement was used only when it was safe to do so (i.e., during issue identification) or when planners were forced to do so by public controversy."[17] Further, the two found that planners tended to bury controversial issues during the planning process rather than clearly identify them to the public. Ironically, these approaches often exacerbated conflict rather than preventing or reducing it. "By burying the issues during the planning process, the [forest planners] merely postponed having to deal with them until late in the planning process, when they were much more intense and difficult to mediate."[18]

Fragmentation of interests, power, and authority makes collaborative resource management particularly challenging. There are literally millions of decision makers influencing the long-term direction and viability of land- and waterscapes in the United States, including some eighty thousand units of government and millions of individuals and corporations. Expanding the requisite scale of activity to the multinational level compounds the problem. For example, the San Pedro River Basin in southeastern Arizona is the location of an innovative partnership among the BLM, the Defense Department, TNC, the University of Arizona, and private landowners to protect the riparian area's unusually high level of avian diversity. While the group has been successful at incorporating a variety of U.S.-based interests, it has not been able to involve managers and landowners around the headwaters of the river in Mexico. According to Dr. Hector Arias-Rojo, a hydrologist with the Institute for the Environment and Sustainable Development of the State of Sonora, "there is no mechanism right now" for a border-spanning conservation project.[19]

Conflicting Goals and Missions

Many times, the different goals and missions of participants hinder collaboration. Organizations have real differences between their goals and missions as defined by statute, tradition, and political realities, and cooperative efforts highlight conflicts between those goals. For example, management of the water resources of South Florida involves numerous agencies with conflicting missions. The South Florida Water Management District is charged with supplying drinking and irrigation water and flood control to the public and commercial interests. The mission of the Florida Department of Environmental Regulation (FDER) is to ensure water quality and wetlands protection. Those conflicting missions have led to differences in assessing the priorities for various restoration activities. The FDER argued that long-term monitoring of agricultural operations was essential, while the district pointed to studies that found no evidence of farming-induced aquifer pollution. Even after joint monitoring showed negligible amounts of herbicides and pesticides in the East Everglades water, FDER remained skeptical of the results.[20]

Sometimes such differences are inherent within an organization and frustrate efforts to foster cooperation inside the organization, as well as with others outside. Many participants in our case studies cited the Forest Service's traditional emphasis on timber production as a key barrier to building collaborative relationships with outside groups. One university biologist commented that "the 'get out the cut' mentality made it difficult to maintain funding and continuity for a threatened species management program," risking the productive relationships with other groups and agencies that had already been established in a joint project. A district ranger noted that those traditional emphases created confusing messages for agency managers. They raised "internal barriers as to our proper role and mission."

Getting agencies with conflicting objectives, traditions, and structures to cooperate is not easy. In some places, the mere number of organizations that need to be involved is problematic. As one contact explained: "We are working with essentially seven different management executives. So we have three regional foresters and four state BLM directors and two Forest Service research directors. Getting that executive steering committee to come together on [a] budget and agree on goals [and] on [the] process is something that requires constant care and feeding."

Inflexible Policies and Procedures

Policy and administrative constraints such as red tape and burdensome procedures are frequent obstacles to collaboration. Lack of administrative flexibility in agency procedures for implementing agreements frustrates many individuals in collaborative efforts.[21] For example, one Forest Service respondent lamented the "inability [of the agency] to provide coffee and snacks at meetings (we pay for these things out of our own pocket) [and the] inability to help defray travel expenses for people who are driving great distances." Many found getting authorization for "special" expenditures such as publishing a pamphlet for the local chamber of commerce to be very difficult and time consuming. Some said that not allowing "field people" to make decisions was a major barrier. Many district rangers expressed the sentiment that his or her hands were tied "because [we] lack the authority to carry out innovative ideas."

Even when procedures allow groups to move forward, red tape makes it difficult for voluntary groups outside agencies to participate in cooperative efforts. One Forest Service district ranger summarizes the situation as follows:

> Frequently these memorandums, agreements, cost-shares, and contracts involve excessive paperwork, follow-up reports, and legal language and are often too difficult to understand. Many times the agreements themselves take too long to complete, complicate a simple project, cost too much in salaries to write, and in effect scare off our cooperators and partners from this level of involvement. We elevate process, rules, and format over the needs of our partners and our agency. Time delays from process often erode the enthusiasm and decrease participation from groups that are ready to work with us now. Involving the public in our programs and management is often hampered by excessive detail and red tape.

Problems due to procedural inflexibility are not limited to public agencies. Nongovernmental organizations (both nonprofit and for-profit) are also bound by standard operating procedures. For example, Kanter observes that "because collaborative ventures often make new demands, managers involved in the relationship must be able to vary their own companies' procedures to make venture-specific decisions."[22] However, few companies or organizations are willing to provide individuals with the leeway and flexibility necessary to participate fully in collaborative problem solving.

Differences in data collection methods and analytic techniques can make it difficult for groups to combine information in useful ways. For example, the Potlach Corporation and the Forest Service have been cooperating for several years on aspects of landscape management, but different ecological classification methods, sampling protocols, definitions, and inventory data sources have affected the effectiveness and efficiency of cooperation.[23] While the development of a common system is possible, managers often are not willing to change systems when they have considerable resources invested in one particular system. "Cross-walking" information from one system to another typically decreases precision and requires a significant amount of time. Besides, different systems reflect varying management priorities and goals. Agreement on a common system requires negotiation of the purposes to be served by the system and inherently requires compromise between user objectives.

Being inflexible about criteria used to evaluate the performance of units or individuals also has been problematic. In a number of places that attempted collaboration, traditional standards for review and evaluation were applied to the new endeavors, which led to high levels of frustration for on-the-ground personnel. For example, an agency participant in one case commented about the tensions in his forest:

> We at the district feel that what we have accomplished has been a success. Rather than going through the traditional process and fighting the appeals, we have something up front that everybody agrees with and everybody thinks should be done. . . . We have a better working relationship with a lot of people in the community, which is very important. [But] the forest super-visor's office thinks that we should have accomplished more than we have. The project has taken too much time, and they haven't seen the products that they wanted to see. They think that we spent too much time dealing with internal issues among the group—what should be done, what shouldn't be done.

This individual expressed frustration at the growing inconsistencies between what the agency asked of the group at the beginning and what was expected of them at the end. At the outset, he commented, there was strong support at the forest level and above because: "It was a pretty thing. It was a pilot project, and the Forest Service was going to try something different." As time went on, however, that support languished, eventually turning to criti-cism as traditional outcome measures were imposed on the group: "A lot of what we were supposed to be doing was consensus-based management, and we don't have that option to be consensus-based if we have specific out-comes that we have to adhere to based on the money that we are getting. They give us a certain amount of money, but they don't want to know that we had a nice friendly group discussion and that we are going to go off and do this and that. They want to know what date you are going to have a com-pleted NEPA document in hand because that is the end product that they are looking for, even though the idea was to get away from that with ecosystem management."

Personnel policies also influence collaborative efforts. Many participants indicate that transfers or retirements of federal agency staff have impeded the development of productive relationships. Indeed, our study that tracked thirty-five collaborative processes over a three-to-five-year period, found that personnel changes affected 42 percent of the original cases.[24] One district ranger commented: "I've been in place three years and am just now making important contact in the six counties and two states with interests in our pro-grams. My superiors are already asking me to consider moving on." A local town official noted that because Forest Service personnel tend to move on after a few years, people "have difficulty believing they care about the community." Similarly, a staff critique of an agency recreation plan observed: "The lack of consistency of the same employees initiating, working on, and following through on a project is a point to be solved in an agency that typically moves employees around every few years." One district-level forester commented: "A lot of stuff depends on people not moving, but with the Forest Service, people are always moving."

Procedures that constrain individuals from acting in nontraditional ways are also problematic. For example, the Federal Advisory Committee Act (FACA) has been a significant barrier to communication and coordination between federal agencies and other stakeholders. While FACA was designed to regulate inappropriate relationships between federal officials and constituent groups, it has created a new set of problems in some cases. For example, one Forest Service employee thought that the biggest barriers to collaborative efforts were the "requirements of FACA, which limit the amount of work that can be accomplished with selected groups without extensive red tape," when they are combined with "the attitude and conservatism of the financial and legal advisors who review and approve these kinds of projects." Creative cooperative efforts such as those prevalent in the Applegate Partnership in Oregon have been hampered by constrained agency participation because of a fear of FACA-inspired lawsuits. (FACA is discussed in greater depth in chapter 13.)

Other government policies affect the ability and willingness of private-sector parties to participate in cooperative efforts. In particular, the Freedom of Information Act (FOIA) and the Sherman Antitrust Act raise concerns about whether corporations should share information with public agencies.[25] Uncertainty about the ownership of information and control over its ultimate distribution is seen as a disincentive to cooperation by firms. In addition, some worry that joint monitoring efforts or data sharing could be subject to FOIA requests by third parties who might use information they obtain from federal sources in litigation against the cooperating firms. The Antitrust Act restricts corporations from sharing production and inventory information for the purposes of price or production fixing in the open market. By fostering information sharing to build a common vision of the future in a landscape with multiple owners, cooperative efforts are seen by some as violating elements of the law. Uncertainty about what is allowed is described as an impediment to the participation of for-profit corporations in cooperative ventures.

Constrained Resources

Respondents in all of our studies cited resource problems as major constraints to cooperative efforts. Lack of time, money, or personnel was noted as an obstacle by respondents in the Building Bridges study more than any other factor. Such a lack was the second most often cited obstacle by both public and private managers in the Ecosystem Management study. As one public affairs officer for the Forest Service noted, "Workloads are increasing, and budgets and staffing are decreasing. Less time is available to devote towards building and maintaining relationships that lead to effective linkages." Nancy·Upham, manager of the Mono Basin National Forest Scenic Area, lamented, "How can we take on something new? The other work doesn't go away—everyone has more meetings and less time." Forest Service District Ranger Elliott Graham commented, "This is the most critical thing we can do to protect the forest. [But] funding is the biggest problem. It needs to be funded, but no one's lobbying the halls of Congress for the money."

Even when funding is available, the way that governments account for and allocate funding tends to hamper cooperative efforts. Line-item budgeting organized along traditional programmatic lines tends to make it difficult for projects that intentionally blur those lines. We received many comments like the following, from a planner and a district ranger: "A project such as this does not fit into our typical budgeting structure," and, "budgets are driven by functional area instead of by total project needs." The fact that many cooperative efforts in resource management are exercises in interagency relations and creative federalism, and involve relationships among local, state, and federal agencies, means that such efforts occur in "a regulatory 'no man's land,' in which no agency possesses clear responsibility for underwriting the process by funding or administrative support."[26] Lag times associated with the federal budget process and budgeting year by year also hinder federal agencies from planning or participating in multiyear collaborative efforts. One Forest Service employee observed, "Any additional projects can't be accomplished to a level of excellence needed to create long-lasting partnerships when we have to wait each fiscal year to see if the funding has been approved and it isn't finalized until April. Our credibility is always at risk when the funding is late or not approved."

Resource constraints are not limited to government agencies. Local citizen groups and other nonprofit organizations often face even greater constraints on the staff and resources they can devote to partnerships. In addition, members of the public participating in a collaborative effort may struggle to find the time to do the background reading and research that representatives from agencies and businesses can do as part of their jobs with support of their organizations' other employees and resources. Disparity in resources among groups can cause resentment. Ann DeBovoise, a small landowner participant in the planning process for the San Diego Multiple Species Conservation Plan, summed it up this way: "To be a participant, fight back, and protect our interests took all of our spare time, evenings and weekends. It was irritating to look around and see all these people were getting paid to do this, especially when their decisions were affecting our land and a lot of other people."

Barriers Due to Attitudes and Perceptions

Attitudes and perceptions held by individuals, groups, and organizations often push people apart rather than foster cooperation. These include a pervasive lack of trust, stereotyped "us-them" images that lead to polarization, organizational norms and culture that result in conflicts even when formal missions are not in conflict, and fear of committing to a collaborative approach because it requires new and potentially risky behavior. How we think affects how we act, and our thinking is often biased against collaboration.

Mistrust

A general sense of wariness and skepticism frequently pervades all sides of the collaboration equation due to past interactions, stereotypes, and a societal context that breeds mistrust. It is clear that the public does not trust government agencies. For example, a Forest Service public affairs officer commented, "Some individuals and organizations do not trust the Service to give fair consideration to their concerns or provide accurate or unbiased information." Another Forest Service employee noted, "I got a fair amount of bad press in the proposal and planning stage. There was distrust of the Forest Service, distrust of the Forest Service–timber alliance, and distrust of our use of the media. People just thought it was a PR move." Past interactions may also foster opposition to new initiatives, even those that are more collaborative and open to participation. One respondent noted, "The public feels they've been duped a number of times [by the Forest Service], and that's why this ecosystem management effort that we're into right now has got such a challenge socially."

The public distrusts the government in general. For example, while landowner participation on most projects is voluntary, it can be difficult to convince the public that the state or federal agencies are not involved for regulatory purposes. A respondent from a project in Colorado explained: "[There is a] fear that the feds have an ulterior motive . . . to discover threatened and endangered species to shut down operations. . . . People outside the project (area landowners, local commissioners, etc.) still are wary that ecosystem management is an attempt by government agencies to control private lands."

This lack of trust cuts both ways. Several respondents cited a lack of trust by the Forest Service toward outside groups as a barrier to collaboration. One employee referred to this attitude as "long-standing paranoia—an absolute distrust of the public and environmental groups by line officers and most management."

While much of the burden of mistrust falls on the interaction between government and the public, a lack of trust appears as a more general theme affecting all parties' perception of others. For example, farmer Connie Young, a participant in the Applegate Partnership (described in chapter 8), recalled her first reaction to the proposal that community members in southern Oregon's Applegate watershed begin working together to solve their shared problems: "At first I was really dubious. I'm like all the other farmers in this valley; I was really suspicious. My guard really went up. Anytime you suggest anything about environmentalists, we all think that you're after our land or our water or something." Even timber industry representative Dwain Cross, one of the initiators of the partnership, admitted to his initial difficulty taking that first step: "It very definitely was hard to sit down and talk to the people that . . . ultimately their bottom line was to put me out of business."

A "lack of trust" is one common reason cited for the failure of strategic alliances in the private sector.[27] Certainly, partnerships involving conservation groups with private-sector partners face a huge hurdle. In developing a partnership with Georgia Pacific Corporation, National Wild Turkey Federation official Ron Brenneman noted, "Forest products companies tend to be somewhat skeptical of new things a lot of times. . . . There was a little bit of skepticism from some of their people . . . that we are going to be a watchdog, that we are going to go to the press and make problems for them."

While a lack of trust takes several forms, including skepticism and fear, opposition to joint efforts is one of the most common. Indeed, opposition by the public and landowners was cited as the top obstacle facing projects in the Ecosystem Management study. Lack of trust also translates into suspicions about others' motives and methods, and even the veracity of each other's data and approaches to analysis. Often one group of technical experts will be suspicious of another group's interpretation of data or methods for analyzing them.[28]

Group Attitudes about Each Other

Intergroup attitudes, such as the ideas about the timber industry held by environmentalists and vice versa, are often exaggerated or false and constrain the communication that is the starting point for building bridges. Groups form identities and boundaries for a variety of sociological and psychological reasons, and those boundaries keep them apart even when they share common interests. Individuals develop cognitive models that help them understand and act on their world, and other individuals with whom they socialize reinforce those models.[29] As a result, a situation may be understood quite differently by different groups, making communication between them difficult and joint action very difficult. Kanter warns that the tendency to explain others' behavior using stereotypes "denigrates individuals and therefore diminishes their incentive to bridge troubling differences." She continues, "Stereotyping polarizes the partners, setting up us-versus-them dynamics that undermine the desire to collaborate."[30] Images of each other are reinforced by within-group socialization conducted in isolation from the other group. Since few opportunities exist to challenge such stereotypes, they can be very resistant to change.

Disciplinary biases foster the creation of intergroup attitudes that affect resource management. Members of different disciplines have different biases that influence their values and color the way they act.[31] Based on research on endangered species recovery teams, Tim Clark and Richard Reading note, "Effective information transfer is further hampered by the different ways in which professionals from different fields communicate (via jargon) and learn. . . . The highly specialized training of experts can thus prevent them from understanding other perspectives." Further, they note that experts "defend their disciplines and discount the opinions of 'outsiders.'" "The challenge," they say, "is to encourage experts to transcend their own expertise and begin to understand both their own disciplinary biases and the way that other experts and nonexperts see the world."[32]

Traditional decision-making processes reinforce group differences and make it more difficult for them to work collaboratively. As Selin and Chavez note, "Organizations that have been bitter adversaries in the past often find it impossible to reach consensus on anything."[33] In recounting a meeting he had facilitated, a Forest Service district ranger said, "Local citizenry was so polarized on forest issues that the initial meeting was volatile and emotional and characterized by name calling."

Extreme polarization can occur when intergroup attitudes are reinforced by adversarial processes. The spotted owl case in the Pacific Northwest provides a great example of such behavior as groups battled to define issues and potential solutions in the media, the public, and the minds of elected officials. Over time, their images of each other became caricatured, so that all sides viewed the others as simple-minded, ruthless, and malevolent. In fact, real differences of opinion and values separated the groups, but the process did little to help them sort those out. Instead, it magnified the pressures at the group level to compete rather than cooperate.[34]

Organizational Norms and Culture

Even when the formal objectives of organizations do not conflict, informal norms of behavior, values, and traditions lead groups to resist cooperation. Collaboration is counter to traditional management styles, appears to undermine the ability of agencies to protect and control their organizational turf, and is feared for a variety of reasons. As Selin and Chavez note, "The institutional culture within many agencies often hinders collaboration."[35] Forest Service District Ranger George Weldon summed it up: "Turf, ego, the human elements—those are the real barriers."

Collaborative management differs from many managers' perceptions of "how we do it." One Forest Service employee commented that "in the past, making linkages just hasn't been a big priority." A state natural resources agency official who has been involved in cooperative projects with the Forest Service cited barriers stemming from what he calls the agency's "tradition of doing whatever they've wanted to do." He said, "There are still the old-timers who think the public is a nuisance." Tom Quigley, manager of the Blue Mountains Natural Resources Institute, noted, "Most people are just used to doing things in a traditional way, and it's difficult to make them change to a new way." Individual patterns of behavior are reinforced by the bureaucratic behavior of organizations. One forest supervisor commented that the process gets slowed down by a "bureaucratic momentum, which works to keep things the way they are." Another noted, "I have spent as much time selling these ideas internally to the Forest Service as I have to the outside."

When these traditions combine with the need for bureaucracies to support and maintain themselves, interorganizational conflicts can occur. For example, Ben Twight documented different norms, traditions, and political outlooks as sources of antagonism between the Forest Service and the National Park Service.[36] He found that historic conflicts between the two agencies prevented the Forest Service from adapting to new political realities surrounding the establishment of Olympic National Park and led the agency to lose jurisdiction over nearly one million acres of public land.

Battles over organizational turf often hamper collaborative efforts. For example, at a site involving the FWS, the BLM, and the Alaska Fish and Game Department, one respondent stated that the problem was "maintenance of turf wars that have been in existence for thirty years." Tim Clark and Ann Harvey described problems in the early efforts to establish a multistate recovery program for the endangered black-footed ferret as partly a result of the Wyoming Department of Game and Fish's (WGF) efforts to maintain control over the program, even if it meant hampering efforts to establish the program.[37] When plans were made to expand a captive breeding program to facilities outside Wyoming, WGF refused to sign the federal recovery program unless a WGF representative chaired the committee that coordinated the breeding program. Participating institutions were forced to sign agreements giving WGF ultimate control over protocols and animals in their facilities and were precluded from receiving federal money that funded breeding activities in Wyoming.[38]

A generalized fear of collaboration on many people's part reinforces these traditional norms and behaviors. Collaboration threatens agency employees because it has "disrupted the comfort level that some employees have developed over the years," according to one agency staff member. "I mean this new style may not be easy for some people to accept," she said. One assistant district ranger stated, "There were a lot of psychological barriers on my part. I've been in the practice of silviculture for ten years. A lot of this goes against my training."

Often these attitudes are rooted in fears of criticism, failure, or losing control. One Forest Service employee expressed this feeling: "At times a fear of taking risks hampers us from building linkages. We may feel that we are giving away power or authority—fear of the unknown." In the words of a representative of a forest products interest group: "They [Forest Service employees] have been beaten up so many times they have become very timid, shy, reticent to move." Others in the Forest Service cited "fear of the public," "fear of having to change how we are doing our job," and "fear of lawsuits" as barriers to collaboration.

Some environmental groups fear collaboration and oppose it on philosophical and tactical grounds. Selin and Chavez point out, "Many of these organizations view compromise as a watering down of their mission. They often feel an obligation to set clear environmental objectives and pursue them with as much vigor and resolve as their opponent."[39] Further, many environmental groups have adopted high-profile adversarial approaches such as litigation and direct action both to increase public awareness of an issue and to gain new members and satisfy existing members.[40]

Several national environmental groups have expressed concern about or outright opposition to resolving environmental conflicts through local collaborative forums because they fear that they lack representation and the resources needed to participate effectively. For some, culture and norms of behavior are rooted in advocacy and a collaborative strategy challenges that identity. According to Sierra Club Chairman Michael McCloskey, "These ideas would have the effect of transferring influence to the very communities where we are least organized and potent. They would maximize the influence of those who are least attracted to the environmental cause and most alienated from it. . . . Industry thinks its odds are better in these forums. It believes it can dominate them over time and relieve itself of the burden of tough national rules. . . . Too much time spent in stakeholder processes may result in demobilizing and disarming our side."[41]

Lack of Support for Collaboration

Fears and conflicting organizational norms often result in lack of broad commitment from an agency to collaboration. For example, even when individuals within agencies have pushed cooperative approaches forward, a lack of support from upper levels of management has sometimes hampered their efforts. As one Forest Service employee noted, "Nothing good will happen without demonstrated commitment by Forest Service line officers. If the forest supervisor doesn't openly support a project, then it's very difficult to generate commitment down the line." Outside groups perceived many of these internal dynamics. One American Forestry Association representative argued that this lack of support stifles potential success: "The field folks want to be leaders in [cooperative initiatives], but if they don't see strong endorsements by the chief and others, projects will get off to a real slow start."

Commitment to the collaborative approach, as exemplified by follow-through of agreements, needs to be evidenced across the multiple levels of an agency. One National Audubon Society representative noted the difficult position the forest supervisor was in as a result of a collaborative planning effort: "The supervisor is caught in the middle . . . the [region] and D.C. office hated the final plan. It was like a cancer to them . . . they tried to undermine it." As a result of this lack of broad agency commitment to implementing the results of the collaboration, "it's hard to get the public involved" in other initiatives.

One example of this lack of commitment comes in the way that agency officials view collaborative activities when faced with resource shortages. While cooperative efforts can be seen by public resource managers as one way to cope with fiscal shortages by sharing resources among partners, ironically, they tend to be one of the first items cut when programs face budget shortages. The agencies often retreat to their core activities, and the time and effort needed to build bridges can be seen as nonessential.

Problems with the Process of Collaboration

Even when groups decide to attempt a collaborative approach, the process can be difficult. Since collaborative resource management fundamentally is a process of communication, problem solving, and decision making, it is not surprising that process-related barriers can greatly reduce chances for success. Ineffective management of the process, limited process skills, troubles in attaining representation of stakeholders, and difficulties in managing the interaction between the collaboration and the world around it can stymie the most well-intentioned efforts.

Unfamiliarity with the Process

Failure to appreciate the importance of the process and spend enough time on process management is an important barrier to collaboration.[42] Collaboration scholar Barbara Gray observes that "convenors and negotiators frequently underestimate the critical role of process in ensuring successful collaboration." As a result, "process considerations are frequently overwhelmed by substantive ones."[43] Forest Service District Ranger Mike Gardner admits that he had to overcome barriers within himself regarding the unconventional process used with the ecosystem-scale Negrito project in New Mexico: "It's not a traditional Forest Service process. I guarantee that. . . . I've been in the Forest Service for eighteen years and I've always had a real structured process for projects." A forest planner involved in the successful negotiation of a forest plan appeal commented, "We are not good at this. I had little or no experience, and I was heavily involved. I had no training, did a lot of groping, made mistakes." Meetings were run "not real well; no agendas, not a lot of structure." Su Rolle, interagency liaison for the Forest Service and the BLM to the Applegate Partnership, observed that collaborative processes are "a kind of awkward dance that none of us know the steps to."

Other efforts failed to understand the time required for building a collaborative effort. Agency managers who pushed to get things done so that they could report accomplishments limited the effectiveness of some efforts. As one respondent noted, "This was a rushed process and didn't involve staff because we didn't have the time. It was not truly bottom-up as it was supposed to be; more like middle-up. Now these actions go back down to the staff level, and we are hearing that some of the actions are too difficult. This input belonged early on in the process and not at this point."

Lack of Process Skills

These problems in managing cooperative efforts suggest the need for effective process management and interpersonal relations skills, yet few resource managers have been selected or trained with those skills in mind. Gray describes a long list of tasks that mediators must perform to assist in collaborative problem-solving processes, including such disparate tasks as establishing ground rules, managing data, creating a safe climate, and displaying empathy.[44]

While collaborative activities and relationships do not all need extensive third-party mediation, most need one or more people to facilitate, and in many cases the skills of the leaders of an effort to orchestrate effective processes were not up to the task. One Forest Service district ranger commented, "Natural resource managers do not typically have public relations skills to the extent that some workers in the private sector do." A Forest Service public affairs officer seconded that comment: "One thing that limits our ability is having the trained persons in people-to-people relationships in the right places to do productive work with publics." Another Forest Service staff member noted, "We have a lot of technically competent people, but they would have done something else for a career if they were interested in people. They are not the best communicators in many instances."

Collaborative processes also require managers to view their roles differently. Selin and Chavez note, "Managers need new skills to move from the expert opinion role in traditional environmental management to an empowerment role as a mediator, catalyst, or broker in the new order."[45] These changes may threaten managers' traditional views of their roles in their organization and make their jobs more demanding and uncertain. "Managers comfortable with the hierarchical decision making of public agencies [need] to cope with the lateral decisions needed to sustain effective collaboration," according to Kanter.[46] She observes, "Managers who are accustomed to acting decisively and presenting full-blown plans (in part to look good to their underlings) need to learn the patience that consensus building requires, and they need to learn to present half-formed ideas for discussion before making decisions. . . . Because the [collaborative] process was far less amenable to packaging or control by any one player, managers accustomed to always having their homework done and their case flawlessly persuasive found that such behavior could be seen as manipulative, disingenuous, and counterproductive."

Managing the Tension between the Process and the World around It

Collaborative initiatives do not take place in a vacuum. Activities "away from the table" affect the interests and strategies of participants. For example, partnerships may be strained when members of the partnership are engaged in conflicts on issues outside the partnership. One Forest Service employee participating in a collaborative initiative observed, "The region is swamped with federal old-growth management conflicts, which involve many of the same players participating here. . . . It has made continued cooperation difficult when we were in conflict in a related and overlapping issue."

Individuals representing groups in collaborative initiatives are often bound by the perspectives and procedures of those groups. One case study of a collaborative problem-solving group noted, "Despite their desire to work together and create a visionary proposal, most members were constrained by their political orientations and the viewpoints of their associations. As leaders of their groups, they represented their groups' points of view, and were reluctant, in this public forum, to challenge or change these."[47] Even leaders or high-level managers of an organization may lack the authority to commit the organization to a specific decision. In some cases, critical interest groups may be unorganized or internally divided, or it may be difficult to find a representative who can speak for the group. In other cases, relevant stakeholders may prefer to remain outside the process and refuse to participate.

Collaborative efforts can be influenced by ongoing activities in political arenas as well, initiated by either noninvolved or involved parties. At times it has been hard to keep political influences from extending into the workings of a partnership. For example, some respondents listed congressional politics as a significant barrier to their efforts to build productive relationships. Forest Service employees cast the problem as "Congress prescribing management." A National Audubon Society representative framed it as: "Things get dictated from Washington, and the supervisor gets caught in the middle." At times, agencies were constrained from acting in ways that their staff and cooperators felt appropriate because of countervailing direction from elected officials. One nonfederal individual noted that the Forest Service's "hands are often tied because of Congress. They are always answering to someone else."

Overcoming Barriers

While many obstacles need to be overcome, collaboration nonetheless does occur. Indeed, many cooperative relationships have developed that are remarkably stable. Examples of cooperative interactions include the "norm of reciprocity" in the U.S. Congress (that is, the pattern of vote trading and many other traditions of helping out a colleague and getting repaid in kind).[48] There are many examples of effective cooperatives, such as farmer's markets and cooperative nursery schools and well-managed common pool resources, including agricultural collectives that allocate scarce water resources and institutions that allocate access to fisheries.[49] University of Michigan political scientist Robert Axelrod describes a fascinating case in World War I in which soldiers in opposing trenches on the Western Front developed a "live and let live" system in which they deliberately avoided doing much harm to the other side, as long as those on the other side reciprocated.[50] This system of mutual restraint developed in spite of the direct orders of officers and the passions of war.

Why does cooperation occur? As noted above, most of the literature on cooperation views human behavior as motivated largely by self-interest, and cooperative arrangements develop because they are mutually beneficial. That is, arrangements develop between individuals so that they can pursue their own interests and because they believe that those interests can be better achieved through collective action. Relying on computer simulations and case studies, Axelrod highlights reciprocity as key to most cooperative interactions.[51] Cooperative behavior develops because the other side responds in kind. If you vote for my pork barrel project, then I will vote for yours. If you fish only your allowed catch, I will do the same. Reciprocity develops through recurrent interactions. The system of mutual cooperation in the "live and let live" situation developed because of the nature of trench warfare at the time. The same small units faced each other for extended periods of time, which changed the prisoner's dilemma situation normally present in warfare (I should shoot you because otherwise you'll shoot me) to an iterated prisoner's dilemma in which cooperative behavior could develop.

Critical to the success of these cooperative arrangements was a time frame that was long enough to allow for iterative decision making. Potential cooperators could test whether their opponents were cooperating, and relationships could be established that could foster cooperation. Axelrod highlights this as one important lesson for individuals seeking to promote cooperative behavior: "Mutual cooperation can be stable if the future is sufficiently important relative to the present. This is because the players can each use an implicit threat of retaliation against the other's defection—if the interaction will last long enough to make the threat effective."[52] Hence, those seeking to promote cooperation should "enlarge the shadow of the future" in two ways: by making interactions more durable, such as by establishing mechanisms that bind individuals or groups to each other; or by making interactions more frequent.

Axelrod points to exclusivity as one way to make interactions more frequent. Specialization, hierarchies, and ways to exclude others tend to make interactions more frequent for those who are included and make cooperation among them more likely. Indeed, "this is one reason why cooperation emerges more readily in small towns rather than in large cities."[53] Axelrod also argues that cooperation could be fostered by rewarding people more for cooperative behavior (or penalizing them for noncooperation) and by teaching people to practice reciprocity and to care more about each other. "Without doubt, a society of such caring people will have an easier time attaining cooperation among its members, even when caught in an iterated Prisoner's Dilemma."[54]

Axelrod's work clearly has some practical lessons for those seeking to promote collaborative resource management. First, it suggests that cooperative strategies once established can endure. The key is to create processes that allow the development of cooperation based in reciprocity. Such processes pay attention to relationship building so that groups can volunteer information and attempt cooperative behaviors in a way that avoids the chance of exploitation. They "enlarge the shadow of the future" by focusing on common goals above the current problem or conflict and seek to build a shared vision. Effective processes seek to provide clarity among the participants through effective communication and agreed-upon rules of interactive behavior. The groups involved in such arrangements need to guard against being exploited by knowing their own interests and by being willing to respond to competitive behavior, yet be willing to trust and work with others if those others appear to be acting in good faith. Over time, involvement in the cooperative effort begins to change the perspective of each of the individuals, so that the benefits of cooperation rise and a noncooperative strategy looks less and less attractive.

It is also the case that humans are much more complex than much of the academic literature on cooperation would have us believe. They form binding relationships that may or may not be supportive of narrow concepts of self-interest, and they act in ways that are only partly explained by their substantive interests. Processes that work at building understanding, trust, and relationships between disparate groups can help create a climate in which collaboration can develop. Some of the problematic aspects of human behavior described above can help. For example, an individual's desire for love and belonging that fosters allegiance to a polarized group also can bind him or her to multiparty collaborative relationships. A psychological need to feel competent, reinforced by norms that promote a view of agencies as technical experts, can become a positive change agent, motivating agency officials to expand their knowledge and their approaches to problem solving.

While the complexity of human behavior makes cooperation challenging, it also suggests numerous ways to promote collaboration. In the next section of the book, we explore eight themes that help explain why many of the collaborative efforts we studied were successful. Building bridges is not easy, but it is possible.

Lessons from a Decade of People Working Together

Chapter 4

Building on Common Ground

The Quincy Library Group formed in November 1992 out of the efforts of an unlikely team of partners: Plumas County Supervisor Bill Coates, a Republican who had historically supported the timber industry; Tom Nelson, a forester with Sierra Pacific Industries; and Michael Jackson, an environmental attorney based in Quincy and a self-described "environmental wacko." The three men were all concerned about the effects on the local economy of sharp declines in timber sales in the Plumas, Lassen, and Tahoe national forests. Coates says, "Our small towns were already endangered. This was going to wipe them out."

Located roughly one hundred miles northeast of Sacramento, California, Plumas County had seen accelerating conflict between environmental and timber interests as local sawmills closed. The Yellow Ribbon Coalition had formed as a grassroots effort by local timber industry workers and their families to draw attention to Forest Service policies that they viewed as the source of timber shortages. The coalition organized truck convoys in Sacramento and San Francisco in 1989 and the early 1990s to dramatize their plight. Acts of vandalism and threats to community members began in 1988, when a spiked board was found buried across a logging road. In 1989, more "nail clusters" appeared on logging roads and vandalism of logging trucks increased. At the same time, environmentalists, including attorney Michael Jackson, received death threats.

In response, Jackson wrote a letter to the editor of the *Feather River Bulletin*, arguing that environmentalists, loggers, and business needed to work together for "our mutual future":[1]

> What do environmentalists believe we have in common with the Yellow Ribbon Committee? We believe that we are all honest people who want to

continue our way of life. We believe that we all love the area in which we live. We believe that we all enjoy beautiful views, hunting and fishing and living in a rural area. We believe that we are being misled by the Forest Service and by large timber, which controls the Forest Service, into believing that we are enemies when we are not.

What can the Plumas County environmental community offer the Plumas County logging community? The Plumas County environmental community has been preparing for the forest planning process for over 10 years. . . . We know what is wrong with present Forest Service activities and we know how to fix it. We know how to do that while preserving all of the local timber industry jobs and potentially increasing them. We know how to increase competition in the forest products industry locally and how to improve the environment and quality of life for all of us. We also know that the logging community has answers to some of our common problems which we may not have considered. We know that for a complete solution to our common goals we need the wisdom of the people who have worked in the woods for the four generations that we have been logging Plumas County.

Coates, Nelson, and Jackson assembled a group that included representatives from local timber interests, environmental groups, and fishing groups, as well as county supervisors and local citizens. The group agreed to meet on neutral ground at the Quincy Public Library, some only half-jokingly noting that meeting in a library would prevent participants from yelling at each other. As trust among the participants grew, they were able to agree to a Community Stability Proposal that was based on an earlier environmental group proposal for management of the Plumas National Forest. This proposal called for more wilderness areas, selective tree cutting, and larger riparian buffers but still allowed for 200 million board-feet of timber sales a year. The QLG plan was intended to "promote the objectives of forest health, ecological integrity, adequate timber supply, and local economic stability." The plan would reorganize timber sales by local watersheds. It would prevent clear-cutting on Forest Service land or in wide protection zones around rivers and streams and would require group and single tree selection intended to produce an "all-age, multi-storied, fire-resistant forest approximating pre-settlement conditions." Under the plan, local timber mills would process all harvested logs. The plan also included provisions to reduce the amount of dead or dying plant material, which the group believed was posing a significant threat of fire to the area.

The full potential of the QLG to be a model collaborative effort was undercut by the lack of participation of some key stakeholders as well as subsequent activities of the Forest Service and the Congress.[2] Nevertheless, the early history of the group highlights several themes about the way in which it and other collaborative groups worked to build on common ground. Many successful collaborative groups emphasize a shared sense of place, defined by a specific geographic location such as a local community. They work to identify their commonalities rather than their differences. In the QLG case, a threat to the economic vitality of the community was seen as a common problem. As environmental attorney Michael Jackson notes, "These people are my neighbors. . . . I want Quincy to survive because I want to live here."

Successful partnerships also highlight common interests or find ways to bridge compatible yet disparate interests. In the QLG case, both environmentalists and loggers were against clear-cutting as a harvest method, but for different reasons. Environmentalists hated clear-cuts because of their environmental and visual impacts; loggers disliked them because they rely on lower-skilled and more automated logging practices, resulting in fewer jobs per timber sale. Both groups viewed the Forest Service and big timber as enemies. They were able to draw on their common interests, fears, and perceptions to craft a joint vision statement in a process that encouraged communication and the development of trust.

These themes—drawing on a sense of place or community, highlighting shared goals or fears, developing a common vision, and capitalizing on compatible interests—are some of the ways that successful collaborative efforts have bridged their differences to find common ground. Coupled with new mechanisms for interaction and some of the themes highlighted in later chapters, these efforts have been successful at improving environmental quality, community health, and the way people interact in many places.

A Sense of Place or Community

A sense of place can help promote collaboration.[3] In a number of successful collaborative processes, strong identification with a geographic location, biophysical feature, or community or neighborhood has provided the foundation on which the cooperative effort was built. For example, the Applegate Partnership, an effort involving industry, community groups, two federal agencies, and environmental groups in south-central Oregon, was built on a strong sense of identification with the Applegate River watershed. Logger Jim Neal, one partnership member, notes, "Once you can sit down and talk about a definable piece of land, you can get beyond philosophy, and things start to fall together."

Field Trips and Community Events

Local watershed groups often enhance a shared sense of place in their communities by taking field trips together or sponsoring community river cleanups. These efforts foster a sense of identity associated with a watershed and encourage participants and citizens to connect their day-to-day actions with the ultimate effects of those actions on river systems. For example, the Huron River Adopt-a-Stream Program in southeastern Michigan seeks "to protect the

Huron River by enabling people to learn about streams and to take care of them." Created in 1990 by the Washtenaw County Drain Commissioner's Office and the Huron River Watershed Council, a coalition of local governments and residents, the Adopt-a-Stream Program has undertaken several activities to foster a stronger sense of community and place around the watershed. For example, when one group of volunteers planted trees along the river, each child in the group "put their name on their tree," in order to "have something there they could go back to," according to program director Joan Martin.

One of the group's successful community-building activities was a gathering called RIVERfest. According to Martin, RIVERfest was used to start the Adopt-a-Stream Program and consisted of a river-long camping and canoe trip. "A number of participants from the Michigan Department of Natural Resources, a number of biologists [were included]," she says, "so we also had more than one session where we talked about 'What are we seeing? What are the issues here?' We had township and county planners there to talk about what are the problems in the county. It was a very useful orientation and discussion as a way of getting things started and making connections. I think that helped a lot in the success of the program." Martin believes that the event helped to foster a sense of community as well as "a feeling of relating" to the river. She notes that being in or on a river or stream is very different from talking about it. In her view, building a sense of place in the watershed is critical to the success of her program because, she says, "Despite all the statutes on the books that mandate water-quality protection, the laws still don't protect rivers. People do."

Places can be powerful symbols that encourage people to reframe their identity and interact with individuals or groups that historically have been viewed as "outside" their geographic, interest-based, or perceptual boundaries. Communities are composed of people whose perspectives and allegiances are framed by their differing individual identities. For example, a single community may contain employees of the Forest Service, ranchers, loggers, a president of a timber company, environmentalists, and other residents. What enables them to begin working together is their recognition of a shared identity with a place. In places like the Negrito Ecosystem in southwestern New Mexico, getting people to identify with a place and not just a set of divergent organizational or personal objectives has been critical to fostering collaborative work. As a key source of the treasured Gila River, the Negrito watershed provides a well-defined and clearly visible target for collaborative work in this rural area in Catron County. Many successful collaborative efforts are able to draw strength from physical or issue boundaries that are clear and understandable.[4]

Sometimes creating a strong project identity can motivate people to be involved. In essence, the project becomes a place. For example, Forest Service project leader Seth Diamond hired a graphic artist to develop a logo for the Beartree Challenge, a partnership to improve the ecological and social dimensions of grizzly bear management in Montana (described in chapter 10). In his view, the logo motivates participation by creating an image with which partners identify. "Now all the cooperators have logos on their caps and their equipment and such. It institutionalizes us."

A Local Focus

Programs that successfully draw on a sense of place are sensitive to issues of geographic scale. Activities that are perceived as "local" in nature are more likely to elicit identification with a place. Collaboration scholar Barbara Gray observes that "collaboration is positively enhanced by the physical proximity of the stakeholders," and that "local level initiatives can best capture the advantages associated with geography."[5] Gray notes that being from the same area makes it more likely that people will have shared values, norms, and language. In addition, when participants live in the same area, they likely interact with one another more frequently and are more likely to recognize their interdependence than participants in a collaboration who are widely dispersed.[6] When participants are from the same place, they often recognize that they will have to continue dealing with one another in the future. This situation is more likely to motivate parties to collaborate than a situation in which people are brought together for a limited amount of time and do not expect to interact in the future. To take advantage of the benefits associated with localism and a sense of place, Professor Charles Foster recommends to collaborators: "Start your region small even though your ambitions may be on a basin scale. Let it grow naturally from there."[7]

A local focus is particularly important in places where people distrust government and are concerned about private property rights. The efforts of the National Park Service to affect land use adjacent to the Rocky Mountain National Park have been hampered by such attitudes. Due to heavy development pressure surrounding the park, The Wilderness Society listed Rocky Mountain as one of the ten most endangered national parks in the country. In response, the park created an outreach position devoted to working with adjacent communities. In carrying out that job, Larry Gamble has learned that efforts to "influence lands outside the park cannot be dictated from above." He says, "People want to know if what we are doing is coming out of Washington or is coming here locally. If it's something that is locally initiated, they're a little more inclined to want to get behind it than if it's something that's coming out of Washington, D.C."

People identify with a "local concern" and feel positively about it, unlike initiatives imposed from elsewhere. The Tensas River Basin Initiative in northeastern Louisiana has been successful in part because it is well grounded in local institutions and staffed by local people. Over 80 percent of that region of the lower Mississippi River Valley has been converted to row-crop agriculture, producing significant water-quality problems and loss of species diversity and abundance. At the same time, high unemployment and poverty characterize the economy of the region. In response, a collaborative initiative has developed that involves local groups, state and federal agencies, and The Nature Conservancy. Critical to the success of the initiative is the fact that a local, nongovernmental group, the Northeast Delta Resource Conservation & Development District, has taken the lead. According to its project coordinator, "The fact that I was a local boy, grew up here, knew lots of folks, and the fact that I didn't have a government uniform on, made all the difference in the world."

As a strategy to motivate involvement, a local focus creates dilemmas when regional or national groups have legitimate interests. But those dilemmas can be managed by involving state or federal agencies that represent nonlocal concerns or by fostering local-scale initiatives that include representatives of regional or national interests. For example, on the island of Molokai, Hawaii, The Nature Conservancy manages a preserve that is bordered by private, state, and federal lands. To achieve its conservation goals on an island-wide scale, TNC has worked to foster understanding and support from the local community, in part by training and hiring local people to work in preserve management. It also formed an advisory committee made up of respected leaders in the community dedicated to protecting the island's natural heritage. According to the program director, "If you want [support] from the community, you have to hire people from the community, someone who knows the community and thinks like the community. . . . I was born and raised here, and this helped me get a foothold here, because people are cautious when new groups come in." These kind of arrangements create two-way flows of information: local concerns and realities can be communicated to TNC, while the Conservancy's sense of the problems and needs can be conveyed to local people.

Clearly, a balancing act is needed to define a sense of place that is large enough to encourage integration of different interests yet local enough to motivate involvement. But many initiatives have been successful precisely because they were able to link association with the local community to a larger sense of place.

Shared Problems or Fears

A shared sense of purpose is equally motivating. Many successful initiatives have sought common ground by focusing on shared problems or fears. Such threats are highly mobilizing. They create a sense of urgency and a common target that allow organizers to generate resources and obtain the commitment of disparate parties to face a common problem.[8] When faced with a common enemy such as an economic downturn or the degradation of a valued resource, people often pull together, as was the case when a jet airport was proposed for New Jersey's Pinelands in the mid-1970s.[9] In another example, a proposed water development project that would pump groundwater from the San Luis Valley in Colorado to urban areas along the Front Range brought a diverse group of stakeholders together to fight the project and protect the area's resources. As one result of this, valley residents formed the Partners for Wildlife Program and increased protected wetlands in the valley by twelve thousand acres in four years.[10]

A Sense of Crisis

The results can be particularly powerful when a sense of crisis associated with a threat overlaps with a sense of place. That situation motivated the formation of the Oak Openings Working Group in northwestern Ohio in 1992. The Oak Openings represent an increasingly rare type of ecosystem: an oak savanna community. This one survives on a belt of sandy soil that covers more than 130 square miles near Toledo. The region provides a home to 179 rare plants and animals, more than one-third of Ohio's rare species. TNC recognized the Oak Openings as one of the nation's "last great places," as land conversion to agriculture and development, hydrological alteration, and fire suppression have destroyed and degraded habitat and allowed non-native species to invade the area.

While portions of the area had been protected by the state of Ohio, TNC, and the Toledo Metroparks District, the Working Group was formed to coordinate the actions of those agencies and to reach out to private landowners and other local governments. The group has been successful in mobilizing a broad coalition of interests in part because of a shared sense of a clear and present threat to the ecosystem. According to Metroparks official Michelle Grigore, who helped form the group, the Oak Openings face multiple threats from increasing development in the area, and that "motivates people to do something now if they think it's going to disappear."

In many other places, the threat faced by a community has been a declining economy coupled with a degraded environment, which resulted in threats to the community's way of life. As described above, that was the situation in the Quincy–Plumas County region in Northern California: sawmills had closed; private timberlands were cut over; national forests, expected to take up the slack, were under pressure to reduce timber supplies; and job losses led to increased anxieties and hostilities in communities such as Quincy and Greenville. As a response to the atmosphere of escalating mutual recrimination, the Quincy Library Group was viewed as one potential way out of a bad situation. Indeed, the sense of a shared problem was expanded by shared perceptions of the Forest Service as a significant source of the problem. It was the agency's emphasis on clear-cutting as a harvest mechanism and an increasing reliance on larger, out-of-region contractors that caused community and environmental disruption. In many ways, the different interests in Quincy had little to lose to attempt a collaborative solution, but the perception of the Forest Service as a common enemy helped provide a starting point to their discussions.

Other Fears

A variety of other concerns have motivated collaborative efforts. Often, organizations join collaborative initiatives because they fear losing control over the direction of an issue. In several cases, agency personnel have helped to form cooperative working arrangements with stakeholders as a means of wresting control over the direction of resource management from a state of impasse. In others, groups have participated because they feared that without their involvement, the cooperative effort would take charge and their interests would be left behind.

In many, a shared sense of uncertainty—fear of what could be—has provided the impetus for groups to attempt collaboration. For example, one of the classic negotiated solutions to a resource management conflict occurred in the Grayrocks Dam case in the late 1970s. A diverse set of parties, including farmers, environmental groups, state officials, and representatives of a large power company, were able to work together to develop an acceptable compromise in this complex dispute over the construction of a dam and reservoir on the Laramie River near Wheatland, Wyoming.[11] After first pursuing litigation, the parties involved eventually worked together to develop a solution while the federal Endangered Species Committee (the so-called God Squad) was considering an exemption for the project from the Endangered Species Act. All parties faced considerable uncertainty about the outcome and decided that a negotiated settlement that they controlled was better than a decision imposed from Washington.

Shared Goals or Interests

Collaborative management does not rely only on fears and threats to motivate involvement. Collaboration is natural when stakeholders recognize that they share interests or goals. For example, the Mill Creek Canyon management partnership between Salt Lake County, Utah, and the Forest Service (introduced in chapter 2) was built on shared goals. The canyon, a popular recreation area less than an hour's drive from Salt Lake City, is a mix of national forest and private and county lands. Over the years, it had seen heavy recreational use, vandalism, and significant degradation of Mill Creek's water quality. "When I started here in 1989, I told friends it was like working in the ruins of Rome," said Jim White, Salt Lake Ranger District's recreation forester. "It was embarrassing to go up there as a manager." Critical to the development of the innovative resource-sharing arrangement that raised funds and allowed better management of the canyon was the perception of shared goals among disparate federal and local agencies. The Forest Service and the county departments of Public Works, Parks and Recreation, Health, and Sheriff's Office all perceived the need to undertake environmental restoration activities to improve water quality while providing higher-quality recreation and decreasing public safety concerns. The memorandum of understanding they developed noted, "The county . . . and the Forest Service . . . have a mutual interest in the protection and management of Mill Creek Canyon."

The Oak Openings project in Ohio also illustrates the power of realizing shared goals. According to project coordinator Michelle Grigore, the partnership "has blossomed and grown, and we try to work together in other ways when we can." The Working Group has grown to include more partners, including the Ohio state Division of Wildlife, which is interested in the Karner blue butterfly restoration, and Bowling Green State University, which sponsors restoration projects carried out by its students. Grigore emphasizes that working together collaboratively does not really require members to dramatically change the way they do things, noting, "All these agencies were working towards the same thing, and it was just getting everybody to sit down and realize we're all working towards the same goals." At the same time, it was critical for the multiple partners to realize that they had to work together to accomplish some of their shared goals, such as effectively reaching out to the public and restoring Karner blue butterfly populations.

Superordinate Goals

Sometimes, to find shared goals, groups are forced to look for objectives above the current conflict. That is, what starts as a battle over a specific proposed action may evolve into a broader look at a community's future. Fostering cooperation by articulating such "superordinate goals," goals above the current conflict, is consistent with classic research on cooperation carried out in the 1950s.[12] Researchers fostered conflict between cabins at a summer camp and then tried to assess the effectiveness of different ways to overcome the conflict. What worked best was to introduce a goal superordinate to the existing conflict. (For example, the camp's water system broke, and the boys had to pull together to fix it. Also, when competing cabins of boys went on a trip together, their bus broke down, so that they had to work together to find a way to get back to camp. The larger and immediate superordinate goal enabled the boys to collaboratively solve those problems despite preexisting differences on other issues.)

Grounding its Upper Stony Creek Watershed project on superordinate goals has helped the Natural Resource Conservation Service restore groundwater recharge and riparian habitat in this area adjacent to the Mendocino National Forest in Northern California. About thirty local ranchers, who own about half of the private land in the watershed, have signed long-term contracts with NRCS to follow certain management practices on their land to protect environmental resources. NRCS Project Coordinator Wendell Gilgert believes that the project has been successful because he and his staff have been able to gain ranchers' trust over time and involve other agencies active in that part of the county. According to Gilgert, his staff has been lucky enough to find ranchers who are willing to reach for a common goal and to take risks to do that. In addition, Gilgert says that the best way to get ranchers and staff from different agencies to work together is to "find common ground." He continues, "That's not hard to do. We all like to breathe clean air. We all like to be around our families. We all like uncontaminated food. [When] we start talking about the similarities, the differences kind of melt away, so we concentrate on the kinds of things we all agree on, and we try to work our way a little at a time on the differences."

The effort by Forest Service District Ranger Pete Tennis to collaboratively develop a recreation plan for the Tongass National Forest's Petersburg Ranger District in southeast Alaska was an innovative and ultimately successful attempt to overcome a history of mistrust and conflict among diverse area residents and the Forest Service. He purposely decided in 1989 to embark on an uncontroversial project, which would help build positive relationships within area communities. By appealing to residents' interests in a goal separate from existing conflicts over timber harvesting, he hoped that polarization and mistrust would diminish, enabling them to progress in the future on more conflict-laden issues.

Common Vision and Mission Statements

While shared goals and interests seem to be an obvious reason for collaborative work, it is not always obvious that goals are shared. Groups or agencies that have not interacted or that have relationships based on disagreements may simply not understand that they share goals, yet perceiving common goals is critical as a starting point in a problem-solving process. Establishing communication between these groups and encouraging them to articulate their interests and concerns can allow points of commonality to emerge. Such processes may simply try to shift parties from describing their positions to articulating their underlying interests. Often they involve developing a common vision or mission statement.[13]

One tool that mediators often use in assisting groups in a conflict situation is a joint problem statement, which seeks to foster agreement on the underlying objectives of the group. These statements are often framed as the question "How can we _____ while also _____?" For example, participants in the Owl Mountain Partnership, a collaborative ecosystem management effort in north-central Colorado, asked themselves, "How can we serve the economic, cultural, and social needs of the community while developing adaptive long-term landscape management programs, policies, and practices that ensure ecosystem sustainability?" The process of filling in the blanks encourages parties to identify their underlying concerns in a way that makes them amenable to a collaborative problem-solving effort.

Common vision, mission, or problem statements can lead participants in a collaborative initiative to imagine solutions to shared problems. The effort of putting together a vision statement produces a sense of accomplishment for the group and starts to build relationships and faith that the group can work together. For example, in mid-1992, the Coalition for Unified Recreation in the Eastern Sierra (CURES) (described more fully in chapter 6) undertook a futuring process with the goal of developing a vision statement of where and what recreation in the Eastern Sierra should look like in the year 2010. This process had its share of tension and conflict. Environmentalists were wary of CURES's motives and feared increased tourism. They had become involved to ensure that environmental protection was stressed as a coalition priority, while the region's tourism industry was driven to expand its capacity as much as possible to attract tourists to the area.

Nancy Upham, manager of the Mono Basin National Forest Scenic Area and facilitator of the initial meetings, sought common ground by focusing the group on a common vision statement. She asserted that the region's carrying capacity should not be exceeded, and the group discussed the concept of marketing some areas and "de-marketing" others that had exceeded carrying capacity for tourists. As the result of this protracted effort, Upham says that there is "true ownership in the final product by divergent groups who may have never agreed on anything ever before." In August 1993, CURES celebrated the completion of its vision statement. The cornerstone of the agreement was that "a sustainable economy is dependent upon a sustainable environment." The coalition's mission statement reads: "CURES is dedicated to preserving the Eastern Sierra's natural, cultural, and economic resources and enriching the experiences of visitors and residents."

Some mission statements highlight improvements in the way that people or groups relate to each other as precursors to improved ecological or community health. For example, the Oak Openings Working Group statement emphasizes improvements in the process of interaction between the diverse landowners and stakeholders involved in conservation of the Oak Openings. The Working Group's mission is to "encourage cooperation, communication, and education among the local community, public agencies, and private organizations in order to create a better understanding of and appreciation for the importance of conservation of the Oak Openings."

One interesting technique used by a collaborative effort to identify a shared vision occurred in a partnership known as the ESL Action Research Project (ESLARP). ESLARP is a decade-long partnership between faculty and students at the University of Illinois and the residents and community-based organizations in East St. Louis, Illinois. Project facilitators gave participants disposable cameras and asked them to take pictures of ten things they liked in their community and ten they did not like. From the information revealed in the photographs, the group was able to identify shared community development objectives.[14]

Compatible Interests

Not all interests or objectives are shared. Indeed, the remarkable diversity of groups interested in and affected by resource management ensures that many different interests will be brought to the table. But groups can work collaboratively in ways that bridge their different interests. Indeed, the literature on negotiation argues that one of the primary ways that parties in conflict can find a settlement is to make exchanges between things they each value, but value differently.[15] This reality is one of the more powerful dimensions of face-to-face negotiation: Since groups are negotiating because of their differences, they can use those differences to craft effective solutions.

Sometimes trading on differences is simply a matter of reciprocity: "I'll support you on this if you support me on that. You can have an off-road vehicle trail here if we have a hikers-only trail over there." Other times, getting to a win-win solution involves integrating the different interests in a way that makes all parties better off. In negotiation parlance, such solutions find "joint gains" by "expanding the pie."[16] That is, rather than divide the "fixed pie" on the table at the start of the negotiation, through creativity they find solutions that make all parties better off than they would be without a collaborative solution. "You say you need a certain level of development at the proposed resort to be profitable. We say we're interested in the jobs but oppose the development because it would damage a historic area. Can you develop a portion of the site at higher density, permanently protect the historic area, and include an interpretive center that explains local history to visitors and uses local people as interpreters and guides? Maybe that would make both of us better off."

Common Goals, Different Benefits

Many collaborative efforts are able to capitalize on compatible yet different interests. The Kirtland's warbler partnership in the jack pine forests of central Michigan (introduced in chapter 2) takes advantage of different interests. While most of the partners are interested in recovery of the Kirtland's warbler, they receive different benefits for participating in warbler management. The potential for warbler-based ecotourism has made local communities "recognize the birds' value, the role they can play, and the uniqueness of this to their communities," according to Forest Service biologist Rex Ennis. An annual Kirtland's Warbler Festival began in 1995 and draws many tourists and bird watchers. Initially, the local chamber of commerce sponsored the event, but now a local community college is sponsoring it. The Forest Service is involved in the planning and implementation of the festival.

The partnership is also successful due to the support of the timber industry. Warblers are dependent on an ecosystem that relies on periodic fires to maintain an early successional jack pine forest, but the extensive matrix of seasonal homes makes it difficult for managers to recreate a fire regime. Instead, trees are removed through selective logging that improves habitat for the warbler while creating commercial opportunities. While warblers will not use an area after the trees are twenty years old, the Forest Service manages stands until they are fifty years old so that they can be commercially harvested. They manage enough area through this treatment that adequate habitat and logging opportunities are both maintained.

Other groups benefit from the partnership in other ways. Former Michigan Audubon Society executive director Terry Yonker perceives tangible benefits to his group: "We live and die by membership concern over our activities. It helps us to be identified with a project like this." The partnership gave Audubon publicity by having its name and logo on booklets and interpretive signs and assured Audubon members that the partnership is actively working to protect endangered species in the state. Similarly, the Forest Service receives benefits from the partnership beyond its statutory goals of protecting listed species: positive public relations and funding to complete projects that would otherwise not be funded.

Different Goals, Compatible Ways to Achieve Them

Other collaborative efforts allow groups to accomplish objectives that are different from one another yet in a way that is compatible with those diverse interests. The partnership between the National Wild Turkey Federation and Georgia Pacific (GP) Corporation described in chapter 2 provides a good example. GP staff members receive training they would not otherwise get, while NWTF's objective of building wild turkey populations is met while building membership. Georgia Pacific sees an economic advantage to the program as well. As GP communications manager Greg Guest explains, "A lot of our land is leased to various private hunting clubs. So obviously, the better the turkey population, the better it is for the hunting clubs to lease our land. And they can help as well with the process. They might go out and do a planting in an area that used to be a logging deck, where the logs were brought out of the woods and were inventoried and stored before they were shipped off to a mill. Or plant an old logging road that is no longer being used with grasses or saw-tooth oaks from which the acorns are good turkey food. I'm sure a lot of members of the hunting clubs are also members of the National Wild Turkey Federation."

NWTF staff member Ron Brenneman stresses the importance of clear communication about motives and benefits at the beginning of the process to develop these kinds of partnerships: "You need to make sure up front that the companies understand what your motives are, what you want to get out of this agreement, and why you are entering into it." He adds, "You need to let the company know why or how it is going to benefit them. Any partnership has to be a two-way street, and both parties have to benefit from it in some way. And if they don't, it won't last, or it won't be effective."

Incorporating Other Issues to Find Common Ground

Sometimes groups can bridge their differences by linking other issues and concerns into an agreement. The partnership that evolved between The Nature Conservancy and the town of Guadalupe, California, began in response to TNC's efforts at preserve management but evolved into finding ways to promote the social and economic development of Guadalupe. As described more fully in chapter 9, TNC's initial efforts to manage the Guadalupe-Nipomo Dunes Preserve, twenty-five miles south of San Luis Obispo, California, were disastrous. By building entrance gates and charging an entrance fee, TNC effectively alienated most members of the neighboring community. The symbol created was of "a place apart," not a place that was a valued component of the local environment.

To turn around the situation, TNC staff started to build on a sense of community and capitalize on compatible interests. After rescinding the entrance fee, TNC started recruiting volunteers to help build a footbridge across a lake and a boardwalk across the wetlands and dunes. The bridge improved access to the preserve while better protecting the fragile landscape, and it also served as a symbol of TNC's efforts to establish closer ties with the community. In another important outreach effort, TNC decided to locate its visitor center for the preserve on the main street in Guadalupe instead of at the preserve. TNC preserve manager Nancy Walker explains, "The people who live in Guadalupe have a really strong identity for that town. And they want to see it revive. So what we are doing is looking at spending this money that we have in the town to meet both their needs for renovation and our needs for connecting with the community to get some good conservation going on. So it serves a lot of different purposes."

TNC also worked with local officials to create a new nonprofit organization that would manage the center to meet the needs of both TNC and the town and become part of the community. Walker notes, "From the beginning we have talked about how this center would function as a place where kids could come for after-school programs. They don't have enough interesting things to do after school, and there is a gang problem developing in Guadalupe. The center can provide a place for youth, which is definitely a common value among all the players."

The Dunes Discovery Center opened in a storefront in downtown Guadalupe in October 1996 as a joint project of TNC, the Guadalupe Historical Society, several city agencies, People for Nipomo Dunes, and the local chamber of commerce. In addition to serving as a visitor center for the Guadalupe-Nipomo Dunes Preserve, the center sponsors adult education classes and art and environmental education classes for local school kids. TNC hired a community relations representative to oversee the Dunes Discovery Center and develop outreach programs to the community.

Rennie Pili, the mayor of Guadalupe, strongly supports the visitor center project. He notes, "It will help to get tourist traffic. Right now, there's not a whole lot to attract tourists to Guadalupe. We envision a bike trail from the center to the dunes and a lot of educational opportunities for the schools and the public." Walker expresses hope that locating the visitor center downtown will "tie the community more to the dunes, promoting the need for stewardship of the dunes to preserve the community." She says, "We want to strengthen the connection . . . that the dunes are part of the reason that [Guadalupe] is such a great place to live."

By crafting a partnership based on common and compatible interests, the economy of Guadalupe and the rare plants and endangered least tern of the dunes are all benefiting. Other collaborative initiatives are producing similar benefits. By building on a sense of place or community, responding to common threats and problems, looking for shared goals and interests, and creating images of a shared future, they are finding common ground among people who never thought it possible.

Chapter 5

Creating New Opportunities for Interaction

The Elkhorn Mountain Range in Montana is small and isolated by western standards, containing 250,000 acres surrounded by low-elevation flatlands. Though it contains several ecosystem types—including mountain grasslands, various forest types, and riparian zones—the entire range is considered one contiguous landscape type, with similar features throughout. Despite this distinct nature, the mountain range is managed by a variety of landowners: the Forest Service oversees 160,000 acres in two national forests and three ranger districts; the Bureau of Land Management manages 70,000 acres; and private landowners own the remaining 20,000 acres. Also, the Montana Department of Fish, Wildlife, and Parks (FWP) has jurisdiction over wildlife in the entire region.

According to Jodie Canfield, Elkhorn coordinator for the Deerlodge and Helena National Forests, this mix of landownerships has led to conflicting management practices, even within the Forest Service: "The three ranger districts all operated on their own, with little cooperation or even communication between them." Communication between the other agencies was even less common. Because of this lack of coordination, the agencies often worked at cross-purposes. With each agency operating under different mandates and working toward different goals for the land, holistic and consistent management of the mountain range was impossible.

A bold attempt to change the situation began in August 1992, when the Forest Service, BLM, and FWP signed a memorandum of understanding titled "An Agreement on Working Together." The MOU designated the entire

Elkhorn Mountain Range as a "cooperative management area" and set forth a process structure for interagency cooperation and substantive management goals. The process involved the creation of two new positions in the Forest Service and several interagency teams and committees. The Elkhorn Steering Committee is composed of line officers in each of the three agencies: forest supervisors of the Helena and Deerlodge National Forests, BLM's Butte district manager, and the FWP Wildlife Division administrator and regional supervisor. Its purpose, according to the MOU, is to "provide coordinated and cooperative management direction, provide leadership for progressive resource management and development of policy, facilitate implementation of management activities and resolution of issues." The implementation group acts on the decisions of the steering committee. It includes employees from the three agencies representing a variety of professional disciplines and is responsible for overseeing on-the-ground management of the Elkhorn.

One way cross-boundary cooperation is being promoted is through a new Forest Service position of Elkhorn ranger, a ranger responsible only for the Elkhorn Mountains. In addition, a full-time Elkhorn coordinator, currently Canfield, works for the Elkhorn ranger and serves "as a public and internal contact person as well as staff to three district rangers." She also chairs the implementation group and coordinates all activities of those involved in Elkhorn management. As coordinator, Canfield says, "I work for all the agencies. The Forest Service pays my salary, but I consider all the agencies to be my employers." Though this scheme may sound confusing, it works well in large part because a common coordinator manages it. As Canfield emphasizes, "It works okay because *everything* goes through me."

The substantive goals of the MOU are based entirely on ecosystem management principles. The MOU states: "Sustaining ecological systems is the umbrella concept in management of the Elkhorn." The document further states that native species management will be emphasized, and that "wildlife values are a strong consideration in evaluating all land use proposals." The MOU contains a vision statement that captures, as the committee put it, "a picture of the desired future." The vision statement reads:

> The Elkhorn Cooperative Management Area is a unique, cooperatively administered geographic area, where management of all lands within public ownership emphasizes sustainable ecosystems. . . . On public lands, a sense of "naturalness" is the pervasive quality of the landscape. Mining, timber, grazing and other land use occur, but are mitigated such that they do not appear dominant. . . . There is a diversity and abundance of wild animals . . ."

The interagency group completed several major projects under the initial MOU and then developed an updated MOU to move the agencies out of the planning phase and into an implementation phase. Among its major initiatives was a joint analysis of the Elkhorn Mountain Range that examines the existing condition of wildlife, water, soil, vegetation, and natural disturbance regimes in the three major watersheds in the Elkhorn Mountain Range. It also establishes goals for the desired future condition of resources in the three watersheds, compares existing conditions with those goals, and identifies management opportunities for reaching those goals. The landscape analysis is used to develop an annual work plan that guides the three agencies' management activities in the Elkhorn Range. The group also developed a joint travel plan for the whole mountain range that determines which roads will be available for public motorized use and in what seasons the roads will be open. The agencies are also completing prescribed burns to improve bighorn sheep habitat, eliminating roads, and implementing new grazing allotment management plans that better protect riparian resources.

Canfield notes, "I've been in this job for over six years, and having the MOU is the difference between night and day in the way we are operating." She says, "The MOU gave us the framework to work together across agency boundaries. It defines the roles of different groups and individuals that are involved in the Elkhorns and how communication and coordination will flow." However, she adds, "I don't think it is so much the document as the ideas behind it that really make it work."

In the Elkhorn Mountains, a common set of issues concerning federal and state agency managers had not been addressed because there was no mechanism to do so. By creating a coordinator position and an MOU, structures were put in place to facilitate interaction, coordination, and collaborative problem solving. Indeed, the success of many collaborative processes can be attributed quite simply to establishment of an opportunity for interaction between parties where one did not previously exist.[1] These opportunities have taken numerous forms. Many have relied on efforts at outreach by lead agencies, groups, or individuals. Some have employed coordinators so that there is someone "minding the store" who can serve as a point person and facilitate connections between groups and individuals. Others have developed MOUs, advisory committees, and nonprofit organizations. While it has been necessary to carefully manage what goes on in these structures, creating opportunities for interaction where none existed was a big step in the right direction.

Working at Outreach through Communication

Most collaboration starts with efforts to establish new lines of communication. "Communicate, communicate, communicate" might be a time-honored solution to disagreements and conflict, stressed by grandmothers and kindergarten teachers. Indeed, Warren Bennis and Patricia Biederman's study of six collaborative efforts that the authors termed "Great Groups" found that "all

Great Groups share information effectively."[2] But doing that takes time, effort, and skills that are often in short supply.

In some situations, communication is not occurring when and where necessary. Although The Nature Conservancy held public meetings about its management plans for the Guadalupe-Nipomo Dunes Preserve (discussed at the end of chapter 4 and described further in chapter 9) in several California cities, it had never held a meeting or done any other significant outreach in the community of Guadalupe, the community closest to the dunes. As a result of the lack of communication with the community, TNC staff did not have even a rudimentary understanding of the community's concerns and were surprised by the community's hostile reaction. The group realized its error following conversations initiated by local community leaders.

In other situations, mechanisms for communication exist but might not be effective at transmitting information accurately and effectively. As described in chapter 3, problematic policies and personalities or the inertia of past practices or relationships can limit communication. All can have a sclerotic effect on the flow of information that can be overcome by creating new relationships or opportunities for interaction, or breathing new life into old ones. By reaching out to talk to others in new or different ways, individuals and groups have been able to start listening, share concerns, and provide a new opportunity for joint problem solving and interaction.

Outreach by individuals or groups has begun many successful collaborative efforts. In the case of the cleanup of the Russian River in Northern California, outreach began with the efforts of Rebecca Kress, a resident of Hopland, California, and a bartender at the Mendocino Brewing Company. Kress undertook a broad set of creative outreach strategies to reach different segments of the community. She also produced a video that she shows at schools and even recorded a song about the river. As a result, the annual cleanup has attracted diverse participants that Kress describes as "a little bit of everybody," including members of the Ukiah Rotary Club, doctors, lawyers, farmers, teachers, recreationists, environmentalists, employees from large companies like AT&T and Wal-Mart, and many other local residents.

In the Beartree Challenge (described in chapter 10), Forest Service project leader Seth Diamond reached out to a broad array of cooperators in order to improve the "ecological and social habitat" of the grizzly bear. The effort sought to improve bear habitat in this area of northern Montana through a variety of restoration techniques. The social habitat was to be improved by creating a partnership among the diverse set of interests involved in the grizzly bear controversy and by undertaking extensive public education and media campaigns. The Forest Service held on-the-ground tours of the project's habitat improvement projects. The high-tech timber harvesting equipment, which featured robotics and had never before been used in the United States, was especially popular, drawing visitors from all over the country. The project also featured "community links" with Boy and Girl Scout troops, elementary and high schools, and universities, as well as ties with environmental education programs such as Project Learning Tree and Project Wild. Some forty or fifty presentations were made in Montana and in Washington, D.C., to educate a wide array of people, from congressional members to schoolchildren.

Forest Service staff also used extensive outreach in the Tongass National Forest in Alaska to collaboratively develop a region-wide recreation plan for the Petersburg Ranger District. The first step of the process was to canvass area communities for their ideas on desired recreation projects. The Forest Service team embarked on an aggressive and highly visible public involvement campaign. It used a variety of mediums to inform the public about the opportunity to share their ideas: brightly colored flyers were sent to all post office box holders, and local television and radio stations and newspapers were used to spread the word. A series of public meetings were also held. According to district forester Maria Durazo-Means:

> We found out that traditional scoping methods such as public meetings were not very effective, so we took a different approach. We tried nontraditional methods such as talking with people informally at post offices and grocery stores, and visiting schools. This enabled us to reach a segment of the public that normally doesn't attend public meetings. . . . We kept the recreation plan in the public eye through the use of various media—television, radio, CB radio to reach fishermen, information brochures to post office box holders, and posting flyers up around town. Eventually, it paid off and people started talking to us.

Durazo-Means says, "[The] community opened up to us. . . . They were excited." Lonnie Anderson, mayor of Kake, agrees, describing the process used by the Forest Service as an "excellent scheme to get involvement." According to Anderson, the "Forest Service coming out one-on-one" to talk to the villagers created "much more enthusiasm" for the plan and helped to generate "consensus." These grassroots techniques proved so successful in Kake that they were also employed in Petersburg, via tables at the post office and at the Octoberfest art show. More than eight hundred ideas for recreation projects were generated through these techniques.

Part of the success of the southeastern Alaska recreation planning effort resulted from starting outreach at the beginning of the effort. While agency staff often fear interacting with the public early in an initiative before they have a specific proposal or decision to air, efforts that leave public outreach to the end work with a self-limited set of information and create a sense of estrangement and lack of ownership that can damage program implementation. One of the key lessons TNC preserve manager Nancy Walker identified from her experience at the Guadalupe-Nipomo Dunes is including money in project budgets for community outreach from the very start. Walker recommends, "You need to have some money up front to do the work with the local communities before you launch your plan. Money for outreach. You don't add outreach on later, like we're doing now. You should do it first." Karen Wood, TNC's community relations representative in Guadalupe, agrees recommending, "Don't try to implement your program without gaining consensus or at least recognition from the other people involved."

Walker and Wood also stress that outreach activities are not one-way flows of information. Rather, successful outreach activities create two-way flows of information, in which citizens learn about the plans of an agency or group, while the agency or group simultaneously learns about the interests and aspirations of the community. Too often, outreach is viewed by agencies as public relations or marketing—selling the agencies' values or products—when, in fact, its best use is as the basis for effective exchange of ideas in both directions.

Establishing New Structures

Organizational, political, or social arrangements that provide opportunities for interaction among members of different groups or organizations can help set the stage for collaborative problem solving. These arrangements can include very formalized mechanisms, such as advisory committees that are formally chartered under the Federal Advisory Committee Act. They can also include simple, informal arrangements, such as a federal or state land manager making an effort to eat lunch once a week at a diner that attracts a large number of local ranchers.

In the successful examples of collaboration that we studied, arrangements included informal relationships, project coordinators, memoranda of understanding between organizations, advisory committees, nongovernmental organizations, and jointly managed facilities. Critical to the effectiveness of these structures was that their core missions included fostering outreach, interchange, and decision making among diverse interests. They established points of contact that were visible and accountable to outside groups. Ultimately, they created a structure through which relationships developed among diverse partners.

Informal Relationships

Some of these structures are simply relationships between individuals that allow interaction between different interests. For example, Janice Brown, conservationist and owner of a guest lodge on the Henry's Fork of the Snake River, and Dale Swenson, executive director of the Fremont-Madison Irrigation District, cofacilitate the Henry's Fork Watershed Council, a multiparty group working to improve watershed management in this segment of the Yellowstone ecosystem in eastern Idaho. The relationship between these two individuals prevented a problem from boiling into conflict in the summer of 1995. As reported in *High Country News*, "Normally by midsummer, farmers along the Henry's Fork are irrigating, thereby pulling cooler, deeper water from Henry's Lake into the river. But continual rain had made irrigation unnecessary, and by July, water in the Henry's Fork was heated to near lethal levels for trout."[3] The relationship already established between Janice Brown and Dale Swenson facilitated a rapid response. Brown called Swenson and explained the situation. In response, the irrigation district and the Bureau of Reclamation "immediately sent 200 cubic-feet per second of cool water down the river, to be captured downstream. In the past, such an action might have taken a week or two—and the lives of many fish—says Brown."[4]

Coordinators

In many situations, positions have been created to coordinate the activities of multiple partners. For example, Gloria Boersma is a full-time volunteer partnerships agreement coordinator for Michigan's Huron-Manistee National Forest. She devotes all her efforts as point person for citizen groups and district rangers alike to facilitate partnerships for completing projects in the forest. Boersma travels to the meetings of different interest groups, to "tell them we're here and provide them with the opportunity" to work with the forest. She acknowledges partner groups once the project is done by creating displays, inviting the press to events, or simply providing recognition awards. Boersma feels that having time to devote to the projects has helped them to be more successful than in forests where individuals combine this role with other responsibilities. Her position has led to increases in the number of projects and their visibility, benefiting both the forest and the partners involved. During her tenure, the estimated value of partnership contributions increased from $129,000 in 1989 to $1 million in 1992.

In the Feather River Coordinated Resource Management (CRM) effort in Northern California, project coordination is provided by the Plumas Corporation, a local nonprofit organization established in 1982 to promote economic and community development in Plumas County. According to Plumas Corporation staff member Jim Wilcox, one of the factors that was "critically important to the success of the CRM here was having a coordinator, whose job it was to keep everyone informed, to write the grants and research various techniques: What's the state of the art and who was practicing it throughout the region? . . . We found talking to other groups that the ones that didn't have a coordinator often folded or are essentially often little more than an advisory body when they wanted to be something more." Wilcox also notes,

"A lot of CRM groups often try to have a coordinator that's working with one of the agencies." This approach can lead to problems because, he says, "That person already has a full-time job and somehow has to try to do all this CRM coordination in addition to their regular job, and it's just not possible." Wilcox advises parties seeking to establish a collaborative group like the Feather River CRM to identify funds to pay a coordinator for at least the first two to four years, even if that coordinator is only a half-time position.

In 1992, Rocky Mountain National Park established an outreach position devoted to working with adjacent communities, landowners, and interest groups outside the park boundaries. According to Larry Gamble, who filled the position, an important aspect of the job is being "at the table early in the development process to express the National Park Service's needs, concerns, and values to local developers and to see what sort of influence we might be able to have on adjacent development." He says, "There's an educational component here that I think is really important, too. If they can begin to understand how important actions they undertake on private property are to the park, then that's where we're going to make the greatest gains, when they're a part of this whole process."

Gamble has worked to build bridges with local landowners and other stakeholders in a number of ways. One of his major initiatives was creating six different task forces to address the following issues: scenic vistas, wildlife habitat, noxious weeds, wildfire potential, night lighting, and trail access. He sent a notice to 1,900 landowners of property within a half mile of the park's boundaries explaining the initiative and inviting them to participate. About 540 landowners expressed interest in the effort, although a much smaller number actually have joined the task forces. Gamble has kept local landowners and local government officials informed of the process through a newsletter that reports on the task forces' progress and upcoming meetings. He also plans to use GIS maps that have come out of the task force process to target specific landowners for future outreach efforts.

Memorandums of Understanding

Many collaborative efforts are facilitated when a memorandum of understanding is developed between the partners. For example, MOUs have formalized interagency relationships in such diverse settings as the Anacostia Watershed Restoration Committee in the Washington, D.C., area and the partnership between the National Wild Turkey Foundation and Georgia Pacific in Georgia (both described in chapter 2). The MOU that provides a structure to the Elkhorn Mountain collaboration has provided a productive forum for those agencies to begin discussing management needs for the mountain range and an opportunity for them to begin coordinating their efforts, according to Elkhorn Ranger George Weldon. It has allowed them to begin capitalizing on differences in expertise and resources among them, promoting their ability to "get more done"; it has been successful in changing attitudes and increasing enthusiasm among land managers; and the processes it created have been effective at "rebuilding trust" between groups that had sometimes had adversarial interactions in the past.

Having an MOU does not necessarily mean that collaboration will come about, however. Often, the development of an MOU becomes a goal rather than a mechanism to facilitate interaction. Many MOUs are symbolic, not functional, and end up having little effect on agency behavior. In successful partnerships where an MOU has been used to facilitate collaboration, it usually was an outgrowth of a collaborative activity, produced as a way to legitimize and facilitate what people felt needed to be done. This was the case in the Elkhorns. According to George Weldon, the cooperative agreement "formalizes the processes."

Advisory Committees

Many collaborative efforts establish steering or advisory committees that explicitly involve different interests in discussing, evaluating, and making recommendations about desired direction. Some of these committees have been established under the auspices of federal or state programs. For example, most of the twenty-one National Estuary Programs (NEPs), authorized by the Clean Water Act and administered by the U.S. Environmental Protection Agency, are administered through multiparty committees. The Barataria-Terrebonne NEP in south-central Louisiana includes two policy and management committees and three advisory committees covering science and technology, citizens, and local government. The latter three committees play an important role in providing opportunities for two-way interaction. They educate constituents on the activities of the initiative while representing constituent interests to the agencies. Similar roles are played by the Resource Advisory Councils created by the BLM,[5] and the NOAA-administered Regional Fishery Management Councils created by the Magnuson-Stevens Act.[6]

Other committees have been established on an ad hoc basis or have evolved in response to shared problems and objectives. For example, the Mt. Roan advisory committee in North Carolina and Tennessee grew out of a long-standing relationship between the Forest Service and local groups, including the Southern Appalachian Highlands Conservancy and the Appalachian Trails Conference. As advisor to the Pisgah and Cherokee National Forests, this committee is particularly concerned with maintaining the region's high-elevation "balds"—grassy, treeless meadows at the top of the Roan Mountain Highlands that are home to at least thirty-four threatened and endangered plant and animal species, along with the largest natural rhododendron garden in the country. In 1988, the group began meeting regularly with the Forest Service and combining forces to monitor change in the balds and begin proactive measures to ensure their perpetuation. One strategy that began in 1992 was to paddock ninety angora goats on the balds to browse on blackberries and other shrubs that threaten to invade the open, grassy areas.

"I have never seen such a diverse group of interests come together in such a cooperative manner," says Forest Service District Ranger Paul Bradley when speaking about the advisory group. The group assists with specific projects and on-the-ground management, and acts as a liaison between the Forest Service and the general public. If someone has a concern, he or she tells it to the advisory group, which then conveys it to the Forest Service during regular meetings. For example, early on some people were concerned that the Forest Service was using four-wheeled, off-road vehicles to travel to the paddock sites. The parties got together and worked out a compromise, nipping a potential problem in the bud. Information also flows the other way. Members of the advisory group help explain to the public the rationale for certain management activities through their ongoing involvement in interpretive activities.

Nongovernmental Organizations

In other situations, nongovernmental organizations have been created to facilitate cooperative activities and ensure their continuation during implementation of an agreement. At times, new NGOs were needed to provide a legal means of accomplishing certain activities, such as acquiring lands or funds for management efforts. For example, Toledo Metroparks official Michelle Grigore helped establish Natural Areas Stewardship, Inc. (NASI), a nonprofit group that acts as a land trust, promotes volunteer stewardship activities in the Oak Openings, and helps prompt agency participation. Grigore notes that NASI "coordinated things and got things off the ground." "Everybody was kind of working towards the same goal," she says, "but it provided a forum, and we also were able to get some grant money to start doing neat things." NASI received a $40,000 grant from the Ohio EPA for a public education project on Oak Openings, which it developed collaboratively with The Nature Conservancy, Metroparks, the Toledo Zoo, and other Working Group members.

Creation of a similar nonprofit organization allowed the development of an innovative partnership between the Saguaro National Park, east of Tucson, Arizona, and adjacent landowners.[7] Development adjacent to the park has resulted in a range of stresses including declining riparian habitat, loss of desert tortoise habitat, and changes in the viewshed from parklands. Conflicts among uses were brought to a head by the proposed development of the

Rocking K Ranch, a large-scale resort that would share an eight-kilometer border with the national park and would contain twenty-one thousand residential units and support a population of over fifty thousand people.

While developers were willing to set aside critical habitat and riparian areas, reduce the development's density, and fund conservation work by imposing a range of fees on homeowners and hotel guests, who could be trusted to follow through on the agreements? The Rincon Institute, an independent nonprofit organization, was created to ensure long-term monitoring, compliance, and implementation of environmental commitments. It would manage open-space lands within the development, provide environmental education in partnership with the National Park Service, conduct long-term ecological research, and oversee environmentally sensitive development and restoration activities. The Rincon Institute was structured as a 509(a)-support organization for the Sonoran Institute, a 501(c)(3) organization that was founded at the same time in 1991. This arrangement ensured tax-exempt status and deductible donations, including an estimated $200,000–$300,000 per year from development fees. Creation of this new NGO made possible collaboration that has a chance of protecting environmental values while allowing development to occur.

The Blackfoot Challenge was also established as a 501(c)(3) nonprofit organization to "enhance, conserve and protect the natural resources and rural lifestyle of the Blackfoot River Valley" in west-central Montana, near the town of Missoula. The group has an executive committee and a board of directors and includes more than one hundred private landowners and representatives from twenty-seven state, federal, and nongovernmental organizations. According to former rancher Land Lindbergh, cofounder of the Challenge, "Before there was no forum by which to handle both the direct and indirect impacts to the river. With the influx of new people and their ideas to the valley, coupled with the different agendas of all the agencies, it was time to get in front of the potential issues and try to deal with them. . . . We are like a roundhouse on a railroad line where issues come in on various tracks and are presented to the board, and then a response is set out on another track to bring together the issue and the individuals or agency that can best handle that issue."

New Facilities

Other partnerships have been facilitated through the creation of new facilities, which provide resources, a focal point, and a new place for interaction to occur. For example, the Trinity Community GIS Center provides training in geographic information systems to residents of resource-depleted communities in Northern California. Established in the summer of 1993, the center is located in Hayfork, a small town surrounded by the Shasta-Trinity National Forest.

The center's core mission is to provide an opportunity for information to flow in two directions: from the community to agencies, and from agencies to the community. According to center director Yvonne Everett, making information accessible to people in the local community can empower them to participate in management decisions. For instance, once people have access to Forest Service maps, "they can see where the errors are, work to improve the errors, and participate in the process of enhancing the information available to everyone." Thus, she says, an important mission of the center is "to try to work with local knowledge and experience and try to bring that into the natural resource management process on public lands." She continues, "We feel it's very important for the community to be involved in the management process, and information is the key to that." She also sees the center promoting "a better information flow between government institutions."

The existence of these opportunities does not mean that effective collaboration will take place. As described in the following chapters, much more hard work is needed to take advantage of such opportunities. Without them, however, it is unlikely that people would find new ways of interacting. By creating new opportunities for interaction, groups have opened the door to collaboration.

Chapter 6

Crafting Meaningful, Effective, and Enduring Processes

The Eastern Sierra, a three-hundred-mile area along the eastern side of California, includes a diversity of landscapes and recreational opportunities, from Mammoth Mountain ski area to the Ansel Adams Wilderness and Mono Lake. It has long been a destination for a range of recreation interests, resulting in a regional economy that is largely recreation-based. Believing that the region needed a focused recreation planning process, Bill Bramlette, district ranger for the Inyo National Forest's Mono Lake Ranger District, initiated a dialogue among federal, state, and local officials and private interest groups. Bramlette thought that plans would best be conceived by the diverse set of recreation providers in the area, having seen the value of partnerships in earlier coalition-building successes in the Mono Basin. He approached Nancy Upham, manager of the Mono Basin National Forest Scenic Area, about assisting him in developing this idea. He sought her participation because of their close working relationship in the past and her strong background in organizing and facilitating workshops.

The group convened for the first time in May 1991 and included representatives of the Bishop and Mono County Chambers of Commerce, Mammoth Tourist Bureau, U.S. Bureau of Land Management, Forest Service, and California Department of Fish and Game. The meeting focused on planning a workshop to discuss recreation in the region, as well as the potential for creating a formal coalition dedicated to the issue. Representatives from the meeting worked through the summer to develop and organize the event, which was held in October. Approximately two hundred people came to the public workshop, about half from public agencies and half from chambers of commerce, private businesses, and environmental organizations. On the second and final day of the workshop, the group brainstormed the type of projects that a hypothetical coalition might undertake, and a long list of ideas emerged. There was strong support for a formal coalition. Participants agreed that the Eastern Sierra's "drawing card" is its natural beauty and that protection of its "wide open spaces" was critical.

During the next six months, newly formed task groups met monthly to develop a range of issues from resource planning to marketing and information strategy. Each group had at least one representative from each of the following interests: private recreation providers, local business, chambers of commerce, elected officials, public agencies, and environmentalists. General meetings of the entire group were also held twice during this time period. By spring 1992, the coalition began calling itself CURES—the Coalition for Unified Recreation in the Eastern Sierra—and had evolved a formal structure and mission statement.

As described in chapter 4, the group began a futuring process in mid-1992 to develop a vision statement for recreation in the Eastern Sierra. Nancy Upham facilitated much of the process and emphasized the common goals of the participants, particularly when the process became adversarial and acrimonious. Humor was very important at those intervals. Upham and others helped move the group through more difficult issues and prevented the process from stalemating. As a result of these opportunities for communication and relationship building, a vision statement was completed in August 1993, following a seemingly endless year of meetings. Participants emerged with a new respect for one another and a sense that the coalition had a sturdy foundation.

CURES has carried out a number of activities. The group created an interpretive guide for visitor centers in the region and published a trilingual activities map. It sponsored three educational seminars for local businesses on marketing techniques. More than two hundred people attended the seminars, and the State Division of Tourism gave CURES its annual "Good Host" award for sponsoring the seminars. CURES also was awarded funds to carry out a marketing conversion study to determine how many people who requested information on the Eastern Sierra actually visited, which is expected to help local businesses improve their marketing efforts. The group also received a $1.5 million federal grant to develop a scenic byway and another grant to install an interactive computer system at a popular visitor kiosk in Inyo County.

In addition to these specific projects, the coalition has served as a model for effective collaboration. When several neighboring counties passed "home rule" resolutions constraining federal agencies within county borders, the Mono County Supervisors passed a resolution calling for collaborative planning between federal agencies and the county government after hearing testimony about CURES and its successes. Greater "trust and willingness to listen" have been achieved among participants. Relationships have developed between seemingly opposing interests, including recreation development and environmental groups. While participants do not see eye to eye on many issues, Sally Miller of the Mono Lake Committee notes that they are nonetheless able to "agree to disagree without attacking each other." Coalition meetings have provided an excellent forum for dialogue. Miller asserts that while in the past opposing interests would often "fight it out through the newspaper," now they have the opportunity to speak directly to one another. In this way, understanding and relationships between environmental groups and the larger community have been strengthened. According to Nancy Upham, "The process is the product."

CURES's success is a direct result of improving the way that people in the region interact, as is the case with many of the successful collaborative initiatives we studied. People invested in the *process* of interaction, not just the products. Processes were developed that were effective at involving people with a range of interests in a manner that was respectful of their differences, and they were well organized and facilitated. Stakeholders viewed the processes as meaningful and legitimate because they were involved in a substantive and ongoing way. Finally, the processes ensured that commitments were upheld and relationships maintained by creating incentives, generating resources, or establishing structures that promoted ongoing interaction. While collaborative efforts succeed for many reasons, taking care of process goes a long way toward improving interpersonal dynamics and can lead to better on-the-ground management of natural resources and communities.

A Meaningful and Legitimate Process of Interaction

It is important to recognize collaboration as an ongoing and evolving process rather than a particular outcome.[1] While "process" is not hard to create, establishing a process that is viewed as meaningful and legitimate by a diverse set of stakeholders is more challenging.[2] The top-ranked factor promoting success in our Building Bridges, Ecosystem Management, and Habitat Conservation Planning studies was the fact that a process was used that differed in significant ways from traditional decision-making approaches. In all cases, the process was more open to real public involvement. In most cases, it evidenced shared decision making in which choices within the group were made by consensus. In most cases, the process was structured to develop ownership of the problem-solving approach and its outcomes by a full range of participants.

Processes established to create habitat conservation plans (HCPs) under the Endangered Species Act illustrate how process design influences the perception of those processes as meaningful and legitimate by the affected groups.[3] More than two hundred HCPs have been prepared under a provision of the ESA that allows for negotiation between a landowner and the U.S. Fish and Wildlife Service. In essence, HCPs are plans that allow development activities in exchange for on-site or off-site conservation activities. Because they generally involve large land areas with multiple affected interests, the HCP process has provided a key opportunity for collaborative land-use planning in places ranging from San Diego County in California to the Massachusetts coastline.

With HCPs, it is clear that different decision-making processes result in different levels of stakeholder satisfaction. In one case involving 170,000 acres of timberlands owned by Plum Creek that are interspersed within a 418,000-acre planning area of public and private lands in the Cascades about one hundred miles east of Seattle, extensive early outreach to the public and agencies managing adjacent lands produced more than fifty public meetings. A full environmental impact statement (EIS) process provided opportunities for comment on draft and final plans. But all of this "process" was not followed up by substantive changes in the proposed plan. As a result, expectations were raised, and many groups expended lots of time and money on the process, yet stakeholders were disappointed in the end. As Charlie Raines of the Sierra Club comments, "At the time we were encouraged; they appeared to be listening. But as it went farther along, you could tell they were smiling and being pleasant, but they weren't changing the substance. . . . The problem with their public participation was that it was as much PR as anything."

Contrast the Plum Creek experience with habitat conservation planning in Clark County, Nevada, which produced a much more meaningful participatory process to create an HCP for the desert tortoise that affected more than 525,000 acres of private and public lands. One of the fastest-growing areas in the United States, Clark County includes Las Vegas and has a population of over a million people. When the desert tortoise was listed as an endangered species in 1989, all hell broke loose as development ground to a halt. The Clark County Board of Commissioners was urged to develop an HCP in order to allow development to proceed. In 1989, the board created an HCP steering committee and invited all affected interests to participate on it. Representation included members from stakeholder groups (environmentalists, ORV interests, miners, developers, ranchers) as well as agencies with decision-making power (Forest Service, FWS, BLM, Nevada state government, the county, cities).

Respondents characterized initial meetings as "violent." Threats were screamed at commissioners from all directions, making front-door weapons checks a standard procedure in the first two years. Yet after many meetings, the process produced a thirty-year Desert Conservation Plan for the tortoise and a multi-species HCP that will affect over two hundred species. All together, the efforts established almost a million acres of preserve, implemented monitoring programs, and improved the ecological conditions and land-use patterns of the region. The most remarkable aspect of the HCP process has been how traditional adversaries have jointly created a land management scheme that acknowledges their varying needs. Indeed, user groups and landowners who once despised the tortoise now participate regularly in implementation and monitoring of habitat protection. As gold miner and committee member Ann Schrieber comments, "This is going to sound crazy to you, but the most important achievement I saw was that a group of people walked into a room hating each other's guts and ready to slit each other's throats . . . and now if you were to come visit those meetings and say something against the plan we've come up with, you're apt to get eaten up by both sides."

Unlike the Plum Creek case, the Clark County steering committee was given an opportunity for meaningful input into decision making. While the county board of commissioners ultimately had to approve the plan, it was the committee itself that crafted the plan. Indeed, one of the critical differences between HCPs that have satisfied stakeholder groups and those that have generated frustration has been in how much decision-making "authority" was granted to advisory groups. As discussed in chapter 13, agencies cannot delegate their statutory authority to collaborative groups, and decision making that affects public resources must be subjected to broader public involvement. However, agencies should take seriously the products of these groups' discussions and commit to implementing them if they meet statutory guidelines and pass muster in subsequent public review. By making that commitment, agencies create a sense of meaning and legitimacy associated with these processes that is sorely lacking in many traditional "public participation" approaches.

Early, Often, and Ongoing Involvement

One simple message from many of the successful collaborative initiatives we examined is that involving the public early and often throughout a decision-making process is more likely to result in more effective decisions and produce satisfied stakeholders. As one district ranger told us about his collaborative planning process, "What makes this project different is that citizens have been involved from the beginning in the development of the plan. By working directly with citizens, managers are gaining greater insight into people's values and needs, and citizens are learning more about the complex issues."

In the Clark County situation, inviting everyone to the table at the outset was the key element accounting for success noted by many interviewees. In contrast, while the Plum Creek HCP effort involved people early, the involvement was not ongoing. One of Plum Creek's critical problems was that the timing of its public involvement efforts was mismatched to the nature of the decision making that occurred on the HCP. Besides extensive early outreach, Plum Creek relied on comments on environmental impact statements as a major part of public input. As a result, the public could comment very early or very late in the decision-making process, yet most decisions and creative problem solving occurred in between those points.

Real, Substantive Involvement

Successful efforts at collaboration pay more than lip service to the benefits of involving diverse interests in decision making. Rather than seeing public involvement as a statutory requirement or something to do because it is politically correct, collaborative efforts that view the ideas and buy-in of partners as integral to finding an effective solution are more likely to achieve good outcomes. Such efforts devise processes of information sharing and decision making that allow for real, substantive involvement on the part of many interests. The success of the Clark County HCP was not just that it provided lots of opportunity for public input, but that it forged a direct link between public involvement and the details of the plan. By all accounts, stakeholders in the Plum Creek case had little effect on decision making, while the Clark County process translated the concerns of stakeholders into tangible changes in the plan.

Most successful processes differ substantially from traditional public participation mechanisms such as public hearings and impact assessments. Traditional approaches usually provide highly controlled, one-way flows of information, guard decision-making power tightly, and constrain interaction between interested groups and decision makers. Often, agency officials use meetings to try to convince the public to accept their plans. One respondent involved in a national forest plan appeal notes, "The Forest Service seemed to think that if they made us sit through enough meetings and listen to them talk about how great their plan is, we would go away. It didn't work."

At other times, public hearings provide a mechanism for grandstanding by interest groups. According to Greg Sherman, a member of the Owl Mountain Partnership steering committee, the partnership sought a collaborative approach "to avoid lawsuits and public hearings." According to Sherman, public hearings "have not been very successful because of the polarization that occurs when you get a lot of people talking. What you don't get are a lot of constructive ideas."

We found that most successful collaborative efforts fostered two-way, interactive flows of information, and decision making occurred through an open, interactive process rather than behind closed agency doors. Such efforts actively involved people throughout a planning or problem-solving process so that they learned together, understood constraints, and developed creative ideas, trust, and relationships. Direct face-to-face interaction between stakeholders and decision-making authorities was critical. In describing one effort that was perceived as a success, an environmental group representative commented, "The Forest Service was successful because its openness was not tokenism. It was sincere. Forest Service leaders were highly accessible to the people. Anyone could call them. They saw themselves as part of the citizenry."

Collaborative processes that provide real, substantive involvement create opportunities for people to make decisions on their own. Just as it is difficult for teenagers to accept the guidance of their parents, stakeholder groups have a difficult time accepting agency-produced decisions that they do not "own" because they have not been involved in thinking through the decision in a real way. They often do not understand the rationale behind decisions and resent having decisions imposed on them.

Consensus Decision Making

Many people involved in collaborative processes highlight the importance of consensus decision making to their success. For example, the Feather River CRM steering committee uses a consensus-based decision-making process, and every project must be approved by all members of the CRM before it is undertaken. The consensus process assures each group that its interests are going to be taken seriously since each can veto a proposal. It also forces members to work harder to craft solutions that span the interests of the different groups. Jim Wilcox, facilitator of the Feather River effort, notes, "The same people who are integrally involved in resource conflicts [outside the CRM process] are sitting down in the CRM meeting room, side by side, and talking about the program and working together on solutions. So they are able to set aside the outside stuff and still come in here and talk and work toward that shared goal." In his view, the consensus process makes "every step of the way on every project" critical to building trust between different people. "Every time you are successful in going through the process of building a solution to a given problem through the collaborative, consensus-building process, we just add another brick to the wall of trust that people can build on."

The experience of the Negrito ecosystem project (described in chapter 7) with consensus decision making suggests that the notion of consensus goes beyond a decision-making rule; it symbolizes a commitment to equality among the participants.[4] Steve McDonald, an environmental representative to the project, feels that the project's consensus approach has been essential to its success. In his words, the approach is "pivotal" and "will make or break" the project. He explains it as "building from a common ground rather than from 'common cause' issue groups with their own agendas." McDonald feels that an "equal partnership" on all issues, including the budget, is absolutely critical: "If any one group controls the process, the project will disintegrate into warring factions."

Consensus decision making clearly involves time and effort on the part of participants and facilitators. For example, the subcommittees and the steering committee for the Owl Mountain Partnership use a consensus approach that requires full agreement from each group member. Stephen Porter, steering committee member and Colorado Division of Wildlife biologist, notes that the group has often been criticized for using consensus due to the fact that decisions often take much longer. "If we can't reach consensus, we will table it and come back or stay with it until we resolve it. We work through it." Porter is quick to point out the strength of decisions once consensus is reached: "If everyone is doing their job, they have to pay attention and communicate back, and the issue is covered so that each person gets a good understanding of the issue. And then we can make the best decision. That is why we have stayed with consensus."

Inclusive and Representative

Successful collaborative efforts also are inclusive of many different interests. Many program coordinators describe their early efforts at soliciting involvement of affected groups as a broad effort to beat the bushes. For example, in order to get the Oak Openings Working Group started, Toledo Metroparks official Michelle Grigore invited the participation of "anybody we could think of that might have land or interest in the Oak Openings." Similarly, Ohio DNR staff member Yetty Alley, a participant in the Darby Partnership effort (described in chapter 2), says that membership was determined by "an open invitation for anyone." Another Darby participant, Kathy Smith from the Ohio DNR, advises, "Try to bring everyone to the table. Don't be afraid to have what you perceive to be an enemy at the table, because if you don't invite them to the table to discuss the issues, it makes it harder in the long run to accomplish what you want."

While open access to a collaborative effort is often important symbolically, making sure that key decision makers, interests, and opinion leaders are represented is critical. Many of the successful collaborative activities we studied implicitly asked the following questions at the outset and throughout their processes: Who is affected? Who has formal responsibility or jurisdiction over the issues at stake? Who controls key resources? Who cares enough to devote time and energy to the effort? Who must be involved to change behavior appropriately? How do we get them involved? How do we ensure that their representative is effective?

In the Darby Partnership, while the process was open to all, its organizers started by focusing on the agencies that needed to be involved. According to Yetty Alley, "Originally, there was more of an effort to get the higher levels of the agencies to meet and come to an understanding for program priorities. After they were on board, we felt it would be easier for the field staff if they had support from their supervisors. Then the upper-level staff pulled back, and it was left up to the field staff." Once agency involvement was assured, other organizations were solicited; their involvement was made more likely due to the prior commitment of the agencies.

In other situations, seats at the table have been assigned to certain interests. For example, CURES chair Chris Plakos, a representative of the Los Angeles Department of Water and Power, notes, "We named positions we wanted filled. . . . If someone leaves, we find someone else to represent that constituency. We didn't want to get to the point that we were so huge and cumbersome that we couldn't get anything done, but you can get good cross representation."

In some cases, interests that need to be represented opt out of a collaborative effort due to a lack of time, resources, or interest, and a variety of strategies have been used to bring them into the process. At times, group members have used personal appeals to aggressively press other groups to participate. At other times, strategies have been used to try to represent interests that were important to the decisions at hand but would not participate on their own. For example, in the Clark County HCP, ranchers chose not to participate in the process since it was likely that preserving habitat for the tortoise would mean losing grazing rights on public lands. In response, the county hired an attorney who was trusted by ranchers to serve on committees as a rural community representative and unofficially represent livestock interests. In another HCP, the Orange County Central-Coastal NCCP in Southern California, the original working group of federal, state, and landowner representatives was expanded to entitle four environmental representatives to participate in discussions with the design team. Those representatives were selected through nominations from conservation organizations and were expected to communicate with their members and other groups during preparation of the NCCP.

In other cases, resources have been provided to enable groups to participate. For example, to facilitate the development of the Alaska recreation plan, the Forest Service paid to fly participants to weekend meetings. The EPA also has a small fund to assist participants having limited resources to participate in regulatory negotiations. Funds are usually reserved for environmental groups or state or local representatives. Appropriate expenses include travel and other costs of participating as well as the expense of accessing expertise.[5]

An Effective Process

Processes created to foster interaction and decision making must be crafted in a way that is sensitive to the demands they place on people's time. Time constraints were cited as significant barriers to collaboration in both the original Building Bridges study and the Ecosystem Management study. Land Lindbergh, landowner, former rancher, and cofounder of the Blackfoot Challenge, advises: "Be aware that people often do not have sufficient time to attend meetings and be involved on a regular basis." To be effective, facilitators often are used to help the group progress. Meetings should be designed and run effectively, and efficient organizational structures developed.

Facilitation

Successful efforts are guided by individuals who are effective at facilitating group dynamics. Collaboration by definition involves interpersonal interactions, and many fledgling efforts die because of poor interpersonal dynamics. Having individuals who can mediate between conflicting positions and troublesome personalities is important to the development of cooperative efforts.[6] As TNC staff member Mark Zankel, a participant in the Nanticoke Watershed Alliance, notes, "It is incumbent upon the group to have a good facilitator. That is something that has improved at the alliance recently versus the first couple of meetings I went to a couple of years ago. Someone who can move the discussion around to people who are raising their hands or whatever. Keep things on track and make people feel like their points are worthwhile."

Often, project coordinators, agency officials, or community leaders provide facilitation. These include individuals like Forest Service staff member Nancy Upham, who worked at keeping the CURES process going in a productive fashion. In the Darby Partnership, TNC staff member Teri Devlin is both one of the partners and the group's facilitator. Her role is crucial to the partnership, according to the other partners. Mary Ann Core of the NRCS says, "Agendas are set a month prior to meetings by Teri. She sends out a call for agenda items, and if there is something out there, she will let us know." Ohio EPA official Marc Smith concurs, "If anyone has a topic that they wish to discuss, they will call Teri and say, 'I want to talk about whatever.' She gets the agenda rolling. . . . She acts as a moderator. If she feels something is not being covered, she will call on someone there at the meeting that could speak to that point. That position has really helped the partnership."

All stakeholders must perceive the facilitator to be legitimate and fair for that person to play an effective role.[7] While simultaneously representing a stakeholder's interests and facilitating the group can be problematic, different strategies have been used to manage that role conflict. For example, sometimes it is possible to have two different individuals from an organization take on the facilitation and stakeholder roles, respectively. In CURES, different Forest Service staff members act as facilitators and as representatives of national forest units.

At other times, nonpartisan, third-party facilitators are used to guide group process, particularly in highly conflict-laden situations. For example, the Forest Service hired and paid for two private facilitators to help achieve a negotiated settlement in a forest plan appeal for the Manti-LaSal National Forest in 1987. The facilitators helped lay out an agenda, encouraged the group to take breaks when they became stuck, and helped the group walk through the points of appeal. Most important, says Forest Supervisor George Morris, the facilitators helped the group "get into resolution mode." Decisions made during a two-day negotiation were made by consensus; if no agreement could be reached, the group moved on to something else and returned to the issue later. Some issues were resolved easily, while others were more difficult. At the end of the session, all but one of fifty-nine issues were satisfactorily resolved. According to Morris, the two facilitators were a big part of the reason for success: "They were relatively low-key guys that made sure everybody had their say, and that there wasn't any badmouthing." According to a nonagency participant, the fact that the facilitators were not Forest Service staff helped legitimize the process considerably.

In other situations, a more forceful facilitation style is needed. Paul Selzer, an attorney who had facilitated HCP negotiations in California, was hired to facilitate the Clark County HCP. A number of interviewees pointed to Selzer's personality and forceful style as elements contributing to the negotiation's success. BLM biologist Sid Sloan comments, "Selzer did an excellent job. He had the personality. At times he could argue both sides effectively and could use his personality and force to get past roadblocks." Selzer, who has no formal training as a facilitator, states, "I admit that some of my measures are rather controversial: I raise my voice often, can use harsh words, and can offend. But I feel a need to push the group towards solutions." Based on his own experience participating in the Clark County negotiations, TNC representative Jim Moore agrees that "it takes a strong personality." He recommends "a facilitator who is well versed in legal issues and can clearly point out sideboards so groups don't go spinning off into [unrelated] matters." The facilitator needs to be willing "to be aggressive at times and ensure a level playing field so groups more powerful because of political connections or economic backing don't get overrepresented."

Facilitators can help a group deal with problematic personalities and uneven power balances in ways that would be difficult for the parties to do on their own. The Owl Mountain Partnership has used outside facilitation, according to BLM project manager Jerry Jack, "when we have a real head-knocking session, and we know some of the more reticent members may get stomped over by more vocal members." Blackfoot Challenge member Becky Garland, local business owner and former vice president of the Big Blackfoot chapter of Trout Unlimited, advises that the group leader or facilitator should be effective at dealing with problematic personalities: "Be someone who is able to deal with the tough people. Put that person on them like a fly to poop until he or she understands."

Well-Managed Meetings

Clearly, one important role for group facilitators is to manage meetings so that they are as productive and efficient as possible. TNC Delaware science and stewardship director Mark Zankel, a participant in the Nanticoke Watershed Alliance, notes: "Forums must be run well. Everyone there has to feel that they will be listened to and are going to be taken as seriously as everyone else."

There are many excellent books on managing meetings that describe various aspects of meeting logistics and timing, agenda formation, and the establishment of ground rules, among other topics.[8] In the successful collaborative processes we examined, many of those items were important to the functioning of the groups. For example, in the Owl Mountain Partnership, establishing regular meetings created a sense of predictability and a momentum that facilitated progress. According to steering committee member and rancher Verl Brown, "When we first started, we just decided to call a meeting whenever we needed one. That did not work, so when I became chair, I changed it to once a month, although we usually don't meet in August, as ranchers are busy and government folks are on vacation. . . . We run fairly loose meetings. We have an agenda, and we try to keep meetings as organized by that as possible." Cochair and rancher Cary Lewis describes the typical process as follows: "Ideas are brought to the steering committee. Whoever brings the idea presents it and gives the pros and cons, usually mostly pros. We then try to tie it back to our objectives. We look for data and input, and then decide whether or not to go further."

In a collaborative effort to create a wilderness plan for fourteen thousand acres in the Lye Brook area of the Green Mountain National Forest in Vermont, facilitator Dick Andrews of the Vermont Wilderness Association believes that meeting logistics contributed to the success of the planning effort: "One of the things we have done at each meeting is to confirm the date of the meeting after that. We always have it at the same time, between 6:00 and 8:00, and that time was chosen by the core team. One thing I made sure to do was start on time, even if everybody wasn't there. And we ended on time, even if ten people stayed and talked for the next forty-five minutes. And

I think people really appreciate that because they know that at 8:00 they can get in their cars and go if they want to." Andrews also called all the team members before each meeting to ask if they wanted pizza, which also served to remind them of the upcoming meeting: "There are a lot of people I know that have never had pizza—and they're never going to have pizza—but they get a call anyway." These arrangements encouraged good attendance at team meetings and helped keep members engaged throughout the planning process.

Many processes start with an explicit discussion of agendas, objectives, and expectations. Based on his experience with the Nanticoke Watershed Alliance, Mark Zankel advises, "Develop a fairly tight mission statement, goals, and objectives. The NWA had kind of a murky mission statement originally, but they have since refined it. It is now a lot clearer what they are trying to accomplish. . . . Have a clear agenda. Defining what kind of commitment you want from people is very helpful. Everyone in our field is way over busy so if you are being asked to go and get involved in something else, you have to know what you are going to get out of it." As discussed in chapter 7, reaching an appropriate problem definition sometimes involves expanding the issues on the table to address the interests of a critical stakeholder. In other cases, the process of defining the problem should narrow the issue to make the collaboration more manageable and focused.

It was also helpful for groups to establish ground rules at the outset, covering the scope of issues to be discussed and how people would deal with each other. Many mediators start negotiations by getting participants to accept basic ground rules such as "no name calling or personal attacks."[9] In the debate over the Clark County HCP, Paul Selzer went beyond rules of communication to bound the substance of the negotiations. He established three ground rules to focus the sessions on the issues at hand: (1) there would be no discussion over the validity of the ESA; (2) there would be no debate over the listing of the tortoise; and (3) everyone had to come to the table willing to "give up something." Selzer also promoted the idea that the process should be "open and transparent." By this he meant that "any problems or inevitable fights in this process must take place at the stakeholder level where they can be worked out before a decision is made at higher levels."

In a number of situations in our research, altering the timing and location of meetings was important to provide adequate opportunity for everyone to participate. When the McKenzie Watershed Council hired John Runyon as coordinator in 1997, the meeting structure was one of the first things he changed. As he recalled, "When I came on board, that was one of the first things I tried to do, change the structure to streamline the meetings, because they would often go on into the wee hours of the morning. They would last for six hours or more, . . . start at 5 and run until 12." Now most meetings last about three hours. Runyon explained, "The way we did that was to transfer a lot of council business and a lot of the up-front framing of the issues to the executive committee. So we have an executive committee that meets once a month before the council meeting, sets the agenda, and frames the issues, actually makes recommendations on what the council should act on."

Most successful processes are designed and carried out with the specific context of the issues and community in mind. With the McKenzie Watershed Council, holding meetings in Eugene is important to facilitate access for rural residents, and sometimes meetings are held in different locations throughout the watershed. According to Runyon, "When we have a meeting where we think there's something of interest to watershed residents, we try to move upriver, especially in the summer."

Such simple things as holding meetings at a time when people can attend can make a big difference in the level and character of public involvement in collaborative processes. For example, one criticism of the working group drafting the HCP for San Diego County was that most meetings took place in the middle of the day. Scheduled to accommodate the work schedules of agency representatives, that meeting time was inconvenient and burdensome for individual property owners and volunteer representatives of nonprofit groups to attend. Furthermore, public comment was reserved for the end of the two- to three-hour sessions.

Successful meeting managers also pay attention to basic human needs. For example, a surprising and frequently mentioned factor that improved participation in the Clark County HCP negotiations was the provision of meals. Many participants noted that working on a full stomach and not having to worry about the cost of meals—covered by developer funds—made long hours of deliberation more bearable.

An Efficient Organizational Structure

Because collaborative efforts by definition involve representatives of multiple interests, many groups in our studies had to struggle to organize themselves as efficiently as possible. They wanted to facilitate involvement but to do so in a way that kept the process of interaction from bogging down or becoming so burdensome that groups would drop out. Ultimately, that means managing the number of participants and organizing their work through multiple committees.

In places like the Anacostia watershed, the sheer number of potential partners can be problematic. The Anacostia River drains some 153 square miles, including some of the Washington metropolitan area's most densely populated regions, before entering the Potomac River along the southern edge of the District of Columbia. While there are four original signatories to the 1988

Anacostia Watershed Restoration Agreement (Maryland, D.C., and Montgomery and Prince George's counties) and two federal partners (the U.S. Army Corps of Engineers and the EPA), the Anacostia Watershed Restoration Committee maintains informal relationships with about 180 other organizations working on protection and restoration of the river basin, including a number of federal landowners.

Rather than expand the committee's membership to accommodate this diversity of interest, the group "decided that it's probably better to keep it a small core of people who are actually members and just do a lot more outreach through technical subcommittees and . . . individual projects with specific parties," according to Lorraine Herson-Jones of the Metropolitan Washington Council of Governments. "Otherwise, it would just be such a huge group, it would be hard to manage." Herson-Jones notes that the group recently added a citizens advisory subcommittee to its two existing subcommittees, the Coordinated Anacostia Monitoring Committee and the Anacostia Technical Committee. The Citizens Advisory Committee reports to the full committee at its quarterly meetings. "It's not a formal membership," she explains, "but it is a way of coordinating and cooperating."

The strategy of using subcommittees that report to a steering committee that ultimately makes decisions works for many groups. Participants in the Clark County HCP effort included county, municipal, federal, state, academic, development, ORV, mining, national environmental, and local environmental interests. Steering committee membership numbered between twenty-five and thirty-five individuals. Clark County staff member Christine Robinson notes, "No matter how frustrating, you must include all stakeholders. Limiting the group for fear of it being too big is never good. On the other hand, controlling the *way it happens,* is something you *can* do." In Clark County's case, the way it happened was managed through the use of subcommittees, which "kept the steering committee from bogging down in technical detail," according to FWS biologist Sherry Barrett.

Separating decision making from technical support through a hierarchical committee structure did not work for the Darby Partnership. Instead, a problem-focused team approach was more productive for the group. According to Ohio DNR staff member Yetty Alley, "There was an interesting split for a while. The partners were viewed as upper management, and they had one meeting while the field staff had another." The two-meeting structure began to lose its effectiveness, however, as some of the agency heads began to lose interest, not many nonagency people came to meetings, communication between the partners meetings and the field staff was lacking, and others just complained that there were too many meetings. After four years of operating, change was needed. According to NRCS representative Melissa Horton, "We had a facilitated meeting, a mini gripe session, then we regrouped to allow members to be more focused." They chose an issue-oriented structure, with teams focused on problem areas: livestock management, communications, land use, stream management. This structure mixed decision makers, technical staff, and other interested parties and helped focus participants in a comfortable setting where their knowledge and skills were most useful.

In Wisconsin, individuals developing an HCP for the Karner blue butterfly, a federally listed endangered species, used a different strategy for managing a large number of interested parties. A consortium of twenty-eight private and public landowners who represent most of the significant large blocks of land within the butterfly's range included county forests, utility companies, forest products companies, three state agencies, and The Nature Conservancy. In addition, other non-landowning interests were involved, including landowners associations and environmental groups. A major challenge that nearly every participant described was the difficulty associated with functioning in such a large, unwieldy group. Fred Souba, a representative of a private timber company, comments, "This was a very large group. You get nothing done in large groups." Wisconsin DNR staff member Dave Lentz agrees: "You can work through [things] a lot quicker with a smaller group of people because you can confront issues and work together to build trust a lot easier than you can in a huge group."

One of the ways the Karner blue butterfly effort sought to manage its size was by dividing interested parties into two groups: *partners* (people with land or other assets at stake) and *participants* (other active members of the public). Partnership meetings were held on a monthly basis, with decision making following a consensus process. While participants did not have voting privileges, the group sought to include their concerns. According to Dave Lentz, "If we have a nonpartner who dissents on an issue, we don't want to just tell them to go away. We want them there. We want to know their position, we want them to try to convince us, and we work to great ends to do that." Partner-only votes were taken on only one or two occasions.

Finally, another way that groups have sought efficiency is in the way they allocate tasks between paid staff and unpaid representatives of various public interests. Forest Service planner Maria Durazo-Means comments on the importance of not asking too much of people, based on her experience facilitating the Alaska Recreation Plan (described in chapter 5): "Care must be taken not to overwork the public if this approach is used. Do as much work ahead of time as you possibly can before bringing the working group together. Although there is more ownership in a product if the working group develops the process used to pick the projects for the planning period, it may be unrealistic to ask them to do that much work. You may want to come to them with a proposed process and let them approve it or improve upon it instead of starting from scratch like we did." In many groups, agency staff do a lot of the leg work between working group meetings—collecting and analyzing information, trying to work through the implications of alternative scenarios. As a result, meetings focus on discussing implications and the acceptability of various alternatives grounded on a common fact base.

An Enduring Process

Successful efforts at collaboration not only establish meaningful and effective processes of interaction, they find ways to make them endure over time. They institutionalize collaboration by creating structures and generating funding that will continue beyond initial partnership efforts. They motivate people to continue to use opportunities for interaction by establishing good reputations and supportive relationships. Ultimately, they are self-sustaining because a structure is provided that facilitates productive interaction, and the partners continue to benefit from it.

The educational partnership involved in Kirtland's warbler management in Michigan (described in chapter 2) provides a good example of an enduring collaborative effort. It has lasted for more than twenty years because, first and foremost, it continues to meet the individual needs of the multiple partners in unique ways. Second, through creative resource sharing, it allows the partners to get work done that would not be possible without sharing information, labor, and funding. Third, the Kirtland's warbler recovery team has provided "a lot of stability for progress to be made," according to Forest Service official Rex Ennis. The team meets twice a year and has fifteen to twenty partners in attendance. According to Ennis, the team provides a structure for work to continue as individuals have come and gone over the years. He also believes that the meetings help to maintain high levels of public support for recovery efforts. Finally, it is clear that the network of relationships that exists between individuals, such as the interaction between Ennis and Michigan Audubon executive director Terry Yonker, helps maintain the collaboration.

Institutionalizing Collaboration

Many collaborative efforts have institutionalized their activities by creating structures, appointing people, or fostering ongoing opportunities for interaction that continue to feed the collaboration long after its early efforts. As described in chapter 5, some of these are formal structures that continue to advance the collaborative agenda as a matter of institutional prerogative. For example, TNC received funding from the U.S. Environmental Protection Agency's Great Lakes National Program to start a regional office that now coordinates the Oak Openings Working Group. Similarly, to implement the

Orange County HCP, a nonprofit corporation was created whose board includes representatives of various stakeholder groups. Three "public members"—one representative apiece from the environmental, recreation, and small business communities—were added to the board to ensure that groups other than landowners had a say in creating and managing habitat reserves.

Other partnerships paid attention to building a funding base and other support for their initiatives as they moved through implementation activities. For example, the Rincon Institute, created to help mitigate the impact of development adjacent to Saguaro National Park (further described in chapter 5), is funded through an elaborate set of fees established through deed restrictions and charged to businesses and homeowners. Nightly surcharges on hotel rooms, occupancy fees on commercial properties, monthly fees assessed homeowners, and real estate transaction fees are expected to generate $200,000 to $300,000 per year for the institute's conservation activities adjacent to Saguaro.

A Sense of Importance and Need

Collaborative efforts also maintain themselves over time through less tangible means by ensuring that involved parties view the initiatives as important. Creating a sense of ongoing purpose or need that transcends the personalities involved has been important to maintain interactions, particularly as personalities change. For example, CURES seems to have taken on a life of its own and is no longer dependent on the involvement of particular individuals, according to facilitator Nancy Upham. In her view, as coalition members move on and are replaced, the group and process will not dissolve because the need to interact will remain.

Building a reputation as a useful and important player in a region has also helped maintain collaborative efforts over time. According to Adopt-a-Stream program director Joan Martin, the good reputation of the Huron River Watershed Council has helped facilitate the program's success. The HRWC "is an organization that people can feel, I think, some confidence in. It's got a good reputation, and it's been around over thirty years," she says. She explains that this positive reputation has been built through its history of success: "It's known throughout the watershed. It's been helpful to communities. So that helps when you call from the Watershed Council."

Self-Sustaining Processes

The Huron River Adopt-a-Stream program also illustrates mechanisms to sustain its activities without requiring much effort from the initiating organization. The program uses a "train the trainer" approach that helps to make the program self-replicating. For example, certain volunteers who have participated in previous stream surveys are invited to become team captains. A few weeks before each stream search, team captains receive in-stream training in collection methods. According to Martin, "the people chosen to 'captain' develop an increased commitment to the program and an increased sense of stewardship." These individuals then continue to guide and motivate other volunteers to participate in stream monitoring and cleanup efforts.

Many groups also create self-reinforcing processes that endure by following lessons described in other chapters of this book. They provide rewards and a sense of accomplishment to participants (chapter 9). They start small and build on their early successes (chapter 10). They follow up on their agreements and stay committed to the process of collaboration (chapter 8). They create networks of personal relationships (chapter 9) and a sense of shared purpose (chapter 4) that become highly resistant to outside attack. Indeed, members of the Quincy Library Group held to their agreed upon direction even when the Forest Service offered a salvage timber sale for bid in an area of concern to the group. The local timber industry was tempted to bid on it but realized that doing so would violate aspects of the QLG agreement. The industry held firm to its commitments, and the sale was eventually withdrawn by the agency. As Bill Howe of Collins Pine Company, a local timber company, comments, "We were under a lot of pressure to break with the group. Industry people were calling, saying, 'Are you crazy or what?' But three years ago, we decided to speak with one voice. It was a matter of principle."[10] Another timber industry participant comments, "A deal is a deal."

As described in chapter 5, many places have created new opportunities for interaction. By crafting meaningful, effective, and enduring processes, the potential of these new opportunities has been realized. In a number of communities, the level and character of dialogue between groups have been transformed and have enabled a new approach to solving a community's problems to take root.

Chapter 7

Focusing on the Problem in
New and Different Ways

*I*n the late 1980s, farmers, government officials, and environmentalists formed an unlikely alliance to address agricultural and environmental concerns in the lands surrounding the Laguna Atascosa National Wildlife Refuge in southern Texas. Managed by the U.S. Fish and Wildlife Service, the 45,000-acre refuge provides a home to many endangered species and is visited by roughly 250,000 people each year. Surrounding the refuge are native habitat and agricultural lands where farmers grow cotton, citrus fruits, and other crops.

In 1988, the U.S. Environmental Protection Agency began evaluating the effect of pesticides on endangered species. After consulting with FWS scientists, EPA proposed significant reductions in pesticide use in South Texas in order to protect the Aplomado falcon. According to Laguna Atascosa refuge manager Steve Thompson, EPA's action "would have, from the farmers' viewpoint, eliminated cotton growing in the Rio Grande valley. About thirty different pesticides were real important to them to make a living. Depending on the year, that's a $125–$350 million industry down there. And because of one endangered bird (which really wasn't around anymore—they were so rare that we didn't even know if we had any), they were putting these restrictions on the farmers." Simultaneously, the FWS was trying to reintroduce Aplomado falcons at Laguna Atascosa. According to Thompson, "On one side we had this bird that was trying to make a comeback, and we needed everybody's cooperation. And then all of a sudden EPA comes down with an edict that you're not able to use these certain pesticides."

Thompson continues: "So the farmers, they received this notice and were frightened, scared, mad, many different things, and sat down in a coffee shop and said, 'You know, we can battle this one through the normal process.' They got a group together, and Wayne Halbert was elected the chairman and Terry Lockamy, who is an outstanding county extension agent, just sat down at a Mexican food restaurant and got a napkin out and said, well, one approach would be to take this standard congressional approach that they have taken a lot, and have been very effective at, and just fight it up through that system and the legal system." Instead, the farmers decided to approach the problem in a new way: They formed a committee to discuss other ways of dealing with the pesticide-endangered species conflict and involved a range of groups, including the federal Natural Resources Conservation Service, federal and state wildlife agencies, agricultural chemical field representatives, and environmentalists.

Steve Thompson describes their thinking: "They came up with this ad hoc committee. They wanted a coalition that was broad enough that they could get enough ideas. They were very hesitant to lose control of the group, though. It was very frightening to invite these people in the first place. Fish and Wildlife Service were all thought of as granola-crunching, tree-hugging crazies that would side with the environmentalists, basically. So they went to the county commissioner at the time and told him about this idea, because they felt like they needed some sort of a 'blessing' to make themselves an official group." The farmers began calling themselves the Cameron County Agricultural Coexistence Committee, and they met irregularly on an as-needed basis, usually no more than about once a month. "They would usually be all-afternoon meetings. It was pretty intense," explains Thompson. "I found out a lot of things that I thought I knew but didn't."

Critical to the development of the group was a joint learning process in which all parties were seen as contributing expertise to the problem at hand. Steve Thompson explains, "Farmers and wildlife people don't normally run in the same circles. As biologists, you tend to watch a special on *60 Minutes* about organic farming . . . and say, 'You guys should all be doing organic farming on cotton.' And [the farmers] would look at you like, 'This guy is loony-tunes. He doesn't know anything about farming.' And [farmers] do the same thing. They would say, 'I went to the library and looked up the Aplomado falcon in the 1952 *Encyclopedia Britannica*, and it didn't say anything about your bird.'" In response, Thompson says, "One of the first things we had to do was to let each of us be our own experts. We quit telling the farmers how to farm. But what we did tell them was that if they used, for instance, granular pesticides, that the other birds were picking that up, and that eventually poisoned the birds. And they said, 'Well, we have another method.' That same pesticide can be injected into the ground, for instance. Or they asked about the rate that was harmful to the birds. We were just using the label rates. And they all looked around and said, 'We never use the label rate; we use half the label rate.' So we ran that through our models and found that wouldn't be a problem. In some cases they could continue to do what they were doing. We just weren't communicating."

Thompson also had to deal with resistance to the cooperative effort from within his agency. "[My staff] were very skeptical," he says. "A lot of people had been there longer than I had, and they had seen these things come and go, and nobody had ever been able to solve them." To address this problem, Thompson explains, "I tried to get them involved as much as I could. We had field trips. I had them go out with me a little bit and see things we were doing. When they actually saw some of the farmers get up in front of the television crews and say some of the things that they were saying, [my staff] were convinced then that we were making some progress. That we were getting information to [the farmers] that was valuable. By the same token, I had a lot of lively, heated discussions at staff meetings, discussing [the farmers'] viewpoints with them. I brought farmers and ranchers into a lot of our endangered species meetings. This spun out into a big bunch of ranchers that we started meeting with. And over a period of several years, people began to see that there were some successes there. They also met some of these people and found that they weren't monsters. But it was slow."

The Cameron County Coexistence Committee represents a different approach to problem solving than had become the norm among agricultural, environmental, and government interests in South Texas. As Steve Thompson notes, "Collaborative problem solving is a different approach than the regulatory two-by-four to the side of the head, and it takes a different mind-set." As in other successful efforts at bridging, the committee was able to achieve that mind-set and take a different approach to the problem. It adopted a holistic perspective, which linked economic and environmental issues across a broad landscape, and focused on the problem rather than predetermined positions or historic procedures. Members worked through a process of mutual learning and used scientific information to bound decision making. In addition, agency personnel were able to rise above their perception of their traditional roles and responsibilities and contribute to a process of joint problem solving. Together, community members, interest group representatives, and agency staff took Robert Frost's road less traveled and found it made all the difference in the world.

A Willingness to Try New Approaches

Most successful collaborative efforts exhibit a different mind-set among those involved, one that includes their willingness to try new behaviors and different ways of interacting. Critical to the ability of the Cameron County committee to carry out a different approach to problem solving was the willingness of its members to try to do so. While this may seem tautological, one of the most common barriers to creative, multiparty problem solving is the unwillingness of groups to set aside past modes of interaction and traditional management practices and consider new approaches. Skepticism about the value of an alternative approach, wanting to stay with old practices because they are familiar and understood, fear of losing control, and a host of other psychological and sociological factors all get in the way of the ability of people to change. One of the biggest fans of the Cameron County initiative, Steve Thompson started out suspicious of the effort and the likelihood that it would succeed. He says he told the group's representatives, "'Well, I'll come to the first meeting. If you're just going to yell at me about the Aplomado falcon and endangered species, then I probably won't attend the second meeting. But if you're serious about working on solutions, I find that very exciting, and I would attend all of the meetings.' So it was up to them to show me that they were serious."

In trying to deal with water-quality problems in the Eel River Delta in Humboldt County, California, researchers from the California Coastal Conservancy met with a mixed response from dairy farmers. According to Dick Wayman, one of the researchers, "There seemed to be a number of farmers who didn't want the problem even mentioned, because they were afraid if it was mentioned that the regulators would come in." In both the Cameron County and Eel River cases, the willingness of a handful of landowners to try a different approach to problem solving provided momentum for a collaborative approach. According to Wayman, "Luckily, however, there were several farmers who were more than willing to face the problem. . . . That was the real key—getting some names of just a few individuals who would be willing to take action on the problem."

Cooperative, Not Adversarial

Successful partnerships are able to establish a noncombative approach to discussions. For example, Dennis Leonardi and other members of the Eel River Delta Sustainable Agriculture Committee successfully created an informal, friendly atmosphere in meetings with state regulators and headed off an adversarial tone by setting an example with their own behavior. They found that establishing a cooperative tone takes time. Leonardi noted that agency staff "often feel like they have some territory they need to protect. They're more used to a combative approach." However, Leonardi fostered a noncombative setting by being open and up-front but nonconfrontational. He encouraged other farmers to talk with agency officials: "Tell them what your fear is: 'We're worried about a regulatory agency coming out on the dairy and fining us or taking some action against our approach, even though we're trying to solve a problem.' . . . By talking about it, they can understand what our concerns are and why we can't do certain things. You may not agree [with each other], but you'll understand what they are trying to say, and that respect has been great. It's worked really well."

At other times, groups can simply agree to disagree on one set of issues and still make progress on others. As negotiation scholar Roger Fisher observes, "You can disagree without being disagreeable." Blackfoot Challenge member Hank Goetz offers the following advice: "Take the time to sit down and build up trust. Find common overriding interests, then focus on what unites the group rather than what separates them. In our instance, it was the protection of the river. Then comes tolerance—having enough tolerance to let other things go by the wayside while concentrating on things in which there is agreement. Agree to disagree on other things."

Based on her experience with management for the Oregon silverspot butterfly, TNC stewardship director Cathy Macdonald notes that groups do not always have to agree about management decisions, as long as they learn to work out ways to accommodate their differences. For example, a disagreement occurred over the extent to which some areas should be burned and mowed to create butterfly habitat. TNC worried that the management activities might harm too many individual butterflies. Conversely, Forest Service staff felt that the level of burning was necessary to protect critical habitat. They could have parted ways in the face of their disagreements, but they did not. Instead, they proceeded with different management intensities on the national forest and The Nature Conservancy preserve and cleared all management actions with the U.S. Fish and Wildlife Service as required by the Endangered Species Act. They closely monitored the results of different management strategies and shared observations and research efforts. In the end, their relationship was kept intact in spite of their differences.

A Flexible, Positive Attitude

People involved in successful collaborative processes also are flexible in considering solutions to problems. In the management partnership for Mill Creek Canyon, a popular recreation area near Salt Lake City, flexibility and adaptation to new ideas were critical to the effort's success. According to Forest Service recreation forester Jim White, "We had our grand idea on how it ought to work, but as we proceeded down the road, it became apparent that the more people got involved or threatened or interested or interfaced with us (the planning team), we realized that for this thing to succeed, we needed to give here and give there and compromise over there. And we ended up changing some basic program operating fundamentals, where I know my tendency would have been to say, 'Hey man, leave me alone. I know what I'm doing.' But by listening and changing and tinkering, not losing sight of the vision but not wanting to lose the opportunity to do this at all, our flexibility helped us to be very successful."

One recipe for success in a difficult multiparty dispute is to have negotiators be "firm on ends but flexible on means." That is, they should be clear and firm on their underlying objectives yet flexible in the ways that those objectives can be achieved. The innovative approach to range management adopted in the Kiowa Grasslands of New Mexico exemplifies this mind-set. Improvements in both the health of the cattle and the land were required. As described more fully in chapter 1, a comprehensive water and grazing management program was developed to achieve those ends. Instead of the usual few large watering holes for cattle, water is piped in to create multiple small watering areas. By having many smaller watering areas spread out over the area being grazed, the rancher can then employ time-controlled grazing, a system that rotates the herd through a series of small parcels for short periods of time. Unlike many traditional ranching systems that apply lower but constant pressure on a large parcel, this system of short but intense grazing, followed by long periods of rest, is believed to facilitate natural revegetation. It was designed to mimic the natural grazing pattern of predomesticated large browsers. The result was a management approach that achieved both of its formerly competing objectives by being flexible and creative in its approach.

As in a number of our successful cases, the partners in the Kiowa Grasslands also manifested a positive attitude—a belief that the situation could be improved. According to Forest Service District Ranger Alton Bryant, a positive attitude to addressing problems is one of the most important ingredients in making a program like this work: "You always hear about how harmful grazing is on the land and how agencies can't seem to coordinate their activities, but we know it doesn't have to be that way." At times, the positive attitude resulted more from a willingness to suspend disbelief than a great deal of up-front faith that a better way was likely. Rather, participants were asked to set aside their preconceptions and see what could be imagined or achieved.

A Holistic Perspective

In many of the situations we studied, groups were able to take a different approach to the problem by focusing on it in a more holistic way. As discussed in chapter 1, much of the literature on innovative land and resource management emphasizes the need to view organizational missions and management problems broadly by employing an ecosystem approach: that is, understanding the variety of interconnections across space and time and between considerations that characterize modern-day environmental issues.[1] Management that focuses on larger spatial or temporal scales, or that highlights interconnections, necessarily involves a greater level of interrelationships among stakeholders and landowners. Many successful examples of cross-boundary management have been able to promote collaboration by adopting a holistic, integrative perspective.

Integrated Geographically

Many collaborative initiatives emphasize the need for landscape-scale geographic integration. For example, when the four public agencies got together in 1988 to form the Anacostia Watershed Restoration Committee (AWRC), "the purpose was to bring them together as a group to look at the conditions of the watershed from the watershed perspective, rather than each of their own local perspectives, and to come up with a strategy for restoring the river across the basin in a way that made sense ecologically," according to Metropolitan Washington Council of Governments staff member Lorraine Herson-Jones. Geographic integration can range from the basin-size scale of the AWRC to the global scale illustrated by the Kirtland's warbler partnership, which has expanded its focus from the jack pine barrens of Michigan to the warbler's winter habitat in the Bahamas.

Geographic integration through collaboration has also characterized efforts outside the public sector. Preservation efforts by land trusts like The Nature Conservancy can no longer achieve conservation goals by simply "purchasing a piece of land and putting a fence around it," according to several TNC respondents. In the case of the Virginia Coast Reserve, a designated UN Biosphere Reserve, TNC's approach is to look "beyond simply identifying, buying, and protecting a parcel to a much broader ecosystem thinking. . . . You need to get out into the community, listen to them, and find common goals rather than focusing on the differences. . . . Otherwise, you end up with little preserves with who knows what surrounding them. . . . You are setting yourself up for disaster. . . . Everything that goes on in the buffer has an impact." Indeed, two-thirds of TNC's objectives for its efforts at the Virginia Coast Reserve are aimed at influencing activities outside its properties by educating area residents, forming partnerships, and enhancing the local economy through natural system protection.

Integrated Functionally

Holistic thinking also implies integration of functional activities on a single piece of ground, and some projects are successful at drawing on that type of thinking. The Kiowa Grasslands case caused a change in the behavior of Forest Service and NRCS staff from working with ranchers separately to working together to simultaneously enhance range and environmental quality and wildlife habitat. Similarly, integration of various agency programs is one of the goals of the Elkhorn Mountains cooperative management effort described in chapter 5. Beyond the various structures put into place to coordinate management among the Forest Service, the BLM, and the Montana Department of Fish, Wildlife and Parks, shifting the perspective of agency staff to viewing the entire mountain range as a cooperative management area has been important to changing on-the-ground management activities. Elkhorn Ranger George Weldon sees it "as a model in terms of how agencies can look across administrative boundaries and do better on-the-ground management." "Those boundaries are just arbitrary," he says. BLM Manager Merle Good agrees: "It's the approach of working together—of not stopping at the boundary—that's most successful. We feel like we're really pioneers in this area."

Integrating Different Elements of a Problem

Most successful efforts also built a perspective that integrated different aspects of a problem. For many, that included expanding the focus from one set of objectives to a broader set, most typically to include both environmental and economic aspects of a situation. For example, the organizers of the Blackfoot Challenge sought to expand discussions from a river-based focus on fisheries to a broader range of issues facing the valley. They realized that the scope of the issues in the valley was outgrowing existing organizations' narrow focus on fish and water issues. The problems required a broader set of interests in order to be effectively addressed. Agencies, industry representatives, nongovernmental organizations, and landowners met to talk about possible solutions for managing the recreational interests, environmental concerns, and commercial uses of the valley.

A keystone of the Negrito ecosystem project (described further later in this chapter), and one that has allowed it to function in the local economic and political climate, is the commitment of all working group members to socioeconomic issues as well as ecological and biological ones. Participants are aware and concerned about the apparent correlation between the increases in unemployment as loggers lose their jobs and alcoholism, spouse abuse, and child abuse in local communities. According to Forest Service timber and recreation specialist Gary McCaleb, the Negrito project's holistic approach was one of the primary reasons for its success. McCaleb says that the reaction of some forest managers to creation of the Forest Service New Perspectives Program was to "rename all timber or grazing projects as New Perspectives projects." The Negrito project was different, however, by being a "holistic, ecologically based ecosystem project" from its inception, not just a "retreaded traditional project."

Problem Focused, Not Bound by Positions or Procedures

Successful collaborative efforts are effective at focusing people's attention on the set of substantive and institutional problems to be solved and moving people away from divergent problem definitions, positional statements of group interests, and constraints established by long-standing organizational procedures. They achieve this problem focus because the managers of the group's process are able to promote a productive approach that effectively deals with all phases of problem solving: problem definition, identification of alternative courses of action, evaluation of alternatives, an explicit decision-making process that relies on agreed upon criteria, and implementation.[2]

Framing Problems Appropriately

Most prescriptions for effective problem solving start with a focus on defining the problem to be solved.[3] Negotiation scholar Roy Lewicki and coauthors note that "the problem identification step is often the most difficult one . . . [particularly] when several parties are involved," and they caution against premature closure of the problem definition phase: "Don't jump to solutions until the problem is fully defined."[4] Resource policy analysts Richard Wallace and Tim Clark highlight the tendency of decision makers to be "solution-oriented" rather than problem-oriented.[5] That is, they tend to choose a desired solution because it fits traditions or organizational priorities, without a careful determination of how it fits the problem or whether an alternative course of action might be more effective or efficient.

The way problems are defined has a huge effect on their solutions.[6] Is the problem "Where should we site new waste incinerators?" or "How do we deal effectively with municipal solid waste?" Is it "How can we get rid of grizzly bears that prey on livestock?" or "How can we protect livestock and enhance grizzly habitat while reducing conflict among ranchers and wildlife interests?" While the first question in these two pairs closes off debate by focusing on a specific solution, the second question in each pair provides a starting point for creative multiparty problem solving. Indeed, mediators often work with groups to reframe problems in a process that organizational theorists Chris Argyris and Donald Schön have called double-loop learning.[7]

Another technique to draw boundaries around a problem is to ask participants to imagine best and worst possible outcomes. For example, the facilitator of the Alaska recreation planning effort, a former Forest Service employee who had received formal facilitation training from the agency, "wrote down working group participants' worst case scenario on a flip chart and their best case." "We got it all out on the table, laid it out in the open, and then just tried to reassure them as best we could that their worst fears wouldn't come true," according to one participant. In so doing, they highlighted baseline realities and possibilities and helped focus participants in a grounded way.

Focus on Interests

Most texts on effective negotiation emphasize the importance of focusing on stakeholders' interests, not their initial positions. "Focus on interests, not positions" is probably the single most important lesson of the popular book on negotiation written by Roger Fisher, William Ury, and Bruce Patton.[8] According to Roy Lewicki, "Interests are different from positions in that interests are the underlying concerns, needs, desires, or fears behind a negotiator's position, which motivate the negotiator to take that position. . . . Although negotiators may have difficulty satisfying each other's specific positions, an understanding of underlying interests may permit them to invent solutions that meet those interests."[9]

The processes used to foster communication in many of the examples of collaboration we studied were successful at focusing on interests and not being bound by initial positions. Throughout the futuring process used to build CURES, facilitator Nancy Upham emphasized the common interests of the participants, urging them, she says, "to get off of their positions and onto interests." In meetings preceding wolf restoration efforts in Yellowstone National Park, environmentalists and ranchers were stuck in familiar positions for and against wolves. Progress in dealing with the real concerns of the groups came when a rancher finally commented, "You need to understand one thing. It's not the wolf we're really worried about. We can deal with him if we need to. What we're concerned about are all the restrictions on how we do our business that come along with the wolf." That realization moved the groups from a polarized situation to one in which concerns could start to be understood, discussed, and addressed.[10]

Rising Above Procedural Constraints

Successful collaborative partnerships in our research did not allow preexisting agency norms and procedures to preclude or limit their efforts. This observation is consistent with conclusions reached by David Osborne and Ted Gaebler in *Reinventing Government*.[11] They highlight the importance of "mission-driven" government, that is, public agencies that have shed the extensive set of rules that control every aspect of behavior, stifle creativity and innovation, and limit the efficiency and effectiveness of solutions.

At times, project leaders have had to push to get around agency procedures. When the innovative fee/cost-share scheme used in the Mill Creek

Canyon management partnership (described in chapter 2) was being developed, resistance from the Budget and Finance staff in the Forest Service regional office threatened to stymie the effort. The proposed fee scheme had not been tried before, and nothing expressly authorized it. Eventually, however, an agency lawyer said, according to Forest Service recreation forester Jim White, "Nothing says you can do this, but nothing says you can't." After gaining further approval from the forest supervisor and the regional forester, District Ranger Michael Sieg moved ahead with the plan. Based on his experience at Mill Creek, White advises, "Don't take no for an answer. We got no's for a year. If you want to make things happen . . . if you gotta bend a few rules, take a few risks—that's probably what it will take."

In a number of our cases, project coordinators went beyond the minimum required by agency rule books or practice. Seth Diamond of the Beartree Challenge highlights the importance of breaking out of the normal government project rut. "We didn't just put a boring government proposal together. We made something that would catch people's eyes." The recreation plan prepared for the Petersburg District of the Tongass National Forest similarly went beyond traditional practice. According to Maria Durazo-Means, "Historically, there has been a problem of just minimally meeting NEPA requirements. We would do the required public meeting, send out a boring letter." This project, however, met the spirit as well as the letter of the public involvement requirements. The public involvement techniques were creative and aggressive and tailored to the customs of the cultures involved. Colorful flyers were sent out and a series of public meetings were held, not just one.

The personal-use firewood environmental assessment process undertaken on the Naches District of the Wenatchee National Forest in 1990 also illustrates the benefit of going beyond traditional agency procedures. The process began in response to a lawsuit filed by a small citizens' organization called Clean Air Yakima, which claimed that the district's sale of below-cost firewood encouraged wood burning in the Upper Yakima Valley and polluted the air. Indeed, the Yakima airshed is a designated federal nonattainment area for particulate matter, 90 percent of which comes from woodstoves. When mandated by the court to complete an environmental assessment (EA) of the effects of its firewood program on air quality in the Yakima Valley, the Forest Service could have done the minimum. Instead, an extensive outreach and analysis program was initiated.

The EA went far beyond traditional NEPA compliance and, in the process, won a Council on Environmental Quality award for "outstanding NEPA compliance." Wayne Elson, principal reviewer from the Seattle EPA office, comments: "Despite the awkward circumstances for preparing the EA, and the observed tendency for agencies to do the 'minimum required' for court-ordered NEPA documents, the district thoughtfully developed and implemented creative mitigation measures for addressing air-quality concerns." He adds, "I thought that they took it further than they needed to for just satisfying the court."

Not Bound by Traditional Conceptions of Agency Roles

In many places, agency representatives participating in collaborative efforts have gone beyond traditional views of how they should interact with the public or other agencies. Rather than being authoritarian, they have been cooperative. Rather than simply consulting with the public to get its consent for a desired agency direction, agency staff have committed to a collaborative approach in which decision making could proceed as a partnership, even though the agency retained the authority ultimately to make decisions. Agency leaders and staff were able to make an often difficult transition to a broader set of roles, including those of expert, stakeholder, partner, facilitator, and leader.

In many partnerships, agency officials were self-conscious about their effect on the decision-making process. As described in chapter 1, agency staff members historically have viewed their role as experts producing technically correct decisions, but the perspective that "we know best" gets in the way of collaborative work and limits information exchange. It also hampers creative thinking and undermines ownership of decisions by regulated parties.

Agency officials who have been successful in collaborative initiatives have been able to provide expertise and retain ultimate decision-making power but in a way that is supportive of the collaboration. Indeed, people usually welcome the expertise of agency representatives in collaborative partnerships because it provides information necessary for effective decision making. FWS biologist Greg Neudecker notes that in the Blackfoot Challenge, "Agency representatives are there to point out the sideboards as to what is and is not feasible." In successful collaborations, agency experts are available but not overbearing; they are forthright about the specific concerns of the agency that need to be addressed and the guidance and constraints provided by law and regulation but open to creative ways to meet those needs.

Agency representatives become more partners and leaders and less dictatorial decision makers in the process of successful collaboration. In the Negrito ecosystem project in New Mexico, the commitment of the Forest Service to a truly collaborative process was critical to changing the dynamics within that area of Catron County, which some have described as ground zero for the property rights movement. According to Forest Service district timber and recreation specialist Gary McCaleb, the Reserve Ranger District of the Gila

National Forest was approaching a crisis situation that demanded an innovative approach, and District Ranger Mike Gardner responded with foresight. "The planning wasn't working. Projects weren't being implemented. We were walking into a meat grinder. He thought a different approach might work," says McCaleb.

A core group of Forest Service staff; environmental, timber, and grazing interests; and the county extension agent began meeting to develop an ecosystem management approach for the 130,000-acre Negrito watershed located at the headwaters of the Gila River. District Ranger Gardner supported the effort fully: "I told them that the only bounds on the group is that their decisions can't adversely affect people who work on the district and they can't conflict with laws and resource directives from Congress. That kicked the door open and people came in."

Part of a leader's job is to motivate and empower others to be creative and take ownership for problem solving. A number of agency officials responded to the challenge of changing their traditional roles by being flexible. For example, Forest Service forester Maria Durazo-Means attributes the success of the Forest Service effort to engage the southeast Alaska community in collaborative recreation planning to the freedom to be creative and innovative: "The ranger gave the group flexibility in accomplishing the project. This is probably why it was accomplished in spite of the glitches. . . . He assigned the project and then let us loose."

Making this transition in agency roles clearly is difficult for agency officials used to operating in certain ways. One EPA participant in a negotiated rule-making process comments: "I've found that we are not trained as effective negotiators; we are trained as engineers, as regulators. We have been trained to say, 'You do it this way.'"[12] From his perspective on the Cameron County Agricultural Coexistence Committee, FWS refuge manager Steve Thompson explains, "A major difficulty, especially for a biologist, was saying, you don't know when you don't know." In addition, staff members involved in partnerships often went back to the office to find a great deal of skepticism and concern. According to Thompson, "When you find a common ground, it really doesn't look quite like what everybody thinks it is going to look like. And so it's difficult. You find yourself being a little bit lonely. When I went back to my bosses at FWS, at first their typical response was 'Well, you must have sold out, or you have done something horrible because they are all agreeing with you. And those are enemy people, you know. . . . There is no way you could have come to an agreement without selling out.'"

Nevertheless, agency personnel involved in collaborative initiatives recognize the need to persevere to overcome such dilemmas. California Coastal Conservancy official Dick Wayman, a participant in the Eel River Sustainable

Agriculture Committee, comments, "I'm a government bureaucrat. It can be real tempting to try to run things yourself, and I think that is a horrible mistake. It's easy to come up with plans that just simply can't work." Often agencies try to protect their own organizations, sometimes at the expense of what is best for the resource. According to BLM manager Merle Good, one of the partners in the Elkhorn Mountains Cooperative Management Agreement, "You must have total commitment to managing for the good of the resource and not the good of the agency."

Learning Together

While there are many reasons that collaborative initiatives are able to achieve a different mind-set, one key step is committing to a process of mutual learning in which participants agree that they individually do not have all the answers. Partners build a common understanding of a problem or situation through shared learning. This process involves sharing expertise, acquiring new information, and adopting a mind-set that more complete understanding is to be found by combining the perspectives of many, not accepting the conclusions of one.[13]

Joint Fact-Finding

Many collaborative initiatives have incorporated activities that built a base of shared information perceived as credible by partners. For example, information sharing and joint fact-finding are central to the partnership involved in managing for the Oregon silverspot butterfly, a federally listed threatened species. The Nature Conservancy approached the Forest Service in 1983 when it found a population of silverspots on its preserve adjacent to the Siuslaw National Forest. In response, the Forest Service staff shared the research and management information they had accumulated over the previous two years and helped TNC carry out a prescribed burn to hold succession at bay. From that point, the two groups decided to collaborate and began to combine research efforts and expertise. According to TNC stewardship director Cathy Macdonald, "Working together has allowed us to compare populations and habitat conditions across sites. These comparisons have improved our understanding of the factors that affect the population dynamics of the Oregon silverspot butterfly and ultimately improve our management of the species. We've learned much more by cooperating than we could have on our own."

Often the efforts at learning together have been shorter in duration than the extensive research in the silverspot case but still highly effective. "Walking the land" and seeing things together provide a great platform for the development of shared understanding. For example, the Beartree Challenge organized opportunities for participants to examine the landscape effects of some timber management equipment, such as single-grip harvesters and for-warders. Bill Jones of Jones Equipment says that environmentalists were "ecstatic" after visiting the project site and observing that management could be carried out in a manner that was relatively "light on the land" and therefore not incompatible with grizzly bear management.

Inventing Options Together

Shared learning also provides the possibility for more creative thinking. As John Stuart Mill noted over 150 years ago, "It is hardly possible to overrate the value . . . of placing human beings in contact with persons dissimilar to them-selves, and with modes of thought and action unlike those with which they are familiar. . . . Such communication has always been, and is peculiarly in this present age, one of the primary sources of progress."[14]

Being creative and "inventing options" are standard mantras of the negoti-ation literature.[15] Brainstorming solutions—identifying as many ideas as pos-sible without evaluating them simultaneously—is a tool used by many meeting facilitators and mediators.[16] In this process, usually more heads are better than fewer, and shared learning processes can result in more creative ideas being identified and developed. As Darby Partnership member Dennis Hall comments, "If we take the time to sit down together and work creatively, we can come up with better solutions than if any of us work independently."

By creating processes that involve opportunities for shared learning, people are released from the burden of having to be "experts" all by themselves. According to Teri Devlin, TNC representative to the Darby Partnership, one of the significant benefits of collaborative approaches is "the realization that you do not have to be an expert on everything. You team up with experts and there-fore can get a whole bunch more done than you ever could by yourself." For agency staff, the shift from an authoritative expert model to a shared learning model often provides a sense of freedom. Staff members do not always have to be the ones with the answers then, and they have an opportunity to advance their own understanding through expertise brought by other participants.

People need to come to their own conclusions, and shared learning processes help them do so. As Dennis Hall indicates, "The Darby Partnership is a place where information can be exchanged without the need for judg-ment, and so people can come to their own conclusions about what the infor-mation means to them." Orange County HCP Working Group member Dan Silver, a representative of the Endangered Habitats League, highlights the need to be involved continuously, in order to understand and trust conclu-sions: "Had I not been part of the working group, I would not have been able to accept the plan. Having that ability to see it as it was developed was criti-cal." He was able to support the final plan, he says, "because I had participated in the working group and been able to understand the constraints and step-wise decision making and hence reformed my expectations for the HCP."

Taking the Time to Develop Understanding

Implementing shared learning processes is challenging. Participants in the Darby Partnership, an effort heavily grounded in information sharing, comment on some of the challenges. Scientific information is "intimidating to many," according to TNC representative Teri Devlin. Different vocabularies stand as barriers between people, according to Kathy Smith of the Ohio Department of Natural Resources: "All of us tend to talk in our own jargon and use terms familiar with us, and that can be a challenge." "A lot of scientists come off as unapproachable or seem esoteric to the layperson," comments Marc Smith of the Ohio Environmental Protection Agency. All of this takes a lot of time, cautions Mary Ann Core of the NRCS. "Science is there—it just takes a lot of time and people to sit around and discuss it."

People involved in collaborative efforts have varying levels of background knowledge requiring a variety of educational and outreach approaches. Jerry Jack, BLM project manager for the Owl Mountain Partnership, advises: "Bring all members along. If because of their background, education, or training, someone doesn't understand, then you have to take the time to sit them down and explain it to them. Go sit down and drink some coffee with them and explain things."

Bounding the Problem with Credible Information

One way that groups involved in collaborative natural resource and environmental management have been able to progress is by using scientific information as a way to bound the problem at hand. In a number of cases, science has provided a playing field that people could agree to and rely on as a means of making fair choices. For some groups, it provides a common language and a set of procedures that enables them to overcome their value- and interest-based differences.

A Base of Scientific Information

Technical information and scientific procedures were critical to the progress of a number of the successful partnerships we studied. For example, Teri Devlin of the Darby Partnership says, "I think the science is integral to everything we are doing—first of all, to prove what we are doing is right and to justify it." Stephen Porter of the Colorado Division of Wildlife, a member of the

Owl Mountain Partnership, agrees: "You have to have a strong scientific component. That is where you will get eaten alive if your protocols are all wrong, if you did not gather good data, if you did not use data accurately in the best means. That is where the scientific community will come in and chop you to pieces." Rancher and Owl Mountain steering committee member Verl Brown comments, "You have to look for the truth and can't be afraid of finding something you don't like."

The Huron River Adopt-a-Stream Program (described in chapter 4) relies on a scientific foundation to ensure its legitimacy. Program staff train volunteer team captains in stream collection techniques to ensure that the teams collect according to uniform methods. The involvement of scientific experts has also been a key element of the program. Program director Joan Martin advises that similar efforts should seek out such scientific expertise. "Make sure you have the resources you need to really know what you're talking about," she says. "You want credibility and respectability . . . as being knowledgeable."

Independent Science

Many groups have used outside experts as a source of expertise and information that is less likely to be biased. In the Cameron County case, "There were a lot of basic questions they asked about this endangered species, and we didn't have much information," according to FWS official Steve Thompson. One way the agency was able to address this problem was by drawing on outside expertise. According to Thompson, "We always tried to find the experts on that, bring them back to the committee, and answer their specific questions, the real questions—not the emotions."

In several cases, ways have been found to involve independent scientists or to insulate scientific fact-finding from decision making. In developing the Karner blue butterfly HCP in Wisconsin, a team of biologists from state and federal agencies and universities developed science-based recommendations, which were then evaluated by the HCP partners for their cost implications and reasonableness. With the Clark County HCP, a technical advisory committee (TAC) provided scientific review and served as an information conduit with outside experts. According to FWS staff biologist Sherry Barrett, "Outside review worked well because we had it early and really all along through the TAC. They [TAC members] also worked as an effective go-between in soliciting views of scientists not on the subcommittee."

In some situations, outreach to outside scientists was used as a way to gather information and ensure that the group dealt with the scientists' concerns at the outset. In the International Paper Company HCP for the Red Hills salamander, International Paper staff involved outside scientists who were very knowledgeable about the salamander and therefore likely to criticize the plan if it were not scientifically sound and credible. According to Joe McGlincy, former section leader for International Paper: "I could anticipate that if we were going to get a whole lot of criticism, it would be from those two or three people." So the company asked them to review drafts of the plan before it went to the FWS in order to ensure that key issues were addressed and scientific understanding was incorporated. As McGlincy observed, doing so would make them "aware of what we were going to do as well as get them on board with us."

An Adaptive Management Approach

Several of the partnerships we studied also were able to proceed by acknowledging scientific uncertainty and using an adaptive management approach. Often differences in people's perspectives arise from varying assumptions about the likelihood of certain events occurring in the future. One person may believe that the chance of a management technique working is 20 percent and another may believe it is 80 percent. Arguing about the probabilities will not reconcile the differences. Instead, an adaptive management approach is the only way to proceed: undertaking experiments or demonstration projects, evaluating them in a credible fashion, and providing a way to proceed in response to the knowledge gained from the experiments. In some cases, a contingent agreement can be fashioned that acknowledges the uncertainty and provides a binding way to proceed given potential outcomes. For example, groups will reach agreements that are quite specific to probable outcomes: "If the outcome is X, we will do A; if it is Y, we will do B; if it is Z, we will do C."

An adaptive management approach was used to deal with uncertainty and skepticism in several cases. For example, many groups used pilot projects as a way to demonstrate the possibility of a different approach. The decision to use goats to graze the balds on Roan Mountain in the Pisgah National Forest in order to maintain the balds as suitable habitat for more than thirty threatened and endangered species was actively publicized as an experiment. The Mt. Roan Advisory Group was involved in decision making and management of the experiment and as a result was supportive. In addition, with the help of interpretive volunteers from local environmental groups, and an honest explanation that they did not know everything and were trying something new, the Forest Service received the support of most visitors to the area.

By promoting the project as an ongoing experiment, Forest Service staff achieved a heightened level of involvement and ownership in the project by outside groups and took themselves off the hook of knowing "the best way" to manage the balds. It was a mind-set that empowered some, relieved others, and allowed for the testing of what Dr. Frank Pinkerton of the National Goat

Research Center viewed as "an environmentally friendly and publicly acceptable management technique." In his view, the goats have been very successful at slowing succession on the balds without mowing or pesticide use, and they have a "soothing effect on people." According to District Ranger Paul Bradley, "a willingness on the part of district employees to try new ideas and an open involvement of any and all interested individuals in decision making" were the two main ingredients that led to the successful and innovative experiment on the Mt. Roan balds.

Achieving an open, flexible, creative, positive, risk-taking, and holistic mind-set that is problem focused and that rises above traditional concepts of agency roles is a constant struggle. Groups use many of the ideas contained in this book to promote this productive mind-set: They appeal to common interests, demonstrate interdependence, employ good process, deal with the people side of partnerships, and take small steps to prove that success is possible. They use changes in personnel as strategic opportunities to change interpersonal dynamics. And they employ processes of mutual learning in which joint fact-finding is used to build an information base and relationships, and science aids decision making. All of this takes considerable effort, particularly given the strength of the alternative views that little change is possible and that any change will be disadvantageous to a group's interests.

Behavioral scientists tell us how difficult it is to "unfreeze" old patterns of behavior yet how uplifting and empowering it can be to do so. In several of our cases, a change in approach—a fundamentally altered mind-set—was critical to the group's progress, and those who achieved a change were exuberant from the experience. In the words of rancher Jim Stone, a participant in the Blackfoot Challenge in Montana, "We have not eliminated cows from streamside grazing in all cases, but now it is done properly. It is that whole educational wheel that I have jumped on, and it is incredible. These projects affect ranchers in a positive way. It saves us money. Everyone is happy, and we are putting more pounds of beef on the hoof because we are managing our ground better." Based on his experience working on economic development projects in Adams County, Idaho, Forest Service District Ranger David Spann notes, "I think there are some folks who just have experienced the power of working together, and when they get hold of that, it's kind of hard to forget it."

Chapter 8

Fostering a Sense of Responsibility and Commitment

*A*n observant visitor to the Applegate Valley of southern Oregon and Northern California will notice that many valley residents sport a small button on their shirts and hats with a single word on it: THEY. A bold, red line slashes across the button, crossing out the word. The symbolism is simple and direct: there is no "they" in the Applegate watershed, only "us." The guiding philosophy of the eight-year-old Applegate Partnership is "Practice Trust—Them Is Us." Members of this unique community have come to realize that if they want an ecologically and economically sustainable future for their valley, the responsibility for making that happen lies in their hands, not in anyone else's.

The Applegate watershed is like many watersheds throughout the West. It contains a patchwork of private ranches and farms, national forests, rangelands, and state and county lands. The social fabric is just as diverse, a rich blend of fifth-generation farmers, newcomer spiritualists, Forest Service foresters, BLM range managers, environmentalists, ranchers, loggers, and timber companies, as well as the myriad small enterprises that provide a foundation for the functioning of its small, rural towns.

The blood pressure of this valley slowly rose during the 1980s as the spotted owl controversy altered management of the public lands in the watershed, and the adverse effects of earlier management practices on the valley's public and private resources became apparent. Tempers flared between loggers and local environmentalists and the supporters of their countervailing perspectives. A Forest Service district ranger captures the adversarial atmosphere of the valley with the comment, "We were dealing here with arch enemies who . . . only met across the courtroom." It was in this social tinderbox that Jack Shipley, an avid environmentalist, and Jim Neal, a long-time logger, did the unthinkable: they began talking with one another. In so doing, these two unlikely collaborators planted the seed for what rapidly grew into the Applegate Partnership.

Shipley and Neal were frustrated with the polarization of resource management issues in their valley and were no longer willing to accept gridlock. They decided that it was worth a try to get people in the valley together to hash out issues face to face. In the summer of 1992, they began discussing with others in the valley their idea of a "different approach to managing the half-million-acre Applegate watershed." To their surprise, they found a receptive yet cautious community that shared many desires and interests in common. As environmentalist Brett KenCairn, a member of the Applegate Partnership Board, recalls: "At the base of it, people really did have this common love and need for a forest that was healthy and intact. That really formed the foundation. And when people saw that, they then could say, 'We do have this overarching set of values or visions that we can work towards. Now, we may not necessarily agree about how we get there, but at least we know that our end goal is the same.'"

BLM range manager John Lloyd echoes KenCairn's observations: "We got to the point where we just had to sit down and start talking. We got to the point where there was something in it for everybody to start talking." As partnership board member Chris Bratt puts it, the group moved away from the frustrating "my opinion against yours; my expert against yours; my laws against your guidelines" dynamic that had dominated their past interactions. Fifth-generation farmer Connie Young summarizes the critical transformation that began occurring in the Applegate watershed and that gradually paved the way for their ability to work together: "In the past it has been 'us' and 'them,' and now it is 'we'—it is all of us together." [1]

Encouraged by this realization, Shipley and Neal organized a meeting in October 1992 with neighbors, representatives from industry, community groups, the BLM, the Forest Service, and several local environmental organizations to discuss a plan to make the Applegate watershed a demonstration site for ecologically and financially responsible resource management. Not wasting any time, this sixty-person group elected a nine-person board of directors whose nominations were based not on affiliation but, according to Shipley, on a willingness to "work toward solutions, leave partisanship at home, put ecosystem health in front of private agendas, and have the time to participate" in meetings. At their first meeting, the group crafted a common vision statement:

> The Applegate Partnership is a community-based project involving industry, conservation groups, natural resource agencies, and residents cooperating to encourage and facilitate the use of natural resource principles that promote ecosystem health and diversity.

Through community involvement and education, this partnership supports management of all land within the watershed in a manner that sustains natural resources and that will, in turn, contribute to economic and community stability within the Applegate Valley.

The overarching objective is to make "future land management in the Applegate Watershed ecologically credible, aesthetically acceptable, and economically viable."

The partnership has implemented or supported numerous on-the-ground projects, including assessments, research and monitoring, environmental restoration, outreach, and public education. One project that was instrumental in establishing the group's identity and commitment was the development of a GIS system that integrates BLM, Forest Service, and county tax lot information. Su Rolle, Forest Service–BLM liaison to the Applegate Partnership, notes that this system for consolidating data on a range of watershed issues provides "probably the greatest amount of integrated information for a half-million-acre area in the whole western U.S." Just as important, it has affected people's perceptions of their interconnectedness and, in so doing, their willingness to work together. As Rolle explains, "Having the whole watershed pop out over and over again—with all of the lands seen as a whole—has really increased people's sensitivity and understanding that we really have to work together. . . . It has significantly reinforced the vision that we are all in this together." In addition to the changed perspective of community members, Rolle has noticed a change in attitude of federal land managers, from believing they were "experts with a mission to convince" to a feeling of "let's see what we can do together." She observes, "We are now part of the system—a neighbor—and we care."

Many refer to the Applegate Partnership as a "project" or an "organization." In reality, however, it is neither. It is a community that has come to recognize its interdependence and has chosen to accept responsibility for guiding its future in a way that is meaningful, legitimate, and sound to all who care about the valley. The people of the Applegate watershed have redefined themselves based on what unites them as a community, not what divides them as individuals. In so doing, they have instilled a sense of responsibility for their valley's future that has spread throughout the watershed and has led to widespread commitment to working together to address shared problems and pursue common goals. They have accepted this responsibility with an obvious pride and dedication and have remained committed to it despite numerous challenges.

As the Applegate Partnership demonstrates, effective collaborative partnerships foster a sense of responsibility and commitment among participants. They work to transform "them" to "us." They instill a feeling of ownership in the resources and issues at hand, the process being followed to address those issues, and the outcomes achieved by that process. Successful partnerships evidence commitment by participants and ensure that the process and its products are honored by all involved. Finally, fair principles guide decision making, and no single individual or group is left shouldering the burden of action.

Transforming "Them" to "Us"

As described in chapters 1 and 3, most collaborative partnerships arise out of adversarial situations in which divergent interests are entrenched in their own camps, focused on the differences that seemingly divide them. Each has its own worldview of who is "right" and "wrong," the source of a problem, and what should be done about it. It is an "us versus them" milieu that is self-reinforcing. The incentives provided by traditional decision-making structures promote polarization and encourage groups to strategically emphasize the differences in their arguments. The expectations and roles demanded by this awkward, often hostile, dance are understood and adhered to by all involved, even if they understand that a different mode of interaction might be useful. Successful collaborative groups in our studies shut down this adversarial dance and helped to transform those involved from self-proclaimed enemies to neighbors and eventually to collaborators. They transformed "them" to "us" and did so in a number of ways.

Unifying Visions and Goals

As discussed in chapter 4, vision statements and common goals provide a guiding mission and focus to a group and help to facilitate the problem-solving process. In the case of the Applegate Partnership, Su Rolle notes, "Articulating the vision has been very, very important for us. We wrote it down in the beginning, and it has really been a guiding light when things got squirrely the last couple of years." By focusing attention on a shared future, such statements and goals unify those involved. They allow groups to recognize that their interests are related and encourage people to acknowledge that they are "in it together": it is "we," not "you." Further, framing common interests encourages individuals and groups to accept some measure of responsibility for solving shared problems and pursuing a common future. After all, if "they" no longer exists, the imperative for action can rest only on "us."

In the cooperative management process for the Elkhorn Mountains in Montana, described in chapter 5, the development of a collective vision among the three land management agencies marked the first time that those government entities recognized the interrelatedness of their lands and management practices. Even though they had long managed adjacent lands, it was the joint visioning exercise that caused them to acknowledge, according to

Forest Service District Ranger George Weldon, that "those boundaries are just arbitrary." The process unified them and instilled a shared sense of responsibility for "integrative, ecosystem-oriented management." As a result, individual landowners such as the Forest Service have changed the way they view their roles. According to Weldon, prior to the agreement the question managers asked themselves was "How do we manage Forest Service lands in the Elkhorns?" Now the question has changed to "How do we participate in the management of the Elkhorns?" Weldon feels that because of this change in attitude, employees are getting "excited about management prospects." "Quality goes up, and we do a better job," he says.

In the Applegate Partnership, the way the process started led to the recognition that interests and responsibility for action were shared. At the first meeting, participants introduced themselves, their families, and their hopes for the future before they were allowed to indicate the interest or organization they represented. This mode of introduction highlighted common interests and individual commitment at the same time that it encouraged joint action. Shared responsibility was needed because it was apparent that there was no lead agency or single individual in charge.

Recognizing Interdependence

Most successful partnerships go beyond a recognition of shared goals to the perception that individual interests are interconnected. They are unable to act unilaterally to advance their individual interests and hence need to work together to achieve their own goals. Collaboration scholar Barbara Gray argues that collaborative problem solving requires stakeholders to recognize and accept that some "fundamental interdependence exists" among them.[2] It is not enough that groups are interdependent; rather, they must perceive this interdependence and recognize that it creates a need for cooperative action.

In most of the partnerships we studied, those involved recognized their interdependence. In order to address the issues that concerned them, groups had to work together as a community. For example, NRCS agent Mike Delano notes that an evolving perception of interdependence caused him, Forest Service District Ranger Alton Bryant, and rancher Ellen Groves to begin collaborating in managing the Kiowa Grasslands ecosystem. He comments: "To manage the resource, we need to work together. We're scattered out over a lot of miles here, and we have to work together in a coordinated effort." According to Grove, there is a feeling now, more than ever, "that we are in this together." "Alton and Mike's doors are always open," she says.

In many resource management cases, geographic isolation helps promote a sense of interdependence. Chris Plakos, chairperson of the Coalition for Unified Recreation of the Eastern Sierra, notes that the Eastern

Sierra is "an extremely isolated community . . . tied together by one two-lane highway. Because of this isolation, we have to work together, even when there are competing interests." As described in chapter 6, CURES has provided participants with a mechanism for working together to ensure that their interests are met. Shrinking budgets have encouraged federal agencies to participate since CURES allows agencies to share costs and obtain grant funding. When CURES first formed, local businesses saw it as an important means of repairing the economic effects of a protracted drought. Environmental groups participated in order to have a voice in shaping the future development of the area. In short, as Forest Service facilitator Nancy Upham puts it, when the Forest Service approached local groups to seek their involvement, "these groups saw it as vital to their interests to participate."

The situation was the same for the Dunes Forum, a series of meetings at which local stakeholders discuss issues relating to The Nature Conservancy's management of the Guadalupe-Nipomo Dunes Preserve in Southern California. Participants in the monthly forum meetings are quite diverse, including local residents; People for Nipomo Dunes, a local citizens group; representatives of the county and other local governments; representatives of the State Parks Off-Highway Vehicles Division, which manages the Pismo Dunes State Vehicular Recreation Area just to the north of the preserve; and representatives of Unocal, which owns a large parcel of contaminated property adjacent to the preserve. As Karen Wood, TNC's community relations representative, says, "I never in my life thought that People for Nipomo Dunes would sit at a table with Unocal and the Off-Highway Vehicles Division of State Parks, because those are the two organizations they are most against." But, she notes, "They recognize that if we don't talk, nothing is going to happen." They acknowledge their interdependence and consequently are working together to enhance effective management of the dunes.

Leading by Example

Successful collaborative efforts usually have one or two individuals who have adopted a "we're in this together" stance that sharply contrasts with previous adversarial interactions. They lead by example and model partnership behavior. Their behavior encourages others to begin conceiving of the issues in terms of shared problems that require joint consideration and action. Certainly, the Applegate Partnership's anti-THEY buttons serve as a gentle reminder for valley residents that they are in it together. Nancy Upham emphasizes that one of the keys to CURES's success is that the Forest Service representatives involved chose to "be a neighbor and a partner to communities we live and work with," thereby transforming, from the agency's perspective, "'the public' and 'the agency' to 'all of us together.'"

Often, but not always, a forward-looking agency official steps forward and captures everyone's attention through actions that break adversarial dynamics. For example, the facilitator in one national forest planning process characterizes the approach of the lead Forest Service participant in this way: "He would say, 'Quit telling the Forest Service what to do. Get in here and roll up your sleeves and [help us to] do it.' And he took a lot of flak for that because [some agency staff thought that] only the Forest Service has skills to write the plan, maintain trails, etc. So he had to fight internally to make this happen." This behavior encouraged people within the agency and other participating organizations to acknowledge their responsibility for ensuring that a sound and legitimate plan was developed. It dramatically altered the nature of their interactions to the point that, as one participant comments, "If the Forest Service folks hadn't been wearing uniforms, you wouldn't have known them from the non–Forest Service folks."

Hiring a nonpartisan facilitator to help run meetings is another strategy that effectively places agency representatives in a partner role and enables them to work together with other parties. Lars Botzjorson, who represented the Green Mountain Club and the Appalachian Trail Conference in the Green Mountain National Forest planning process, comments: "Having an independent party to run the process . . . was a key factor for success. It's not the Forest Service directly that's leading the meetings. We're all in the same boat because there's someone else standing in front of the room."

Focusing on the Problem, Not Who to Blame

Often the first response to a problem by individuals and organizations is to blame someone else, and the claims and counterclaims that result from the "blame game" can limit the possibility of collaborative problem solving. Successful partnerships are able to step back from the issue of blame and focus attention on the problem or issue at hand. For example, Rebecca Kress, the entrepreneur behind the successful effort to clean up California's Russian River, was careful to avoid getting caught up in the often polarizing debate about resource management issues in the diverse communities where river cleanups take place. Instead, her strategy has been to say, "Hey, the river belongs to everybody. It's going to take everybody to clean it up. I'm not pointing any fingers." She feels this approach has helped her attract a broad range of volunteers, and she notes, "Taking a nonadversarial role has become one of the most productive things I could have done for this."

Similarly, Kim Rodrigues, the coordinator for the North Klamath Bioregional Group in Northern California, recognized that the "common mistrust of state and federal agencies" shared across local communities had to be circumvented before collaboration could occur. Her strategy was to shift attention from the debate about agency actions or inactions that had created problems to focus on "local needs," thereby fostering "more people working together for local solutions and decreased polarity within our community." By focusing on the problems that concerned local communities and how those problems might be solved, people began to realize, she notes, "that it is not 'us versus them' but 'we' that will bring success."

When the Forest Service lost a lawsuit claiming that its sales of firewood contributed to air pollution problems in the Upper Yakima Valley (see discussion in chapter 7), District Ranger Donald Rotell could simply have halted all firewood sales, thereby ridding the Forest Service of any culpability for air-quality problems in the valley. Instead, he acknowledged that an air-quality problem existed in the Yakima Valley, and while no one was wholly responsible for it, there was no way that a single agency could resolve it alone. According to Rotell, "As a result of the lawsuit and public reaction, it became readily apparent that this was a major issue on the part of the public. We didn't really feel we could afford to do anything but the best job, so we put some of our best people on it and gave them time and resources to do the job. . . . They took a very objective look at the whole program. They let it take them wherever it would. We found out a lot of things we didn't know at the start."

Noting that air pollution was a problem shared among many individuals and organizations, and that responsibility for acting on it must also be shared, Rotell initiated a collaborative approach by forming an interdisciplinary team to prepare the EA and conducting extensive outreach. Framing the problem as a shared community concern encouraged others to help solve the problem, rather than criticize and fight Forest Service proposals as had been the norm in the past. Rather than asking how the Forest Service might do the minimum to satisfy the court's ruling, Rotell asked himself who needed to be a part of an effort to address the whole problem, and how they might be engaged in a process of problem solving.

Ownership of the Problem and the Process

People take care of what is theirs. When they "own" something, they pay attention to it and protect and nurture it. As Harold Simonson has observed, "We vandalize, pollute and plunder what is separate from us; we revere, protect and cherish what we belong to."[3] Fostering a sense of shared ownership was critical to the success of many of the collaborative efforts we studied. People who "owned" the resource or the problem felt compelled to find ways to take care of it. Successful efforts also instilled ownership in the collaborative process. Through involvement in the process, participants came to own its outcomes and consequently ensured that decisions were implemented. If a problem arose in the process, they did not look for whom to complain to, they took care of it themselves. They made the process work.

Ownership of the Problem

Successful collaborative partnerships establish a direct, personal connection between individuals and the problems at hand. In facilitating involvement in restoring the Oak Openings ecosystem of northwest Ohio, Michelle Grigore of the Toledo Metroparks Department emphasized a sense of common ownership of a special place. The group's educational materials describe the Oak Openings as "*our* Oak Openings" and "Toledo's Oak Openings" and make the point that the area is home to a unique and threatened ecosystem of local and national significance. Grigore comments that this sense of common ownership helped build a sense of shared responsibility for doing something about the problem. The partners' realization that "If *we* don't do it, it's going to be gone" has become an important cornerstone of the effort. As groups became involved in restoration efforts, their activities built a sense of pride that reinforced their feelings of ownership. Many volunteers now return to sections of the Oak Openings where they worked on restoration projects to see how *their* area is doing.

Similarly, one of the strategies of the Huron River Watershed Council's Adopt-a-Stream program is to build a sense of ownership of the river system in the local community. In Program Director Joan Martin's view, people "are more committed when they feel an identity" with the resource. She has seen that once people get involved in the Adopt-a-Stream monitoring efforts, they become more interested in the watershed as a whole and seek additional ways to help protect and restore the ecosystem. Active volunteer stewards play an important role in raising awareness and getting others involved in creek protection. Martin notes, "The [Adopt-a-Stream] stewards I hope will be the spokespersons for the creek to the community because it's the community's creek, and that's going to make the difference as to whether it's protected or not."

Ownership of the Process

As discussed in chapter 5, early and proactive involvement of diverse interests facilitates successful collaboration by building understanding, relationships, and trust among people. At the same time, this early and meaningful involvement fosters ownership of the process and leads to a greater commitment among those involved to making it work and following through with its results. As Dick Andrews, facilitator of the Green Mountain National Forest wilderness planning process, observes, "It appears that when people are in on the takeoff, they're generally a lot happier about the landing. . . . Having a chance to participate all the way through makes people happier with the results."

The same early, ongoing, and integral involvement of all parties in the Negrito ecosystem management effort fostered their ownership of and commitment to it. The Forest Service held group meetings to help set priorities and develop proposals on how to apportion funding for the project. As Forest Service range and watershed staff member Chuck Oliver comments, "If it is just a project that the Forest Service has sponsored, funded, and done, it is just another Forest Service project. But if it's a project that the group brought forward, got outside and internal funding, everybody was a part of the planning process, and it was carried through to fruition, then folks can feel like they have done something. It has to be a part of everyone."

Because people often assume that agencies are supposed to take charge of problems, a special role for agency staff in promoting ownership is to reinforce the point that resource problems are shared. For example, Forest Service District Ranger John Baswell engaged the Clifton-Choctaw tribe in a community development project but not by agency dictate. Baswell emphasized to the tribe that he was willing to help with the application process but that the tribe should decide on its own what project it wanted to fund. Baswell comments, "I kept repeating that I didn't know what kind of project they should do . . . but was there to help out with any logistics. I kept telling them that I didn't know what they needed, but that this program was available and this was the information they needed to apply to the Forest Service to get the ball rolling. I made them come up with a proposal."

Providing people with the latitude to make creative decisions is critical to fostering ownership of the process and its outcomes. According to Lonnie Anderson, mayor of Kake, Alaska, residents were particularly pleased about being included by the Forest Service in all phases of planning and selection of recreation projects for the St. Petersburg District of the Tongass National Forest: "For the first time it gave outlying communities an opportunity for input on the type of recreation projects we would be interested in. . . . It becomes the people's recreation area, not just the Forest Service's." Building this sense of ownership is just as important for agency staff as for outside groups. Having the opportunity to solve a problem rather than implement a predetermined solution is energizing. As one forest planner expressed with great pride, "It was *our* choice; nobody from above told us to do it this way."

Commitment

In the successful collaborative partnerships that we studied, individuals and organizations lived up to their commitments. They did what they said they would do. They abided by the terms of the decisions and agreements reached and worked diligently to diffuse that commitment through their agencies and constituencies. People translated their sense of responsibility for a problem and a process to a commitment to acting on that responsibility. Quite simply, they kept their promises to one another in a variety of ways.

In our study of twenty national forest plan appeals settled through negotiation, commitment stood out as the single most significant difference between successful and unsuccessful negotiations. Since we interviewed participants six or more years after the negotiations were completed, success was judged against a backdrop of real experience. That is, success was not just reaching a signed agreement, but achieving a management situation with which groups were satisfied over time. Commitment to the process of collaboration and its products contributed most to respondents' satisfaction levels. For example, one nonagency individual who participated in negotiations on three different national forests shares this observation about why two negotiations succeeded while the third failed:

> The [X] and [Y] forest plan appeals were settled because all parties were committed to the process, all were willing to consider compromise, and all parties tried to understand each other's concerns. The Forest Service took a positive leadership role and was honestly willing to make major changes, if necessary, in the forest plan. The [Z] National Forest involved many of the same non–Forest Service players. However, the supervisor and his staff offered no leadership, were not interested in any substantive changes in the plan, and in the end stonewalled.

A different nonagency respondent who also participated in more than one national forest plan appeal negotiation (on a different set of forests) offers a similar explanation for why one succeeded while two others did not:

> It worked because it was not facilitated by the U.S. Forest Service, and the new forest supervisor had a high degree of integrity, vision, and broad mindedness. . . . [The] other negotiations have not gone well at all. The Forest Service has not lived by many written agreements, tried to renegotiate numerous times, and ignored brewing problems.

Commitment to a Collaborative Process

Those involved in the successful negotiations we studied evidenced a broad, conceptual commitment to the collaborative process. They were collaborating not because they had been told to do so. Instead, they were philosophically committed to the approach. Negotiation was not chosen for strategic reasons but in the belief that it provided a more appropriate context for addressing issues of concern. One forest planner comments that the appellants' "allegations were so widely disparate that the only way to resolve them was to do it all around the table together at one time." A supervisor of a different forest comments: "It's the only way. Only mediation looks at interests [vs. positions] by design."

On yet another forest where negotiation was judged successful, the agency planner describes the inability of the traditional appeals process to either build understanding of or effectively resolve the issues of concern. He comments that the official "responsive statements" used by the agency to respond to the formal issues raised in an appeal do not help the forest to actually understand the issues in the terms that the appellants care about them. He states that he simply "did not know how [the agency] could have done it through the responsive statements." Negotiation was the only way he knew to bring out the issues and address them, as opposed to, as he describes it, "running paper around the response statements." Furthermore, he comments, "The real issues are often social issues," and the only way to raise and address those issues is through dialogue.

In these cases, commitment was more than simply fulfilling the terms laid out in a written agreement. Not only did the agency do what it promised, but it remained committed to the fundamental tenets and spirit of the collaboration and the relationships that had been established through the negotiation process. One forest planner captures this sentiment when she emphasizes the importance of "keeping the faith with the folks that participated in this thing." She goes on to say, "It is very fair to say that this settlement is thought of as the Bible."

One simple way that agencies demonstrate their commitment to the collaborative process is by maintaining continuity among those involved in order to preclude wavering commitment as staff changes. At times, continuity simply means continued staffing of the effort when the initial staff members move elsewhere. Successful partnerships replace agency representatives in a timely fashion and work to maintain continuity in their understanding, dedication, and commitment. Given the level of personnel transfers in the federal lands agencies, maintaining continuity is often a challenge, but doing so provides an important message to participants in collaborative processes. As noted by Forest Service planner Maria Durazo-Means, based on her experience in the Alaska Recreation Planning case, "The importance of following through on promises cannot be overstated. Responsible land management begins with responsiveness to those we serve."

Building Support within Agencies and Constituencies

Collaborative decision making takes place among representatives of agencies, organizations, and groups. The individuals at the table are representing the interests of their broader constituencies in addressing issues and solving problems. Hence, to solve problems in an enduring way, decisions must be consistent with the interests of those beyond the table, as well as understood and accepted by them. A sense of responsibility and commitment must also be diffused among these broader organizations and the key decision makers within them. In successful collaborative initiatives, individuals maintain communication with their organizations and help build support for the collaborative efforts "back home."

In collaboratively developing a recreation plan for the St. Petersburg District of the Tongass National Forest, planner Maria Durazo-Means recognized how critical it was "to keep every level of the bureaucracy (forest supervisor, regional office, etc.) involved at each step and make sure they buy into the project." This level of involvement would help prevent the project from getting stopped later by the "higher ups." As Durazo-Means notes: "It is just as important to keep your organization informed as the public. This helps to build internal support. It is easier to sell the public on what we are doing when we have in-house support."

Similarly, one of the factors promoting success in the Elkhorn Coordinated Management case was that there were people throughout all of the agencies dedicated to the idea and willing to work toward its realization. The idea for an MOU began with a forest supervisor and filtered all the way down in the agency. District Ranger George Weldon notes the importance of this broad-based commitment: "You've got to have a communicated direction and mission from the top all the way to the bottom—all the way through the organizational structure." He believes that this occurred in the Forest Service in this case. The BLM's Merle Good agrees that the MOU was a result of "a lot of work on a lot of people's part" in all the agencies, not just those directly involved in the on-the-ground collaborative management activities.

Maintaining Communication

Collaboration is people working together, and commitment can start faltering when people stop interacting. This does not mean that formal meetings need to be scheduled every day, but it does mean that mechanisms are needed for easy, periodic interaction among partners. Participants need to be kept abreast of discussions and decisions that have been reached and the progress of implementation activities. Ongoing communication fosters an understanding of what is going on and assures people that others are abiding by their promises such that commitment is sustained.

Most successful collaborative efforts in our studies created mechanisms for ongoing communication among participants in the collaborative group as well as with their constituents. As Su Rolle observes of the Applegate Partnership, the group's frequent meetings have been critical to maintaining communication, thereby building the trust and personal ties among participants that have sustained their commitment to the effort. She notes that the group tried meeting twice a month rather than every week, "but then people miss each other and people feel like they are losing touch, and we aren't getting as much done anymore, and so it cranks up again."

Jim Wilcox, Plumas Corporation coordinator for the Feather River Coordinated Resource Management group, learned over time that the importance of communication "can't be overstated." He says that it is critically important to "keep members in the loop to a sufficient level that they'll always feel involved in the decision-making process and comfortable with the decisions that are made." Wilcox has found that this can be a challenge, particularly as the Feather River CRM has grown in size and scope. However, despite how busy he and his staff get, he says, "We constantly have to remind ourselves, 'Hey, we've got to keep everybody informed,' and take the time to do that."

Ongoing communication is important among more than the immediate participants in a collaborative partnership. Many efforts find ways to involve members of constituent groups at various stages in discussions and implementation in order to build understanding and support for group efforts. For example, while the Negrito ecosystem management effort relied on a core group of a half dozen people to develop and refine its proposal, it relied on an informal working group of about twenty-four people from a variety of backgrounds and interests who participated in four or five all-day meetings to help in developing the project's philosophy, scope, and issues and concerns. Group participants serve as information "conduits" to the organizations and people with whom they have relationships in the community. As Chuck Oliver, of the district's range and watershed staff, explains, "We have a wide cross-section of people who are working with us and discussing the problems and benefits related to these projects. So when the project finally comes to fruition, there is a large majority of people outside the group who are buying off on it." He continues, "The group members go back to their constituents and say, 'Hey, we worked hard on this, and it's a good project.'"

Backing Up Field Staff

For a collaboration to achieve on-the-ground outcomes, it must be paired with the funding and other support that allows agreements to be implemented. Successful collaborative efforts build the broader agency and organizational support necessary for those involved to follow through with their commitments. For example, the Adopt-a-Stream program has been an ongoing success because of the sustained support of Washtenaw County drain commissioner Janis Bobrin. The commissioner endorsed the original idea and provided initial funding for the program through funds available under the federal Clean Water Act. According to director Joan Martin, the support and personal dedication of Bobrin have been critical to the program's success. The program's budget is fairly small, with only one and a half staff members devoted to the project. Adopt-a-Stream does, however, have a "healthy equipment budget, which is very important and is not often the case [in such programs]," according to Martin. These funds have provided the program with sufficient resources to obtain quality scientific equipment, which has been an important factor in the program's success.

Similarly, the Forest Service demonstrated commitment to the Blue Mountains Natural Resources Institute (BMNRI) by continuing to fund the institute when faced with budget cuts in the mid-1990s.[4] Focused on a 19-million-acre area in northeast Oregon and southeast Washington, the institute is a cooperative venture whose goal is "enhancing the long-term economic and social benefits derived from the natural resources of the area in a way that is ecologically sensitive and sustainable." Overseen by an independent board of directors representing twenty organizations, the collaborative effort was funded as an attempt to avoid the kind of forest management conflicts evident elsewhere in these two states. Continuing commitment to the effort by the Forest Service has been important. According to BMNRI manager Tom Quigley, "In a time when budgets were being downsized, [our] budget was not cut. So those actions are walking the talk. They're literally putting their money where their mouth is."

Fairness

People want to be treated fairly. They are usually willing to do what they believe is fair and follow through with their commitments as long as everyone else does the same. In successful collaborative efforts, considerable effort is made to craft decision-making processes that are perceived as fair and outcomes that are judged equitable. Establishing procedures to assure "fairness" guards against people feeling that they have been "taken" and allows them to share information and make commitments. Greg Parsons of the Animas River Stakeholders Group in Colorado, a collaborative group convened in response to the threat of Superfund designation, offers three words as the key to building trust and respect: "Treat people fairly."

Fair Principles

Structuring a decision-making process that is seen as fair is a first step. Beyond the measures suggested in chapter 6, adopting decision-making criteria that are grounded in fair principles is important to helping people move beyond positions. Using objective criteria for decision making is a standard element of most texts on negotiation and decision making.[5] Establishing objective decision-making criteria allows people to discuss their interests and concerns with fewer worries about being exploited for revealing information honestly.

The most difficult step in the planning process used to construct a recreation plan for the Petersburg Ranger District of the Tongass National Forest was choosing how projects would be selected. The working group came up with criteria, such as safety and public service, by which they ranked all of the proposed projects. A point system was developed to indicate how well projects met each criterion. According to Mary Clements, recreation forester for the district, it was not easy for the group to agree on which criteria were most important and would distinguish projects from one another. She says, "It was an all-day session. We just kept going at it. We finally got to the point where no one was sure it was right. So, we tried it out on a couple of clear-cut projects to see how it would work." By getting agreement on the criteria for choosing which projects would make it onto the list, the final choice became straightforward, and different groups viewed it as fair.

Shared Costs

Beyond process fairness, it is important that outcomes be viewed as equitable in that costs are shared. The opposite situation, in which some groups come to be seen as "free riders," can damage an effort over time. As Nancy Walker, manager at TNC's Guadalupe-Nipomo Dunes Preserve, comments, "There are still an awful lot of people looking at us as, 'Yes, let's work together—you do all the work.'"

A vivid example of burden-sharing on a fairly large scale comes from Canada's Alberta Province. University of Michigan political scientist Barry Rabe analyzed the siting of hazardous waste facilities in the United States and Canada and found two dramatic success stories in which Canadian communities voluntarily cooperated in the siting process and supported siting decisions. According to Rabe, deliberate efforts to distribute the burden of hazardous waste management across the province rather than concentrating the burden on one or two communities played a key role in the successful collaboration that occurred in the two cases. Host communities were "reassured that a central part of the siting process involved special commitments to distribute the waste burden for waste management efforts more fairly."[6] Those commitments included import restrictions that limit (and in some cases ban) waste facilities from accepting waste generated in other provinces or outside Canada, the creation of regional waste storage and transfer stations in other communities, and widespread implementation of waste reduction and recycling programs.

The measures also promoted a sense of ownership of a shared problem needing a solution. One local citizen noted that before participating in the siting process, "I had no idea that so much waste was generated in Alberta and that so much of it came from our own town, and our businesses and homes."[7]

Treating communities equitably encouraged them to take responsibility for finding a solution rather than seeking to shift the burden to others.

As in the Alberta case, creating a process where people felt they were being treated fairly helped stakeholders in the cases we studied participate in decision making that was often painful and frustrating. Successful initiatives were able to foster a sense of shared ownership of community problems and collaborative processes. They pushed participants to commit to keeping faith with their agreements and the process itself. In many places, the most significant outcome of the collaborative efforts has been a reborn sense of shared responsibility for the problems people face and for finding ways to treat others with respect and dignity. "We're all in this together" may sound simplistic or trite, but traditional decision-making processes push us apart rather than bring us together. Processes that build a shared recognition of interconnectedness among people and the world in which they live allow them to address shared problems and work toward sustainable futures.

Chapter 9

Partnerships Are People

The sand dunes bordering the town of Guadalupe, California, are a central feature in that community's identity. As Nancy Warner, manager of The Nature Conservancy's Guadalupe-Nipomo Dunes Preserve, explains, "Guadalupe lacks a plaza—the traditional center in Latino villages and towns, the place where people come to visit and stroll, where young people meet and children play. The dunes were the nearest open space and therefore were serving the function of a plaza, providing a community gathering place."

In 1992, The Nature Conservancy staff worked long and hard to develop a master plan for their new dunes preserve adjacent to the town of Guadalupe. Located twenty-five miles south of San Luis Obispo, the preserve encompasses an area of huge shifting sand dunes along the Pacific Ocean that provide habitat for the endangered least tern and for rare blossoming plants. The preserve managers wanted to restore and protect this natural feature and thought the best way to do so was to regulate public use. They constructed an entrance gate and imposed a new $4 entry fee to fund stewardship and management efforts. Unfortunately, they had neither informed nor involved the town of Guadalupe in this planning effort, and the community immediately banded together in protest. As one local resident put it, "We saw The Nature Conservancy as scientists who wanted a preserve on the beach that you don't step on. *They* would do it; the local people weren't smart enough to protect it. They didn't go to the schools. They didn't prepare us for this. We started a little revolutionary work: Free Guadalupe Beach." Someone vandalized the new entrance structure, painting on it "Nature Conservancy Get Out." In the wake of the protests, TNC rescinded the entrance fee and began to look at what had happened and how to fix the situation. Warner admits, "We were blindsided by the public reaction."

Trust and communication between these two neighbors had been shattered. It took many apologies and some time to begin reestablishing relationships and restoring the trust necessary to start the preserve planning process anew. As Warner commented, "It didn't all happen in one meeting, . . . but it did take saying, 'We screwed up. We made a mistake.' And it took saying I'm sorry quite a few times, in a lot of ways."

Although TNC had held public meetings about its management plans for the preserve in Santa Barbara, San Luis Obispo, Sacramento, and San Francisco, it had never held a meeting or done any other significant outreach in the town of Guadalupe, the closest community to the dunes. Warner notes, "Our offices are in San Luis Obispo. We weren't in Guadalupe; we didn't know Guadalupe. The people, when they were writing the management plan, didn't hang out in Guadalupe. They were interested in the dunes. And they didn't know how important the beach was to people. And I sure didn't realize it until I'd been on this job for a little bit. They use the beach like their back yard, and we didn't realize how important that was to the community because we weren't spending that much time in the community in the planning process."

Warner organized a series of meetings with local stakeholders to discuss revising TNC's management plan. She met with Guadalupe's mayor, Rennie Pili, and Ariston Julian, a board member of the Guadalupe Recreation Commission and coordinator of a local boys and girls club. She remembers, "We started mending fences ever so quickly at breakfast one day. Rennie and I talked about a lot of things, got past this anger in a hurry. I think I had a couple of breakfasts with him and Ariston, and we talked about the dunes and the community and what kind of potential there would be for working together. And then Chuck, my husband, [and I] ended up going to a boys and girls club banquet with Rennie and his wife. It was easy to start working with people down there. It's just getting to know people and building trust. That's what we had not done—we had not built trust."

There is no magic recipe for building trust and relationships. Warner notes, "I think you just have to do a lot of one-on-ones with people," and warns that it is a slow process. Just as TNC invited community members out to learn about the natural and cultural history of the dune preserve, TNC staff needed to learn about the interests and concerns of the local community. "Communication made [our eventual] success possible," suggests a TNC staff member who recalls the strategy of stopping in at "the Far Western, which is the local hangout, to see if we couldn't make some personal connections as a way to try to get these people to not be threatened by The Nature Conservancy."

In the case of the Guadalupe-Nipomo Dunes Preserve, TNC learned the hard way that partnerships are people joined through relationships. While people may represent organizations, agencies, or occupations in a collaborative process, they are fundamentally individual human beings. The relationships that form the core of collaborative partnerships are between those individuals, not between organizations. Yet people are only human. They can get angry, be affronted, and become discouraged. Hence, human emotions and fears and the tendency to develop stereotypes and misperceptions pose challenges to effective collaboration. On the other hand, the development of understanding, empathy, trust, and motivation can foster collaborative interaction. In most of our cases, participants became increasingly aware of the human dimension that underscored their efforts. They offered comments like "It's the relationships that matter," "It gives a big boost to the spirit," and "People just began to believe."

Effective collaborative processes support the individuals in the effort. They shatter misperceptions and foster understanding while building productive relationships. They motivate the involvement of diverse individuals and pay attention to the cultural dimensions of the issues and of the people involved in the process. In the end, collaboration succeeds because the projects acknowledge that partnerships are people and deal with their needs effectively.

Shattering Misperceptions and Fostering Understanding

Dealing with the baggage associated with past history is the first challenge facing any collaborative venture. Participants bring a variety of perceptions and misperceptions into a collaborative effort. Some perceptions are drawn from prior experience with the adversarial interactions that characterize most decision making. Others are based on presumptions about people's intentions, styles, or attitudes. Many of those presumptions are extreme caricatures of reality. As discussed in chapter 3, we develop stereotyped images of others for a variety of reasons but partly to establish our own identities by contrasting their behavior with ours. Building the level of understanding needed in collaborative problem solving requires that stereotypes and misperceptions be shattered. At times, it requires individuals to see themselves in someone else, and that can be difficult.

In considering the start-up of the Cameron County Coexistence Committee in South Texas, FWS official Steve Thompson notes the challenge inherent in moving beyond preconceived notions about the parties and the issues. "I went into that first meeting with fifteen years of baggage," he recalls. In addition, the negative perception of the Fish and Wildlife Service held by many farmers and members of the public clouded and complicated the early discussions of the committee. According to Thompson, "The public and farmers do not recognize the different branches of the Fish and Wildlife Service. They just see it as one agency. Their perception was that the refuge did have a lot of influence on the final decision." In reality, he stresses, "We didn't have any direct power over [the farmers] . . . but the public and the farmers saw us as the bad guys—the one that was feeding all the information that was making their lives miserable. . . . It's hard to negotiate with someone if you think they're a policeman, if you think they are going to use everything you say against you." To get past these initial attitudes, Thompson emphasizes the importance of being open-minded and building trust.

Successful collaborative efforts create the opportunity for those involved to begin breaking down stereotypes and misperceptions. As Jack Shipley of the Applegate Partnership observes, "We are much more similar than we are different, although we perceive all of the differences in one another. We emphasize the differences. It's almost like we have prided ourselves in our differences—the John Wayne independent mentality. There's a tremendous opportunity to work together for solutions." "What we're finding," in the Applegate watershed, notes Shipley, "is that those people we've perceived as enemies for so long are just like us. They just have a different perception, and what we need to do is start working towards communicating with each other so that we can understand where each other lies, instead of through the broadbrush generalities that we seem to work with."

Successful collaborative initiatives do what Thompson and Shipley suggest. They devote considerable time to fostering a shared understanding among all participants of the situation, the issues, and the interested individuals. Over cups of coffee or through formal visioning processes, the participants begin to get to know each other as individuals and begin setting aside the stereotypes and misperceptions that have defined and strained their interactions. Rather than responding to issues with animosity or despair, participants set out to develop a shared understanding that can provide a more solid foundation upon which they can work together.

Socializing Informally

Early efforts to connect with other participants and get to know them as individuals help break down stereotypes, foster understanding, and build trust. Rosabeth Moss Kanter notes, "The time spent chatting over coffee and donuts . . . before a meeting is not just 'filler' until the meeting begins but a helpful adjunct to the process, a signal that people are willing to make gestures towards one another as people."[1] Clark County official Christine Robinson, a participant in the Clark County HCP case, emphasizes, "Anytime you can increase the informal aspect of the process and make opportunities to just talk, that's good. Having lunch together and field trips to conservation sites meant more opportunity for personal communication and the building of mutual respect—and I thought that was key to eventually dealing on an honest level."

Teri Devlin, a TNC representative to the Darby Partnership in Ohio, also encourages development of personal relationships early in the process: "At a very personal level, to get a farmer in a canoe with a regional planner, normal relationships that would not normally occur happen on the canoe trip. And it is happening in the habitat. . . . It is very powerful." Similarly, FWS refuge manager Steve Thompson describes some of his early interactions with another member of the Cameron County Coexistence Committee: "We had a few informal lunches together. We even went on a fishing trip together, me and a county agent. And I found out then that that guy and I shared a lot of common ground. I saw that his personal goals and his professional goals were not that different than mine. . . . You don't build trust until you actually get to know people a little bit."

The process for developing the Lye Brook wilderness management plan in Vermont's Green Mountain National Forest built upon existing relationships in a way that allowed people to move beyond basic trust and understanding to real camaraderie and friendship. The meetings were informal and, according to Assistant District Ranger Ed Toth, "a lot of fun." The team often held dinner meetings, at which they would order pizza. "We took a lot of time to socialize," planning team leader Diane Strohm says. Toth concurs: "We didn't forget the human aspect." District Ranger Michael Schrotz notes, "Friendships developed even though there was lots of disagreement. Spending quality time together in relaxed atmospheres I think had something to do with the success." Asked if there were any differences or disputes between the groups during these informal gatherings, Toth remarks: "Only over what kind of pizza and beer to buy."

Focusing on Individuals, not Organizations

Informal lunches, meetings over coffee, fishing trips, and pizza and beer allow individuals to get to know each other as individuals, not as representatives of organizations. Since stereotypes often are attached to organizations or groups, it is important to de-couple the individual from his or her organizational label. As Mario Mamone, Forest Service wildlife biologist on the Applegate Partnership, notes, "Once you get agreement, then you can get beyond some of the barriers and deal with people as individuals rather than as the timber industry representative or environmental representative or Forest Service representative. We're individual people with our own beliefs, and we learn to accept that." Based on his experience with the collaborative process used in restoration planning for the East Fork of the Quinn River, extension agent Dave Torrell comments, "When you start with data, people get afraid and move to positional bargaining." Instead, his approach focused on "people skills . . . strategies for cooperation and consensus building." Once everyone involved "began to realize they were working with individuals, not bureaucracies," he says, then they could begin to work productively together.

As stereotypes and misperceptions are relaxed, a more robust understanding of a group's interests and concerns can be built. Through the early conversations among participants in the Cameron County Coexistence Committee, Steve Thompson recalls, "I started to discover that many of the farmers and ranchers . . . weren't trying to do something to hurt animals, or hurt other people, they were just trying to make a living. And were looking for a way to do it in a responsible way and in an environmentally safe way, if they could."

Similarly, Steve Corbitt, a business representative to the Nanticoke Watershed Alliance, indicates, "I have learned a lot . . . about different points of view. My attitude has become adjusted by being able to see things from another person's point of view. Case in point is the farmers. There are things that they are doing that I thought they were not doing. That it is tough with the poultry industry. I have been able to adjust my preconceived notion of what was going on here. The boat traffic study is another. Hearing from boat operators, some of their concerns. I had always thought of them as people spewing out pollution, and they saw it as a lot of people presenting hazards to them on the river due to increased traffic. It was hard to do his or her job without killing someone. They were concerned about the environment. I have had to create a new sense of respect for them. They face challenges every day that I do not have to think of."

Building and Sustaining Relationships

While enhancing people's understanding is an important step, collaboration ultimately takes the form of interpersonal relationships. Successful human relationships in a family setting, a work environment, or a civic endeavor such as a collaborative process share several characteristics. They are honest, sincere, compassionate, committed, understanding, respectful, and caring. Over time trust is demonstrated by the individuals in the relationship. Effective collaborative partnerships recognize the need to build and sustain productive relationships between those involved and take steps to establish those linkages.

Capitalizing on Established Relationships

For many partnerships, the fact that they are not starting from a blank slate is a big help. Relationships established in the past can have a major impact in allowing collaborations to move forward. For example, Greg Neudecker of the Blackfoot Challenge comments that his effectiveness was rooted in earlier projects that he had conducted with a number of the other participants: "When the Challenge started, people already knew who I was. To them, I was not just a U.S. Fish and Wildlife Service representative, I was also Greg Neudecker." Prior to his work with the National Wild Turkey Federation, Ron Brenneman worked for eleven years for International Paper. "I had a pretty good background in what the forest industry was doing," recalls Brenneman. "The experiences I had helped immensely in just knowing people in the business, having a feel for the economics involved, the constraints and pressures that the foresters are under out there." This prior experience helped build trust with his industry partners, setting them at ease in their new relationship. "I think it helps with them," notes Brenneman. "Knowing that I came from that background . . . it made them feel more comfortable."

Preexisting personal relationships often provide seeds for collaborative efforts. For example, the Environmental Protection Agency and Amoco conducted a groundbreaking joint study of air emissions at Amoco's Yorktown facility that provided information on how EPA can regulate industry more cost effectively. The idea for the joint study was formed during a chance meeting between two old college friends on an airplane: one now a senior EPA official and the other a senior executive at Amoco.[2]

Fostering Trust and Respect

As discussed in chapter 3, many collaborative interactions start within a context of deep-seated distrust. Su Rolle of the Applegate Partnership notes, "There is distrust between environmentalists and the timber industry; and certainly between agencies and communities; and agencies and environmentalists; and agencies and industry. The sense of distrust feeds the conflict and makes it very hard to focus on the issues." Innovation expert Michael Schrage notes, "Successful collaborations don't require friendship or even that the collaborators like one another very much. . . . However, there must be a minimum threshold of mutual respect, tolerance, and trust for a collaboration to succeed."[3] Successful collaborative efforts do not try to sidestep a lack of trust but instead begin taking steps to build that trust.

Trust is not easy to come by, however, especially in situations where longstanding distrust and hostility have characterized interactions between the parties. Even the Applegate Partnership, in many ways the "poster child" collaborative partnership, given its long-standing success and high-level endorsement by the Clinton administration, continues to struggle at building trust. Logger and sawmill owner Dwain Cross notes, "Total trust in the Applegate has not been achieved." The eight-year-old group continues to place a high priority on that objective and accepts that it will occur only in a process that promotes respect for one another, patience, and a willingness to try to understand. As environmentalist Brett KenCairn reflects, "Trust was certainly the objective from the beginning, but you can't magically create it. The only way you can build it is by sitting together—a lot—and by going through all kinds of issues. And by seeing each other in our sort of worst moods and behaviors, and almost giving up and not. And witnessing another person's real deep pain and fear and not turning away."

A starting point for building trust is to create a situation in which people act the way Grandma said they should: being respectful, honest, and fair. As Rosabeth Moss Kanter suggests, "People will take the time to understand and work through partnership differences to the extent that they feel valued and respected for what they bring to the relationship. . . . Respect that builds trust begins with an assumption of equality: all parties bring something valuable to the relationship and deserve to be heard."[4] In response to the question of what has sustained the Nanticoke Watershed Alliance, participant Larry Walton, president of Chesapeake Forest Products, comments, "It is respect. Those people, whether they agree with me or not, over the length of time, we develop a respect for one another. I consider a lot of those folks friends of mine now, and I am sure vice versa. I know that there are things that we would go toe-to-toe on, and I think that they realize that. They respect me for my position and vice versa."

As discussed in chapter 6, a carefully structured and facilitated process can create conditions in which respect and trust can emerge. Steve Corbitt, a business representative to the Nanticoke Watershed Alliance, advises: "Take it slow. Be respectful. Encourage people to speak up. Don't be judgmental. Put a positive spin on everything that is said and try to see everything in the best light as possible. Keep hammering away on making progress. Get to know each other. Do meetings in different places once in a while." Roy Packer, BLM representative to the Applegate Partnership, says, "Realize that facilitation doesn't make trust, but it can help produce ideas and create conditions that develop relationships." Trust emerges slowly in situations where people treat each other with respect and are patient and willing to understand. As Sharla Moffat, a timber industry representative to the Applegate Partnership, sums it up: "It takes a lot of patience. And it takes tremendous commitment from each of the participants. And it takes sharing a lot of yourself to be able to make it work."

Gaining the trust of the community posed a major challenge for Rebecca Kress in her efforts to clean up the Russian River. To build trust, she spent a lot of time networking and was careful not to take sides. She remembers: "The first year, no one knew me or knew what I was about or what I was going to do. Neither did I. I'd never done anything like this before." Gaining the trust of the landowners was particularly important, because 95 percent of the land along the river was privately held. Moreover, gaining trust and broad participation was difficult because people in the community were extremely polarized on environmental issues. Members of one local environmental group had been shot at while clearing debris from the river. Kress comments that "everyone was suspicious" and says that people would ask her, "Are you on the landowners' side? Are you on the timber owners' side?" In such an atmosphere, she cautions, "You have to be really super careful about what you say . . . and what you do, because once you get the label, you're labeled." She advises, "You get a lot further if you don't make enemies. You need to look at both sides of every group you are working with and find common ground."

Over time, people came to trust Kress in part because she demonstrated her trustworthiness. Obtaining liability insurance was one tangible step in her efforts to assuage landowner distrust. "The landowners were reluctant, the city managers were reluctant" to support her river cleanup proposals, she notes. "Nobody wanted to sponsor me, they were worried about liability. Once I got insurance . . . that was great. . . . I provided a copy to all the landowners. After the first couple of years, they saw we came in, we cleaned up, and we got out of there; we didn't bother their property."

While building trust in places like the Russian River, the Nanticoke watershed, and the Applegate watershed required a lot of effort, it ultimately established the capacity to productively address issues that emerge over time. Lisa Jo Frech, a Nanticoke participant, comments, "I think that what we were able to accomplish in the long run is far greater because we have trust. There is not a player in this watershed that I do not trust. There is not anybody that I would not call at the drop of a hat at work or at home and say, 'I heard a rumor—would you verify this for me?'"

It Takes Time and Energy

Of course, individuals do not immediately become understanding, respectful, and open. Jack Shipley chuckles when he recalls the first meeting of the Applegate Partnership: "First thing that came out of Dwain's mouth was: 'You're walking a fine line with me, you SOB.'" It takes time to develop relationships grounded in trust and respect. Moreover, it takes a willingness to try to see and understand the world as another does and to acknowledge one's own biases and preconceptions, and to then move on. "We all come to this table with a bias," commented one Applegate partner at an early meeting, "Whether it's from our organizational connections or our personal biases, [we've] got to acknowledge them and move forward." Doing so takes time and, as another Applegate partner notes, "a lot of humility." BLM staff member Roy Packer concurs: "Don't be surprised if this takes years."

Steve Wiles, one of the partners in the Three-Quarter Circle Ranch CRM in Wyoming, comments, "You've got to have time. It's that simple. Without the relationships between stakeholders that the passage of time allows, you get people holding back what they are willing to do because they fear they'll be giving too much. In our CRM, knowing what process the other guy is going through is also very important because it helps to know where they fit into the issue and where they don't." Similarly, George Grier, a landowner and cochair of Oregon's McKenzie River Watershed Council, emphasizes: "You need to have an incredibly long-term view of things if you're going to gauge success by collaborative processes. This is kind of like the analogy of filling the pipeline: You know you don't get anything out the other end until the pipeline's completely full, and in this case filling the pipeline takes a really long time because it's relationship building, and it's building a knowledge base, and it's networking, and there's a lot of complicated stuff that goes on that has to do with human dynamics."

Nurturing, Honoring, and Respecting Relationships

Like all human relationships, a collaborative relationship needs to be sustained, and that comes by understanding the need to respect and nurture the relationship and not presume it will be self-maintaining. Sometimes it requires giving a little of oneself: giving way on an issue, giving time, or giving support of a variety of kinds. At other times it simply requires vigilance about the relationship at play in a situation. For example, Toledo Metroparks official Michelle Grigore suggests that a good way to look at partnerships like the Oak Openings project is as a family: "Sometimes you love them, and sometimes. . . ." Just like a family, successful collaborative efforts pay attention to the bonds that unite them and respect them even when tempted to find fault or turn away.

Steve Thompson recounts an incident he faced while he was Laguna Atascosa Refuge manager that could easily have severed the relationships established through the Cameron County Coexistence Committee:

> We had an ocelot; they are endangered cats. And they were poisoned by the use of temic—it's a very toxic pesticide that's used in citrus crops, and I think to a certain extent on cotton, and it's extremely toxic. If you even touch your hands on it, it can go through your skin and actually kill people, also. The way they use it, they inject it into the ground . . . if you use it properly, it is very effective. But some people were taking some of this stuff, and, because they were mad about the lack of predator control, they would make kind of homemade remedies. They would put some in some meat and toss it out to kill coyotes and raccoons on private property. We were radio-tracking an ocelot, and it died, and we went through a bunch of analysis, and it turned out that it looked like this was a temic poisoning case. And we wanted to catch the people that did it.
>
> My first reaction before would have been to say, "Temic is horrible stuff— I hate that stuff—it just killed one of my endangered species, so I'll use my press contacts to get this on the front page of the paper. And we'll blame the citrus growers for this." Well, since I had several people from the citrus community on this committee, I called [one of] them before I did this. I told him what happened, and he said, "That's horrible—that's really bad. What can we

do to help?" And I said, "Well, I'm going to need some reward money, probably, to flush this person out or maybe catch him." So they volunteered $1,000 of reward money. The cotton growers did the same thing, and then I combined that up with some federal money, and we were able to offer a $5,000 reward.

Then I also told him that I was going to call the press, but I was going to tell the press to contact them so they could tell their side of the story and say that they were also very upset, that this was an illegal use of the chemical, not an intended use, and they wanted to catch those people just as badly as we did. So that's the story that came out of the newspapers. And it was a totally different spin than we would have had before we had known each other.

The situation had the potential to undermine the relationships that had gradually developed through the interactions of the Cameron County Coexistence Committee. But by discussing the event with his partners, Thompson was able to capitalize on the relationships that had been established and circumvent a potentially unfortunate turn of events. Members of the Cameron County Coexistence Committee took care in other ways to respect their relationships within the partnership while recognizing their commitments to their constituent groups. Thompson provides an example in which groups balanced these roles in a manner that respected the collaborative relationship: "They would also stand there with us in front of the press and talk to television crews and the newspapers. Sometimes they couldn't say everything that I would want them to say; they kind of had to put a farmer spin on it, but that was fine. And they would call us ahead of time and tell us, 'I'm going to rip on you a little bit here, Steve, but I haven't got my group fully behind me yet. I understand what you're trying to do, and I'm all for it, but it's going to take me a little while to get the information out to my following.' And we all had that problem."

Relationships are fragile and when damaged are hard to rebuild. Indeed, TNC preserve manager Nancy Warner notes how long it takes to build trust versus how quickly one can lose it, based on her experience at the Guadalupe-Nipomo Dunes. Also, Larry Gamble, Rocky Mountain National Park planner, cites a case in which park staff failed to consult with local county commissioners before objecting to a development near the Rocky Mountain National Park. As a result, he says, "That bridge was burned, and we have not been able to totally rebuild it." Once relationships are damaged, it can take years and even require a change of personnel to regain trust and reestablish partnerships.

Managing Transitions in Relationships

Successful collaborative efforts also manage the transitions in relationships that inevitably occur as individuals move, retire, or simply become unable to continue participating for whatever reason. As Larry Gamble comments, collaborative relationships tend to "ebb and flow" over time, and the parties involved need to understand that reality and find ways to maintain the relationships that underlie the collaboration. He notes that the National Park Service's practice of moving personnel from park to park as they advance in the agency's hierarchy can make it difficult to sustain partnerships. In his view, it is important for a local office to have long-term staff that can maintain relationships and partnerships "over the long haul."

Partnerships in our studies dealt with turnover in a variety of ways. In some cases, new individuals were eased into partnerships by overlapping with the individuals they were replacing. At a minimum, current representatives made a considerable effort to introduce new representatives to others in formal and informal ways. Jim Wilcox notes that the Feather River CRM group effectively incorporates new members into the process in a couple ways. First, new members typically meet and sometimes work with the group for some time before becoming official participants. Thus, they are already familiar with how the group operates and people in the group know them before they officially join. Second, people who are leaving an organization represented in the group brief their replacements and say, "Hey, this is a good deal. You need to work with these people; you can trust them." As a result, such turnover has been "virtually painless" even though the group has been in existence for more than ten years.

Motivating Involvement

Collaboration is not easy. At times the task can seem impossible and the prospects hopeless. People can become discouraged and overwhelmed. Sometimes they lose energy and focus when they are hungry or tired. They may feel hopeless when faced with particularly complex or controversial issues. Successful collaborative efforts consciously deal with the need to motivate people. Making the process tangible and fun, instilling the hope that success is possible, and acknowledging the efforts of those involved help provide motivation. An understandable, predictable, and straightforward process also helps. People pick up on the emotions of others, so that the motivation to continue can result from others demonstrating their commitment, for example: "If Jane is willing to persevere in the face of this adversity, then so am I." Ultimately, projects succeed because basic human needs are met.

Fun

A striking characteristic of successful partnerships in our studies was the energy, enthusiasm, and optimism of those involved. People were working hard, but they were having fun at the same time. This "fun" was partly rooted in the sense of accomplishment that came from making progress in the face of great odds. To a large extent, however, the work was fun because people made it so. Rebecca Kress not only organized diverse groups of people to clean up California's Russian River, she also got those people to play together at the same time. She sponsors a big one-day barbecue after the cleanups that includes sky diving, live music, volleyball and other games, and lots of food donated by local businesses. Kress admits that there is "lots of reward and personal gain" for herself and others in improving the Russian River resource, but also that it is undeniably "a lot of fun."

Similarly, Joan Martin of the Huron River Watershed Council initiated a RIVERfest celebration for the Adopt-a-Stream partners that she labeled a "wonderful" event for those involved. She enthusiastically recounts: "It was a camping and canoe trip that covered the entire river. We did a walk at the headwaters where it's too small to canoe and then started in where we could in Proud Lake and spent eight days canoeing as a group of over one-hundred people. . . . We canoed the whole river and stopped to celebrate with all the communities along the way, who threw a party and a meal, and usually then gave us a place to camp."

Participants in the Coalition for Unified Recreation in the Eastern Sierra process have made a point to celebrate major milestones in their effort. The first party was thrown in August 1993, when the CURES vision statement, the first major accomplishment of the group, was completed. Nancy Upham of the Forest Service recalls, "There were people there who never thought they'd party together!" Participants in the Green Mountain National Forest wilderness planning process share frequent potluck dinners with one another. Consequently, according to Dick Andrews, a participant from the Vermont Wilderness Association, "They don't seem to be getting tired of the work—they seem to be enjoying it."

Instilling Hope by Demonstrating Success

After years of adversarial conflict, often people doubt that a collaborative effort can succeed or even that the problems themselves can be solved. A history of inaction has produced a legacy of despair. Successful collaborative partnerships recognize this initial skepticism and instill hope by working on the smaller, more manageable issues first to demonstrate that progress is possible. By instilling a glimmer of hope early on, partnerships are able to motivate those involved to persevere through the first major substantive barrier to their effectiveness. For example, one of the first projects the Anacostia Watershed Restoration Committee funded was an inventory of potential restoration projects. That initial effort was chosen strategically to shatter preconceptions that nothing could be done to help the river. From creating the inventory, committee members learned that possible projects existed that could make a difference in the environmental quality of the Anacostia River system.

Once the group began cooperating, members came to believe that progress was possible and strengthened their commitment to the effort. Metropolitan Washington Council of Governments staff member Lorraine Herson-Jones explains, "Once they cooperated together on a watershed basis and looked for solutions, they were convinced that there really were some potentials for real restoration in the watershed that would make a big difference." According to her, "The actual benefits I don't think have been the real motivator. It's more that they just began to believe that something could happen, and that kept them together." Over time, the Anacostia River began to show some improvements in water quality and biological indicators, including expanded acreage of submerged aquatic vegetation, increased diversity of fish that are not pollution tolerant, and some reductions from peak sediment levels. The positive feedback encouraged further collaborative efforts among the committee members.

Hands-on, Tangible, and Nonthreatening

As logger Jim Neal of the Applegate Partnership comments, "Abstraction is death for a partnership." Effective partnerships in our studies grappled with issues in a tangible way by visiting sites and grounding their discussions in hands-on experiences. They implemented on-the-ground projects together. They got their feet wet and their hands dirty. By developing a sense of personal and group satisfaction, they stimulated further steps and created the foundation to take those steps together.

Volunteer-based, hands-on restoration activities have formed the central core of the Oak Openings Working Group outside Toledo. Such projects have helped promote a spirit of cooperation among the diverse partners and have motivated their continued engagement in the process. Andy Clewell, president of the Society for Ecological Restoration and an Oak Openings participant, observes, "Picking, pulling, planting gets you away from the environmentalism of white and black hats and confrontation. You're doing something personally, and it gives a big boost to the spirit." Michelle Grigore, a cofounder of the Oak Openings Group and an employee of the Toledo Area Metroparks, notes, "When we are most successful at working together is when people are willing to put their egos aside and not worry about who is getting credit for what and just work towards achieving the goals that we have set." She believes that this is best achieved when everyone is able to "work together and pull as a unit" in the field.

Steve Thompson of the Cameron County Coexistence Committee emphasizes how motivating it was for all of the partners to have a hand in reintroducing the endangered Aplomado falcon to the Laguna Atascosa National Wildlife Refuge. He encouraged the direct involvement of local farmers in releasing new falcons: "We would bring falcons in from Boise, Idaho, and [the farmers on the committee] would come to help me pick them up from the airport. And then we would go out to these hacking towers, and they would stand up there with us and put the birds up in the top. It became part of the reintroduction process. They were just as interested in getting them up flying as we were. Each year we had a few birds coming down. We were able to increase that to about twenty-five birds after the committee got going."

Acknowledging and Rewarding Efforts

Most collaborative efforts succeed because the partners devote time, energy, and resources to the effort. Not surprisingly, people appreciate receiving thanks for their contributions. One motivating factor for the San Gorgonio Volunteers Association (SGVA) on the San Bernardino National Forest has been the district's visible appreciation of the volunteers' efforts. Each fall the district puts on an awards ceremony for the volunteers at a mountain lodge, and every volunteer receives an award. As Barb Ward, Forest Service interpretive specialist, explains, "It is a very important part of the volunteer program. They all really look forward to it." The SGVA's contribution was recognized nationally in 1991 when the group was granted the Forest Service Chief's Award. Two members of the group were flown to Washington, D.C., to receive the award.

People take great pride in having been recognized even in small ways. We were struck by the number of times participants in collaborative partnerships mentioned that their group "was nominated for an award" or that "we received a letter from the chief commending our efforts." Gloria Boersma, the Volunteer Partnerships Agreement coordinator on Michigan's Huron-Manistee National Forest, does a number of things to acknowledge partner groups once their projects are completed. She creates displays, invites the press to events, or simply provides recognition awards to those involved. Jim White, a forester on the Wasatch-Cache National Forest in Utah, was quite enthusiastic about the recognition his group has received within the agency for developing the Mill Creek Canyon partnership. "They love us!" he exclaims. "This is a model. People go, 'Why don't you do this? Look at what they did at Salt Lake.'"

Cultural and Community Differences

People vary in their values, attitudes, and norms community to community. Such cultural dimensions add another layer to the people element of a collaborative partnership, and they also need to be recognized and accommodated if a successful interaction is to occur. At one level, simply dressing appropriately for the culture of a community can facilitate success. As Jim Moore, The Nature Conservancy participant in the Clark County HCP process, comments, "You really have to find the right individual to match the culture of the communication needed. You can't just send a person in a three-piece business suit into a community where the culture is ranching and ·mining. That just doesn't work."

Collaboration is a different kind of management process and, as noted in chapter 7, takes a different mind-set among participants in order to succeed. Depending upon their own community culture, people come to this understanding in different ways and at different speeds. District Ranger Steve Williams had to proceed slowly in developing a "shared vision" for the Quinn River restoration partnership. He notes that the biggest barrier to that process was skepticism about the visioning process and the personal reflection and expression that it requires. As he observes, "For a lot of rural ranchers, that's not their style."

Particular attention must be given to culture when different languages, practices, or beliefs are at play. For example, in developing the Russian River cleanup project, Rebecca Kress made special cleanup T-shirts with a slogan in Spanish as well as English to relate to the Hispanic community. In the Guadalupe-Nipomo Dunes case, the culturally symbolic use of the dunes as a town plaza was what sparked community concern, yet it was not an element of TNC's initial analysis of dunes management issues. A renewed planning process was structured with the community as a partner in a way that allowed local culture to be expressed and accommodated.

In the Alaska Recreation Planning case, Forest Service planner Maria Durazo-Means tailored her public involvement strategy to the specific needs and customs of the cultures associated with the many communities affected by national forest management. She notes, "In a native village, public meetings have historically not been a good forum, so other methods were used such as setting up tables and booths at grocery stores, at the post office, and talking one-on-one to people to get their input." In addition, an archaeologist who had worked with the residents of Kake recommended that the Forest Service try to reach adult residents through their children. The district put on Smokey Bear and Woodsy Owl skits about recreation for the schoolchildren and sent them home with information about the recreation plan for their parents. School-wide assemblies were held in middle and high schools to collect project suggestions. Native American communities were contacted individually and were directly involved in the archaeological facets of the planning process and its implementation.

In seeking to assist the Clifton-Choctaw tribe with improving economic opportunities (as described in chapter 2), Forest Service District Ranger John Baswell took care in how he initially approached the tribe and was patient as both he and they learned about each other's interests. He did not presume that the agency had all of the answers but instead let the tribe define the project in a way that best fit its unique needs and cultural context. As a result, the project's goals and work plans melded easily with the operations of the tribal council and the tribe's traditional customs and methods of doing business. Sensitivity to the cultural context allowed an effective project to be initiated while developing a relationship between the tribe and the agency. According to Anna Neal, Clifton-Choctaw tribal coordinator, "We would love to do more projects with the Forest Service. . . . The Forest Service is the first government agency that truly appears to be interested in self-determination."

Like other successful collaborative efforts, the Clifton-Choctaw project recognized that partnerships are composed of people, and people are only human. The successful efforts worked at developing a heightened level of understanding and respect for each other's differences and concerns, including those arising from cultural factors. They paid attention to various ways to motivate involvement and dealt with psychological barriers to collaboration. Over time, trust emerged among the partners and provided a foundation for the development of new or improved relationships between parties that had often been at odds in the past. While collaborative relationships need ongoing nurturing, ultimately they provide the possibility of a new form of community-scale discourse and action. For many places, their most significant legacy is hope.

Chapter 10

A Proactive and Entrepreneurial Approach

The Rocky Mountain District of the Lewis and Clark National Forest in remote northern Montana abuts Glacier National Park on its northern border and stretches for one hundred miles along the east side of the Continental Divide. The district is considered one of the Forest Service's premier wildlife districts, featuring bighorn sheep, elk, and wolves. Half of the district is in the Bob Marshall Wilderness Complex, and the remainder is designated as roadless in the forest plan. Grazing and recreation far outweigh logging as a dominant use. With a population of six thousand people, the district has a density of human beings only slightly higher than that of the eighty to one hundred endangered grizzly bears that also inhabit the region.

The presence of grizzly bears is considered a big problem in the surrounding ranching communities for both economic and personal safety reasons. A Forest Service employee explains, "We had a problem of deteriorating ecological habitat: buffaloberry bushes and whitebark pine were disappearing due to fire suppression. This meant less food for grizzlies on national forest lands, which meant they spent less time feeding there, which meant they spent more time eating on ranchers' land. . . . It's easy to see how this ecological problem became a social problem." The situation was exacerbated by the fact that the Rocky Mountain region features large ranches that provide an abundant supply of sheep, cattle, and pigs, which are vulnerable to hungry bears. Linda Holden, a rancher who raises cattle with her husband, John, describes their fear of grizzlies: "John used to be able to go fishing on the creek. Now he won't go at all unless there's somebody with him to watch for bears, with a gun. You just don't feel safe anymore." Grizzlies have bothered their neighbor's sheep and ripped apart a seat in one of their vehicles. She maintains that the bear population has increased and that recent years of drought have caused the bears to come down into the valleys and be less scared of people.

This situation became quite heated. Ranchers, upset about not being able to kill a federally protected species that preyed on their livestock, focused their anger on the federal land managers in charge. Pro-wildlife groups, on the other hand, opposed any disturbance of the bears. Seth Diamond, a resource assistant for Wilderness, Timber and Minerals in the district, decided to try and solve the dilemma. He explains his thought process in taking action: "The grizzly bear has the ability to stimulate great interest. Let's transform it into something positive—to grizzly bears, ranchers, environmentalists, and the general public. Let's do something positive and use it to bring people together."

Diamond's solution was the Beartree Challenge, an innovative partnership involving a broad array of cooperators—timber interests, environmentalists, ranchers, and educational institutions—on behalf of the grizzlies. The program has a dual purpose. One goal is to improve the ecological habitat of the grizzlies by fostering the growth of the nuts and berries they eat as a way of encouraging them to stay on national forest lands and not stray onto private ranchlands. The second is to improve the bear's "social habitat"—minimizing and resolving the conflicts surrounding grizzly management by "break[ing] down the barriers that polarize people over the grizzly bear issue."

The ecological goal was to be achieved by improving one thousand acres of bear habitat over a five-year period through the use of controlled burns, plantings of whitebark pine, and limited tree harvesting to open the overstory canopy to let in enough light to stimulate growth of the buffaloberry bushes. To accomplish those goals, Diamond solicited volunteer assistance and machinery from loggers, timber companies, and timber equipment dealers. The machines used in the habitat improvement work are considered to be "light on the land" because they do away with the need for road construction. Their wide tires help reduce soil compaction. Single-grip harvesters cut, delimb, buck, top, and pile the trees, and forwarders are then used to gather the logs and haul them away. Since logs are processed on the spot, they can be hauled away rather than dragged across the ground. All of these features help minimize ground disturbance. In addition, since the machines are fairly quick and efficient, they can minimize the length of time during which cutting operations in grizzly habitat disturb the bears.

The Beartree Challenge's social goals were to be achieved through collaborative work carried out by the diverse set of stakeholder groups, as well as extensive public education and media campaigns. Diamond also promoted the project within the Forest Service. After four years, there was "a much more collaborative atmosphere surrounding grizzly bear management—much more positive," according to Diamond. "Ranchers used to have a 'shoot, shovel, and shut up' approach and now they have a 'wait and see' approach." According to rancher Linda Holden, the project was a "good option to keep bears away from people. . . . The Forest Service has done a good job."

In Seth Diamond's words: "Three years ago, the district was at a crossroads. We could continue to manage grizzly habitat by reacting to conflicting demands, or we could grab the reins and develop a program that made the grizzly the focus of collaboration, not conflict. We chose the latter approach, and the Beartree Challenge is the realization of that vision. With the Beartree Challenge, we have seen the grizzly bear transformed from a symbol of controversy to a symbol of cooperation." By "grabbing the reins," Diamond helped to transform a bad situation into a better one.

Like the Beartree Challenge, many collaborative partnerships have gotten underway and succeeded due to the efforts of dedicated, energetic individuals who worked at being proactive and entrepreneurial. These people have established relationships, secured resources and institutional support, marketed the efforts and pushed for effective implementation. They have taken advantage of opportunities for collaboration and have used small footholds in a conflict to chart a pathway to greater involvement. These efforts have built on preexisting networks of people in communities and have used the incentives facing individual stakeholder groups, and the symbolic power inherent in being seen as an innovator, as leverage to motivate others to get involved. Many started small and built from their successes, simply sticking with it through difficult times. These people took a chance on a different course of action and found it worth the risk.

Dedicated, Energetic Individuals

Many projects succeed because they rely on the efforts of a small set of dedicated, energetic individuals who catalyze an activity and drive it forward. Clearly, the Beartree Challenge benefited from the efforts and energies of Seth Diamond, its creator and biggest cheerleader. As Forest Service staff member Dave Whittekiend notes, "Seth was the one that made it happen. He didn't let anything get in his way." Indeed, the project changed considerably after Diamond left in 1994 to work for the Intermountain Forest Industry Association.

Individual Leaders

Many participants in the collaborative management efforts we studied highlight the importance of individual effort to the success of the group. Nanticoke Watershed Alliance member Mark Zankel advises: "Have one or a couple of people who have a lot of energy to round up people. You need a cheer-leader, in a sense, who has the right personality and energy level and compo-sure to say, 'Come and join this party because there are going to be long-term benefits of doing so.'" Larry Gamble, the Rocky Mountain National Park land-use specialist who works with communities adjacent to the park, agrees that a critical factor leading to successful collaborative relationships is "local champions: people that network other agencies and organizations to find people of like interests and like mind and then hold those people together."

The literature on collaboration and cooperation also highlights the impor-tance of a strong leader or interested party "whose energy and vision mobi-lizes others to participate."[1] Once collaborative efforts are established, dedicated individuals also help to make them successful on the strength of their personality and energy.[2] Bennis and Biederman write in their study of successful collaborative efforts: "Every Great Group has a strong leader. This is one of the paradoxes of creative collaboration. Great Groups are made up of people with rare gifts working together as equals. Yet in virtually every one there is a person who acts as maestro, organizing the genius of the others. Within the group, the leader is often a good steward, keeping the others focused, eliminating distractions, keeping hope alive in the face of setbacks and stress."[3]

In our cases, project leaders, community leaders, agency field staff, landowners, and elected officials all played a leadership role in various projects and often kept projects alive despite a lack of resources, political support, or agency direction. Such individuals serve as a source of motivation for change and foster stakeholder trust and support for project goals. The roles they play include cheerleader-energizer, diplomat, process facilitator, leader, convenor, catalyst, and promoter. These people are not superhuman; rather, they put a lot of energy into moving projects forward. According to one participant, "It always boils down to key talented people [who] are willing to invest them-selves over and beyond the call of duty."

This type of leadership can emerge naturally or be deliberately fostered in an organization.[4] In many cases we studied, individual entrepreneurs emerged from inside agencies. For example, biologists on the Siuslaw Nation-al Forest in western Oregon took the initiative on recovery efforts for the Ore-gon silverspot butterfly, a federally listed threatened species. They collaborated with Oregon State University entomologist Paul Hammond and began pioneering research on the butterfly, cataloging and observing it in an effort to better understand its needs and habits. Simultaneously, Forest Ser-vice staff began experimenting with on-the-ground management practices to control succession and protect habitat in a thousand-acre "silverspot manage-ment area." They built a partnership with The Nature Conservancy, private landowners, and the Oregon Department of Transportation. According to

Hammond, the "above and beyond" efforts of individuals in the Forest Service have enabled continued progress to occur: "Nothing would have happened without their personal effort and commitment."

Local Champions

In many other situations, projects were pushed forward by the efforts of "local champions," and our respondents highlight the necessity of finding such people. Guadalupe-Nipomo Dunes Preserve manager Nancy Walker points to the importance of identifying the "doers" in a community. Mark Zankel of the Nanticoke Watershed Alliance advises: "Get local leaders to champion your cause. You have to connect with the people who live there and have them understand that you are trying to make this place more livable for everyone. . . . In rural areas it helps to have someone local who is doing that. People in southern Delaware are fairly insular and skeptical of outsiders."

Forest Service District Ranger David Spann, who spearheaded the community development effort in Adams County, Idaho (described in chapter 11), reiterates the importance of local leadership and highlights the need for training to enhance the capacity of local leaders. He emphasizes the need to build leadership capacity within the community so that the agency's role is not so central. He asks, "If I were to croak or move tomorrow, does the organization continue? Within the community, we have a few good leaders. I should have brought someone in and brought them along (on earlier projects)." To further this idea, several individuals were identified in the community for potential training for leadership positions.

Extraordinary Effort

Many of the individuals who lead collaborative efforts have gone well beyond the call of duty. David Spann was president of the Adams County Development Corporation for two years and arranged his work schedule to consist of four ten-hour days so he could devote the fifth day each week to rural development projects as a volunteer. When Rebecca Kress started organizing the Russian River cleanup effort in Northern California, she put hundreds of miles on her truck just driving and talking to different groups and people about the cleanup days, encouraging their involvement.

Often people have persisted in spite of considerable personal risk. Seth Diamond says that the biggest hurdle to the Beartree Challenge was "skepticism within the organization that this was crazy, that it wouldn't work." He indicates that he "didn't get overwhelming support from his district ranger at first." Diamond recalls him saying something to the effect of "If this blows up, I hope you have a big umbrella." Diamond was not dissuaded, however: "I just did it. Just showed results. Built partnerships. Put myself in a position that they couldn't say no."

Proactive, Not Reactive

Successful partnerships are proactive. They lead. They make something happen. Groups anticipate problems and do not just react to crises. They take the first step and are willing to take risks in order to improve a situation. In doing that, they often start a process that reduces conflict, improves relationships, and enhances the quality of on-the-ground management.

Being Proactive

In the case of the Oregon silverspot butterfly, Forest Service staff on the Siuslaw National Forest believe that a serious long-term commitment to the silverspot in 1980 made all the difference. Forest Service biologist Michael Clady says that Forest Service staff "were serious about doing it and stuck to it" regardless of what other agencies and individuals were doing: "We were leading, not being dragged along—it was very proactive." Because of this sincere commitment and "lead by example" attitude, other groups were more comfortable signing on and offered valuable time and resources to it. Most participants believe that if the Forest Service had not started early and stayed committed, the silverspot population at Rock Creek (the only known population in the national forest at that time) would most likely have been lost.

Similarly, it was the Petersburg Ranger District's willingness and desire to try something different in the way it approached recreation planning that changed the dynamics in that area of the Tongass National Forest. As described in the recreation plan, "In the past, recreation project planning has been a bit like the job of the lonely Maytag repairman. A lone person or two trying to think of new ways to serve that big public out there. This plan represents our effort to break loose from our Maytag mode." Its effort to reach out to the community (described in chapter 5) attempted to lead the community and the agency into a different mode of interaction. In many ways, the district planners followed the advice that Seth Diamond provides from his vantage point in the Beartree Challenge: "Look at where you have conflict. Identify the root of the conflict. Then think of some middle ground, some positive way to engage the different parties."

Formation of the Eel River Delta Sustainable Agriculture Committee in Humboldt County, California, was an attempt to get out ahead of emerging water-quality issues related to dairy farms. Dennis Leonardi said that he and a small group of other dairy farmers "decided that we should probably take a proactive approach and see if we couldn't come up with a set of guidelines and a set of definitions of what the problems are and what the end results are supposed to be, before we have a regulatory hammer upon us." The farmers formed the committee as an offshoot of the local Resource Conservation District. They could either anticipate problems and try to lead a response or sit back and react to others' framing of the problems and solutions. In Leonardi's words, "I, for one, would rather have some choices and determination of where I'm going, rather than have someone tell me what to do." Bill Potter of the Blackfoot Challenge reiterates that theme of self-determination: "We realized that if you do not make the rules, someone is going to make them for you. It is a lot easier to follow your own rules."

Taking the First Step

Many collaborative efforts start because someone is willing to take the first step. On the surface, initiating an activity appears to be easy enough. But in places with years of conflict and mistrust, where proposals for collaboration and information-sharing may be viewed as a sign of weakness, the first steps are some of the hardest to take. Inertia and limited resources are significant constraints to new modes of action. Psychological dimensions of past relationships, including stereotypes and a need to save face, raise even higher hurdles to getting started. Besides, it is never certain that the new activity will result in improvement. As Mario Mamone, a Forest Service wildlife biologist and participant in the Applegate Partnership, recalls about his initial reaction to the formation of that group, "I thought to myself, this could never work. How can these people with such diverse interests ever sit down and agree to anything? I guess it's like anything else: you have to take that first step; and once you've taken that first step, the second one is a little easier."[5]

Keith Hudley, governmental affairs manager for Weyerhaeuser in North Carolina, took the first step by making a phone call to Bill Holman, the state lobbyist for the Sierra Club's North Carolina chapter. He asked if the Sierra Club and other state environmentalists would be interested in learning about a new practice that Weyerhaeuser was thinking of implementing on its corporate lands in Plymouth, North Carolina. The company wanted to start spreading boiler ash from its mills on its forest lands instead of burying it in the company's landfill. Hudley explained the purpose of the invitation:

> We decided that in this particular situation, because there had been some discussion of what might be in the boiler ash, that we would simply invite some of the environmental activists from our neighborhood to come in, take a look at what we were proposing to do, and in some cases, what we had already done on a practice basis, and get them to react to us. We told them that we weren't asking their permission, because the permission was already granted

from the state to do it, but we wanted them to be absolutely and positively aware of what was going on, and even asked them to tell us some things that they saw that could be a problem that we may not have seen in being too close to the situation.

Holman and five colleagues visited Weyerhaeuser for a half day in the fall of 1994. During the visit, the environmental representatives were able to see and ask questions about the area where the ash would be applied and examine samples of the ash and analyses of the samples. According to Hudley, "We showed them everything that day, warts and all. And it turned out that any serious questions that were there were answered that particular day." The environmental representatives felt that spreading the ash would not harm the environment and noted that keeping the ash out would save landfill space. In addition, the meeting helped open lines of communication. According to Hudley, "It showed us that we can work with environmental organizations, or at least with some people who represent those organizations, without having fear of being sued tomorrow afternoon." Holman says he feels that a degree of trust was created among the groups involved: "If a company comes and says, 'We're thinking about this. What do you think?' and seems to be operating above board and in good faith, then we basically give them the benefit of the doubt."

Willing to Take a Risk

Being proactive also means being willing to take risks by trying nontraditional approaches. One of the primary reasons for success in the Beartree Challenge was simply that participants were willing to try something new. According to project coordinator Seth Diamond, "People haven't taken risks to try to do something like this before. No one has ever developed a grizzly bear habitat improvement program, let alone addressed the social problems." In the Kiowa Grasslands, Alton Bryant encouraged local ranchers to take a risk and experiment with alternative ranching techniques. At the same time, he tried to absorb some of the ranchers' risks by backing up the experiments with technical expertise and interagency cooperation.

The innovative Elk Springs timber sale on the Targhee National Forest in the Yellowstone area also showed a willingness by Forest Service leadership to take a risk. With numerous clear-cut stands regenerating and a high degree of animosity from environmentalists, Assistant District Ranger John Councilman decided in 1991 to try a different kind of timber sale. Councilman's primary aim was to plan a sale that would include a minimum of clear-cutting, utilize existing roads, and take plant and animal species more fully into account. He also wanted the timber to be sold in small parcels to local timber operators. To accomplish his goals, Councilman collaborated with the Idaho

Department of Fish and Game, small timber operators, and environmental groups including the Greater Yellowstone Coalition.

Councilman's plan involved significant risk. The Elk Springs area is primarily lodgepole pine, which, when clear-cut, regenerates well and is not susceptible to disease or windthrow. With the other harvest methods Councilman planned on using, disease and windthrow could have been a problem. But he was willing to take a risk. He decided to do something that had not been done before and that conflicted with traditional practices on the Targhee. This risk-taking set him up for potential criticism within the agency if difficulties occur. Given the tense situation between environmentalists and the forest, however, he believed it was worth a try.

Taking Advantage of Existing Opportunities

Most successful collaborative efforts look for many different ways to advance their agenda. Some have been able to overcome internal resistance by strategically linking their efforts to existing programs. Leaders and facilitators of partnerships have often adopted an entrepreneurial mind-set and sought to advance their activities by taking advantage of small windows of opportunity for change, using preexisting programs and networks of relationships in communities, and aggressively marketing their efforts. Selling the possibility of achieving joint gains—the win-win component of alliances that can make both parties better off—can be an important entrepreneurial activity. For example, in the Beartree's case, timber companies participated because the collaboration provided opportunities for them to demonstrate equipment that minimized the environmental effects of logging.

Using Government Programs as Catalysts and Support

Proponents of collaboration do not have to start from scratch. Federal programs such as the Forest Service's New Perspectives and Challenge Cost-Share programs; the National Estuary Program and the Remedial Action Planning Process administered by the EPA; the FWS-administered Partners for Wildlife Program; the North American Waterfowl Management Program and the Habitat Conservation Planning provision of the Endangered Species Act; and the BLM's Coordinated Resource Management process have provided opportunities for numerous projects. Similarly, state programs such as California's Natural Communities Conservation Planning process and ecoregional planning efforts by nongovernmental organizations such as The Nature Conservancy have facilitated the development of collaborative initiatives. Indeed, in our study of ecosystem management, more than half of the projects were initiated in response to agency programs and policies.

While preexisting programs can catalyze collaborative efforts, equally important is their ability to provide individual agency entrepreneurs with a platform and the internal "political cover" to try something different. The Forest Service's New Perspectives program, a precursor to the agency's efforts at ecosystem management and collaborative stewardship, provides a good illustration. New Perspectives was intended to be a seedbed of innovation in the Forest Service. It was designed to help the agency substantively by testing out new ideas and politically by demonstrating responsiveness to pressures for change. Several of the successful cases that we examined had been developed because of the existence of the program. People used the program as a source of funding and a way to legitimize their activities within the agency. With the Elk Springs timber sale, Assistant District Ranger Councilman used the New Perspectives program as a way to try something innovative: "I thought, 'Hey, here's an opportunity to try some of these ideas.' This sale was a recognition that not every stand has to be a sterile environment of fast-growing trees."

Seth Diamond also used New Perspectives as a way to advance the Beartree Challenge. The effort originated as a Challenge Cost-Share project using money and personnel from timber companies and organizations. But when the New Perspectives program started, the Beartree Challenge "fit New Perspectives to a tee" and "met all the New Perspectives objectives of sustaining desired ecological conditions, participation, integration, and collaboration," so it became a part of the New Perspectives program. Indeed, Diamond made sure that it was highlighted as a showcase project under New Perspectives partly to justify the project within the Forest Service. In other cases, linking new initiatives to existing agency programs has enabled entrepreneurs to override internal opposition.

Exploiting "Seams in the Bureaucratic Wall"

Lack of precedent is a common idea killer. The attitude that "we've never done it that way before" or "we don't do it that way" often closes the window for innovation. Yet individual entrepreneurs can overcome that barrier by looking for what Seth Diamond calls "seams in the bureaucratic wall," that is, small opportunities to do things that lie in the somewhat ambiguous interface between agency rules or procedures. According to Diamond, "If you have an idea and no one has done it before, don't think you can't do it." As an example, he cites how the Beartree Challenge group worked around a rule that prohibits cooperators in a project from making any economic gain from it. The agency established an "administrative sale" so that it could sell the logs harvested as a part of the habitat improvement project to local ranchers who were plagued by a local shortage of posts for fencing. Providing the logs at a reasonable cost was an invaluable relationship builder.

Sometimes opportunities for change emerge when people responsible for an issue change. Individual personalities can make a huge difference, particularly in agencies like the Forest Service, where a considerable amount of discretion exists at the ground level. Every Forest Service employee knows the difference that a change in the forest supervisor can make. Such staff changes can open a window of opportunity for changing the way decisions are made; they are a seam in the bureaucratic wall. For example, in mid-1987, the forest management plan for the Manti-LaSal National Forest in Utah was under appeal by several environmental and recreation groups. Limited opportunities to participate in the plan's development had alienated and angered these groups. Into this conflict-laden situation came a new forest supervisor, George Morris, who had transferred from the White River National Forest in Colorado, where he had gained some experience in dispute resolution. It appeared to him that the issues in the appeals were resolvable.

Since the plan had been written and appeals filed before Morris came to the forest, his appointment provided an opportunity for the agency to back off previous positions and begin to find a collaborative solution. According to Morris, "I didn't have any real ownership of the issues being appealed." Since he had not worked on the plan for four years, he "wasn't in love with the thing," and he believes that freed him to communicate more openly and effectively with the appellants. He decided to approach them and try to solve the disputes. To begin, Morris says, "I picked up the phone and introduced myself to the appellants." He says at the time the appellants "were angry . . . because we hadn't been talking to them. . . . They weren't happy campers to start with, and they wanted a little communication." Morris began communicating and started a collaborative process that resulted in resolution of the appeals.

Using Community-Based Social Networks

Successful cases of collaboration also make use of the networks of social relationships that always exist in communities. People know and trust others, and power is structured in communities by local politics, wealth, and traditions. Tapping into those preexisting social networks enables project leaders to create effective communication links, mobilize support, and achieve a legitimacy that they could never achieve on their own. For example, agency personnel involved in the Blackfoot Challenge in Montana highlight the importance of finding the "elders" and the opinion leaders in the community and getting to know them. According to FWS biologist Greg Neudecker, "Not only do the ideas have to come from people in the community, they have to come from people who are well respected in the valley. If Jim Stone thinks that it is a good idea, then it must be. Sometimes it takes a long time to figure out who are the elders in the community. But once you do, they will take the whole project and run with it."

FWS staff member Steve Thompson speaks from his experience with the Cameron County Agricultural Coexistence Committee: "To be successful, it has to start from the farmers and ranchers. . . . Every community has a leader farmer. Several of them meet at a coffee shop, and they know what is going on. . . . A [Fish and Wildlife] Service person could take a report [describing successes elsewhere], go sit down and have a cup of coffee, and hand it to the guy and say, 'No, you don't know me, and you probably think I'm an enemy, but I heard about some of these other stories that have worked, and we've got a big problem here. Would you just read this, and get back to me sometime and let me know what you think?' I think you can set the seed a lot of times that way. . . . You have to do this very informally and catch a leader in the community."

Two strategies that build on preexisting relationships have been used to increase the awareness of local landowners in Northern California's Upper Stony Creek initiative. Local cooperative farm extension agents have been used to convey the group's message. In many cases the agents have worked in the county for over thirty years and are trusted by the ranchers, which has improved the effectiveness of the education program. In addition, NRCS staff have involved respected landowners as demonstration cases to gain credibility with other members of the community.

Seeing Opportunities in Crisis

Finally, successful partnerships can be facilitated by an entrepreneurial mindset that recognizes the opportunities inherent in a crisis. Since change occurs primarily in response to conflict and crisis, the most successful leaders take advantage of the window of opportunity that problems create. In other words, one person's crisis is another's opportunity. For example, in Cameron County (described in chapter 7), when the EPA proposed eliminating the use of pesticides involved in growing cotton so as to protect the endangered Aplomado falcon, the farmers could have sought a solution through the courts or through political channels. But, as FWS refuge manager Steve Thompson relates the story, "They were tired of that. It takes a lot of energy and time and money, and you don't really always get your best solutions that way." Instead, the farmers seized the opportunity implied by the crisis to develop an ad hoc committee to work through the issue more productively.

Nothing Succeeds Like Success

People and groups want to be part of a success; hence, one way to motivate involvement is to demonstrate success. In many of our successful examples of collaboration, projects were structured to provide participants with an early, tangible success: They started small, produced results, and went on to bigger issues and efforts. By taking small steps, success was more likely. Nanticoke Watershed Alliance member Mark Zankel advises, "Accomplish things and show people what you have done. People are hesitant to get involved, but once something is up and running, they do not want to miss the boat and seem like they are out of the loop. Success really sells." Michelle Grigore of the Oak Openings Working Group agrees, "Everybody wants to be part of a success and part of a winning team."

Building on Small Steps

The value of starting small is reinforced by scholars who write about collaboration. For example, Rosabeth Moss Kanter notes that the most successful collaborative agreements between companies "incorporate a specific joint activity, a first-step venture or project." She says, "This project makes the relationship real in practice, helps the partners learn to work together, and provides a basis for measuring performance."[6] Early small successes help build trust among participants and increase their confidence in each other and the process, thereby allowing the group to address more complex or controversial issues later. Successes also build support for the collaborative effort among the public and others who provide resources or otherwise aid the collaboration.

In some situations, taking small steps means working on "easier" issues first. Particularly in complex negotiations dealing with disputes, finding a way to demonstrate the possibility of success can help parties muster the courage to deal with more difficult issues. For example, the Clark County HCP effort attempted to resolve more approachable conflicts as a starting point. Participants describe this strategy as the pursuit of "the lowest hanging fruit first," which allowed the group to make incremental progress toward more central issues. Going at the biggest issues first was considered impossible with such diverse issues on the table. One interviewee described the conflict as "just too exhausting, mentally and physically, so we started to look for areas of good discussion that didn't lead to shouting." Ultimately, the Clark County process produced a short-term HCP for the desert tortoise, followed by a thirty-year HCP for the tortoise, leading to the development of a long-term multispecies conservation plan—an incremental process in which one step facilitated the next.

Several projects chose uncontroversial activities as a step toward improving decision making on more difficult issues. In developing the Alaska Recreation Plan, District Ranger Pete Tennis deliberately chose recreation, a fairly noncontroversial forest use, rather than responding to a preexisting polarized conflict such as timber harvesting, to avoid becoming hamstrung by controversy and to demonstrate success. Based on her experience with the Darby Partnership, TNC staff member Teri Devlin recommends: "When you form a group, one piece of advice is not to get caught up in the issues that are hot that have brought you together. Slow down, so you keep trying to see who is there, who is missing, who should be there, how we are forming our relationships with each other."

The Blackfoot Challenge started by focusing on a topic that obviously needed a coordinated response. Land Lindbergh advises: "Start with issues that will mean something to everyone. [In our case] noxious weed control was just that example. Weed control got the Challenge into the minds and hearts of landowners because it was easy for landowners to see the critical importance of a coordinated approach in tackling this problem. Moreover, it was something in which the ranching community could relate and in which they welcomed a group approach. Focusing on weed control has now spilled over into other issues (albeit slower than the group would like). Younger ranchers have been particularly keen once they got some experience under their belt with using the Challenge to help them deal with some problems."

Other efforts work on controversial issues but do so in a step-wise fashion. For many, small steps lead to bigger endeavors. For example, in the case of CURES, the recreation partnership in the Eastern Sierra, a single two-day workshop began a long series of activities that established the new organization, multiple task groups, and a set of implementation activities. According to Forest Service facilitator Nancy Upham, "You gain confidence when you find out that it really does work and that there are tremendous benefits derived by having strong relationships with external entities. With that confidence, you can go forward and try to build more linkages."

Some efforts get off the ground by starting as small-scale demonstration programs. In the Kiowa Grasslands in New Mexico, a small yet significant success encouraged others to become active. Rather than implementing a large-scale program aimed at all grazing permittees on these public grasslands, a handful of ranchers were identified as possible candidates for an integrated program of rangeland improvement and environmental restoration. By ensuring that training and technical advice were available, monitoring was put into place, and problems were handled promptly, this targeted program produced significant results. Such an image was very powerful for other ranchers in the area, and record numbers—both grassland permittees and those that ranch on privately owned land—are currently seeking aid and advice from the Forest Service and the NRCS.

One reason starting small makes sense is that it avoids raising expectations overly high given that "success" is usually defined in relation to a baseline of expectations. Dr. Yvonne Everett, director of the Trinity Community GIS Center in Hayfork, California, cautions that people involved in community-based partnerships need to "walk a fine line between needing to publicize so that people know you are there, yet not putting out a huge blast of publicity before you can actually put your money where your mouth is." She warns against promising more than can be delivered in order to avoid damaging credibility, especially in rural areas where word tends to spread quickly. Her own philosophy is to "be low key, work along, and then do the fanfare" once you have accomplished some things.

Using the Symbolic Power of Innovation

Being seen as an innovator has a symbolic power that can propel collaborative efforts along. While some fear involvement in something new, many others are excited by the prospect. There is a palpable energy associated with involvement in something new and different. For participants, taking risks by moving down a less traveled path on which the destination is not clear quickens the heart. It may be hard to get people to commit to trying a different approach, but once engaged, they tend to hang together in part to rationalize their past involvement. Successful project entrepreneurs have used the psychological power of innovation to encourage others to get involved, motivate people to stay involved, and secure funding and other resources.

The Anacostia Watershed Restoration Committee was partly stimulated by the successful efforts of several government agencies in addressing water pollution problems on the nearby Potomac River. As Metropolitan Washington Council of Governments staff member Lorraine Herson-Jones explains, "Probably another indirect motivator of all this is that there was such a success story in the Potomac, and at least two of the jurisdictions [on the AWRC] were involved in that effort." Additionally, "There was actually pressure from citizens who said, 'You've done a lot with the Potomac. Why aren't we doing anything with my river?' which was the Anacostia," she says. "So that was kind of an odd motivator, but I think it did work." Notably, the Potomac River flows alongside Washington's historic Georgetown and other affluent neighborhoods, while the Anacostia runs through some of the District of Columbia's poorest areas.

The Anacostia project also gained momentum from being seen as an example of a new approach to resource management being pushed by the Clinton administration. When the administration seized on ecosystem management as an alternative to multiple use, it looked for places that could demonstrate the innovation. On an administration priority list that included the Chesapeake Bay, the Everglades, and the old-growth forests of the Pacific Northwest, the Anacostia was one of the only areas that was predominantly urban. As a result of its selection as a priority site, several federal agencies signed a memorandum of understanding in 1994 agreeing to give "full support to the Anacostia River Demonstration Project as an opportunity to apply ecosystem management concepts in an urban environment." The administration's Interagency Ecosystem Management Task Force highlighted the effort in its report. This attention to the project as a visible demonstration of innovation helped to propel the project forward and secure funding for it.

In several cases, a sense of being new and different helped cooperators line up funding for their projects. Oak Openings participant Michelle Grigore notes that funding agencies like partnerships: "You definitely need partnerships if you want to get that funding for your project. We've been successful [in fundraising] because of the partnership." The same dynamic worked for the Darby Partnership. According to Teri Devlin, "What the partnership did was twofold. First is if you get that many people from all those agencies together talking about one area, it gets a lot of attention, and attention is a magnet for more attention, which means more resources, more ability to work on things, which all translates into success."

The sense of doing something different—of being an innovator—also helps to reinforce positive group dynamics, as partners begin to transform their perception of "us against them" to "us as innovators against the possibility of failure." In describing his involvement with the Cameron County Agricultural Coexistence Committee (chapter 7), Steve Thompson, manager of the Laguna Atascosa Wildlife Refuge in Texas, explains how the group dynamics associated with being a pioneer tend to promote higher levels of effort and commitment:

> It took a lot of guts, I guess. There was a sort of group bonding. You get to the point where you have gone out on a limb enough, trying to convince people that this thing is worth doing, that it might work. And then all of a sudden you realize you are kind of out by yourself. You are with this group, not your traditional group. You have a fear of failure. So I think you do some things that are a little riskier. You are willing to say things that are a little tougher to your own group. And once you get hammered by your own group, you tend to come back. Either you are going to bail out at that point, and stay with the same group that you're comfortable with, or you are going to come back to our ag/wildlife group and be more dedicated—and more convinced that you *have* to solve this thing because your credibility is hanging out there, and your reputation.

Success Begets Success

Successes are emulated by others in comparable situations and have led to the proliferation of collaborative efforts. For example, the Russian River cleanup has gained attention throughout the state. The California Conservation Corps started participating in the cleanups, and Rebecca Kress's efforts have inspired other individuals to organize cleanup days along rivers in their communities. The Cameron County Coexistence Committee became such an effective group that it began to be "respected in the community for all kinds of problem solving," says FWS participant Steve Thompson. "We were always asked to solve another problem." Thompson and farmer Wayne Halbert also have been asked to share their experience with numerous agencies and organizations across the country.

Ron Brenneman of the National Wild Turkey Federation has leveraged his successes with Georgia Pacific to develop partnerships with other companies. According to Brenneman, "When you can start showing other companies some of the giants in the business that have signed an agreement, it certainly makes the other companies feel a little more comfortable. . . . It's at the point now that we have companies coming to us, saying, 'Hey, I heard about this partnership program that sounds great. How can we get involved?'"

The success achieved in the Kirtland's warbler partnership also has given Forest Service staff the confidence to pursue other collaborations. According to Forest Service wildlife biologist Rex Ennis, they learned from the initial education program partnership how to find and take advantage of partnership opportunities. "We have actively sought out additional partnerships" because this one was successful, says Ennis. "It has further instilled in us that this is the right way to do business."

Persistence Pays Off

Since small steps are often needed to build momentum and establish new relationships, achieving significant on-the-ground management outcomes may take a long time. Indeed, the Kirtland's warbler effort developed over a twenty-year period. The Negrito ecosystem project was also extremely time-consuming and "awkward and unwieldy" at times, according to Forest Service staff member Gary McCaleb: "We had to spend a lot of time bringing people up to speed. . . . We had to teach them everything the Forest Service has learned over the past one hundred years." In addition, the consensus approach made progress "very slow and agonizing," which, McCaleb admits, was "frustrating to implementing-type bureaucrats like us." Steve Thompson also stresses how much time and effort collaborative efforts can require, drawing on his experience with the Cameron County Coexistence Committee. At the start of the process, he says, "I had no clue how much energy, time, and emotions would be tied up in this thing. But I'm almost hesitant to tell others, because if you let them know what they're getting into, they might not do it."

Be Patient

While these respondents bemoan the amount of time and effort that goes into partnerships, they also are strong advocates for collaboration and highlight the challenges implied by lengthy, energy-consuming processes: being patient, staying interested in the effort, maintaining group members' motivation, and learning from experiences along the way. The chronology of these efforts suggests that their time requirements are high at the outset yet tend to diminish over time. Program entrepreneurs need to hang in there and not give up when faced with initial skepticism or ongoing challenges. Our cases suggest that the results are worth it.

With the Alaska Recreation Plan, one of the first obstacles the Forest Service team had to overcome was how to get people to participate in yet another planning effort. "Why should we talk to you?" asked area residents. "You asked us the same questions six months ago. You're obviously not listening to us." Forest Service planner Maria Durazo-Means's response was to be patient but persistent. "The public is leery of our sincerity and won't be ready to immediately start talking to you. Be patient with public involvement," she advises. In her view, "The key was persistence. We wouldn't go away."

The same message of patient persistence comes from other cases. Rocky Mountain National Park outreach coordinator Larry Gamble says that apathy was a difficult obstacle to overcome, but that it is important to keep "plugging away" with those people who are willing to participate and to work to raise the awareness and interest of other members of the community. Similarly, it was difficult to get some agencies and organizations that were critical to the success of the Oak Openings partnership to commit to collaborative work. To overcome their resistance, project supporters were persistent in their efforts. According to Michelle Grigore, "It took a lot of badgering and a lot of stressing that this was one of the best areas in the state . . . and if you were going to preserve rare species, you really had to look at this area." These individuals also secured coverage in local newspapers and published newsletters and brochures to "bring home the message that all the agencies need to make this area a priority."

Learn from Failures

Being persistent also means being willing to learn from failures and move forward while adapting to what you learn. While early successes were important to gaining trust and building support in the Upper Stony Creek watershed project in Northern California, NRCS project coordinator Wendell Gilgert emphasizes the importance of learning from problems that occur. He says, "You cannot be afraid of failures. Don't try to hide them. One, because other people will find out about them. Two, you learn critical things from them and allow other people to learn from them."

Fortunately, while collaborative initiatives require continued care and feeding, the early steps take more effort than later stages, as important relationships and communication channels are established at the beginning that pay off throughout the life of the partnership. In the successful examples we studied, project proponents were able to persist and get through the difficult times. For example, Ron Brenneman had to deal with considerable skepticism on the part of Georgia Pacific's staff and worked hard to make sure the company understood the National Wild Turkey Federation's goals and motives. "We probably worked longer to get the agreement signed with Georgia Pacific than any other company we have worked with," he notes. Once those initial barriers were overcome, however, the reception "has been excellent."

Other partnerships have similarly moved forward through the persistence and hard work of individuals like Brenneman, Seth Diamond, and Maria Durazo-Means, who reached out to face situations proactively. They used opportunities strategically and drew on the latent power of innovation as a symbol that can mobilize people to act. Small steps yielded larger benefits over time. Ultimately, their efforts at entrepreneurship helped forge durable relationships and a belief that change was possible.

Chapter 11

Getting Help, Giving Help

The East Fork Quinn River, located within Nevada's Humboldt National Forest, flows out of the Santa Rosa Mountains approximately eighty miles northwest of Winnemucca. One of the few perennial creeks in Nevada, it provides an oasis for livestock during the arid summer months. Because it is situated on the outskirts of the Santa Rosa Ranger District, it had long suffered from insufficient management attention. Unauthorized and excessive grazing in the large pasture surrounding the creek had caused serious erosion and thermal pollution problems. The East Fork Quinn had historically accommodated 1,300 fish per mile of river, but that figure had dropped to fewer than 25 fish per mile by the mid-1980s. Tensions arose between ranchers and Forest Service employees, each perceiving the other's interests and actions as antithetical to their own.

This situation came to a head in 1986 when the Sierra Club and other environmental groups appealed the Humboldt National Forest plan, arguing that it did not provide adequate standards for riparian habitat. Forest Service officials were aware that the agency was not adequately fulfilling its stewardship mandate. Increased concern about the status of the Lahontan cutthroat trout, a threatened species that had been sighted in the upper reaches of the creek, provided added incentive for the Forest Service to take action. Ranchers with grazing permits in the area began to realize that overgrazing was hurting them as much as anyone.

Rangeland management specialist Steve Williams knew that something needed to be done about this situation, but he did not know exactly what to do or how to do it. Whatever was needed, he could not do it alone. So he looked beyond the agency's boundary for help.

Williams recognized at the outset that resources would be needed to undertake restoration of the East Fork Quinn River and that the Santa Rosa Ranger District did not have resources for such a project. So he applied for funding for a riparian demonstration project under Section 319 of the Clean Water Act. CWA funds are distributed through the relevant state agency, in this case the Nevada Department of Conservation and Natural Resources. Williams knew that he would need to work closely with local ranchers because it was their activities that needed to be monitored and modified. However, the agency's relationship with those ranchers was quite strained, and he was uncertain how to begin working with them in a positive and productive manner. He enlisted the help of Dave Torrell, an educator with the University of Nevada Cooperative Extension who was also a skilled facilitator. Williams knew Torrell through his work facilitating general needs assessment meetings with the agricultural sector in Humboldt County. With the Clean Water Act funds in hand, and Dave Torrell at the helm, Williams began a collaborative dialogue with the ranchers, the Forest Service, and other agencies about how to begin restoring the East Fork Quinn River.

Torrell used a process he had developed called "shared vision" to help the parties begin working together. The process emphasized consensus, "avoiding blame and fault finding," and assigning an equal voice to all involved. Each participant was asked about his or her needs, desires, and expectations for riparian management of the East Fork Quinn. Each person was heard equally, and his or her response was summarized and discussed by the group. Individuals came to realize that they shared the same goal: riparian and riverine improvements. They began to see each other as individuals rather than "the other side." Williams says, "I think the 'shared vision' focuses people on the positive rather than the fears or negatives. If you can focus on the positive and where you want to go, it tends to open up people and their barriers."

In a one-year period, starting in the summer of 1989, Torrell facilitated five or six meetings involving a Forest Service interdisciplinary team consisting of Steve Williams, two district rangers, and a forest hydrologist and ranching interests including representatives from Circle A Ranch, which owned approximately thirteen ranches in the area, and NJ Ranches. The Forest Service also held some less formal meetings with grazing permittees. In the initial meeting between Forest Service representatives and ranchers, it was decided that a fence should be installed to control grazing in the area. The Forest Service bought the materials, and ranchers built the eight-mile fence, creating a riparian pasture. The Nevada Department of Forestry arranged to have juniper and other brush cut to be used in stabilizing riverbanks. Boy Scouts and other volunteers planted fourteen hundred willow saplings. The Forest

Service and fisheries biologists from the Nevada Department of Wildlife then jointly monitored the effects of the East Fork Quinn demonstration project, hoping to see the river return to blue ribbon status. The monitoring activities were financed through an EPA grant sought by Williams, who recognized that the Forest Service's limited budget would otherwise make monitoring unlikely.

The East Fork Quinn restoration process is considered by those involved a success on many grounds. It established lines of communication and broke down long-standing barriers between traditional adversaries. Not only do those groups understand each other's needs and interests better, but they also better understand how to communicate with one another and how to address mutual problems. When asked whether the participants came away with a greater trust in one another, Williams responds, "Maybe not trust, but certainly understanding." From a management standpoint, restoration practices have been initially successful, and Forest Service monitoring has eliminated most unauthorized grazing in the area. The ranchers see obvious on-the-ground success in this project. According to rancher Jim Fair, "It is clear that the benefits to cattle operations will outweigh the costs" of the ranchers' investment. He says, "We'll get higher calf percentages, heavier calves, and healthier cattle." Moreover, he is quite pleased with his involvement in this process, arguing that "the resource will be easier to maintain over the long term."

Restoration of the East Fork Quinn River could occur only through the joint efforts of the Forest Service, state agencies, ranchers, and others concerned about responsible long-term management of the resource. The collaboration would never have been possible, however, if Steve Williams had not sought help from a number of sources along the way. Acknowledging the lack of agency funds for restoration, he sought support through the Nevada Department of Conservation and Natural Resources. To promote dialogue with the ranchers, he enlisted the help of a professional facilitator. To conduct the restoration work, he partnered with local Boy Scouts and other volunteers to supplement the core work provided by the ranchers. He also enlisted the technical support of the Nevada Department of Forestry, consulted with Nevada Department of Fisheries biologists during monitoring, and sought EPA funding for that phase of the activity. By getting help from others, he created a successful collaboration to restore the East Fork Quinn River that others can emulate today.

Seeking help is not a natural tendency for agencies long accustomed to being in charge—to being the experts with the knowledge, skills, and authority to get the job done. Looking to others for help takes a different outlook, one that is more humble yet also more realistic and aggressive. Many successful collaborative partnerships have moved forward because people sought and acknowledged the assistance of others. They got ideas from others and accessed expertise wherever it could be obtained. They sought external funding and enlisted the assistance of those who could help manage the process of interaction between groups when they were unskilled or unsure about how to begin. They built public and political support, which led to the necessary authorizations and resources and allowed their efforts to proceed. Just as important, successful partnerships are reciprocal: they recognize when it is important to *give* help to enable others to do things that they would otherwise not be able to do. By seeking and giving help, stewardship of public resources is advanced.

Resource Mobilizing, Not Resource Constrained

It takes resources—money, equipment, humanpower—to get things done. As noted in chapter 3, many things never happen simply because resources are not available. Few of the cases highlighted in this book were do-it-yourself projects. Most succeeded because someone took the initiative to find the funds and other assistance to make them work, wherever those resources might be available. Successful collaborative partnerships are driven by people who are neither naive nor foolhardy but simply say, "The glass is half full; let's fill it to the top," rather than "The glass is half empty; therefore, it can't be done." They are resource mobilizing, not resource constrained.

Different organizations have different types of resources to offer a collaborative venture, including dollars, equipment, labor, and expertise. While many think of partnerships based solely on common interests, building relationships with groups that have needed resources is also critical. Michelle Grigore of the Toledo Oak Openings Working Group advises that those forming a partnership "may want to pull in other groups that can bring benefits to the table, whether it's volunteer help, the ability to publish a newsletter, they've got a xerox machine . . . everybody can bring something to the table." Those involved in successful collaborative processes work in many different, innovative ways, building bridges between government agencies, nonprofit organizations, companies, and individuals to piece together the resources necessary to take action on issues of concern.

Equipment

In the Beartree Challenge (described in chapter 10), Seth Diamond looked for organizations that had the technical capability as well as the direct incentive to help out. Improving grizzly bear habitat required planned burns, planting whitebark pine, and opening up the overstory canopy. To accomplish those tasks, Diamond solicited volunteer assistance from loggers, timber companies, and timber equipment dealers. Seven timber industry organizations and companies agreed to lend equipment, technical advice, and $100,000 to the Forest Service over a four-year period. Bill Jones of Jones Equipment estimates his contribution at about $20,000 annually for several years. Jones had an incentive to lend this helping hand to the Beartree Challenge. As he explains: "The visibility with the public . . . to show them what the equipment does, to work with environmental groups which are so down on management and logging and such." He explains further that "companies want to demonstrate that their equipment can do more than just cut timber for timber's sake."

Funding

Most partnerships seek funding from multiple sources. In some cases, they have applied for funds through government programs established specifically for projects like those contemplated. For example, the Eel River Delta Sustainable Agriculture Committee in Northern California, a partnership between dairy farmers and several state agencies, was formed to address a range of water-quality issues. The committee sought and received a $30,000 grant from the California State Water Board and additional funds from the EPA to underwrite a planning process and fund water-quality tests throughout the delta in order to acquire reliable baseline data. In addition, farmers and agency resource specialists conducted joint fact-finding in the field to determine the floodplain level and establish methods for water-quality regulators to evaluate dairy operations. Finally, the nonprofit California Coastal Conservancy, the Resource Conservation District, and the Sustainable Agriculture Committee worked together to obtain a $188,000 implementation grant from the State Water Board. The grant funded experimental measures to control runoff on ten demonstration farms, including new containment structures, riparian restoration work, and new management practices.

Similarly, the Trinity Community GIS Center, linking data across landscapes in Northern California and providing access and training in sophisticated GIS to residents, was initiated with a mix of funding from the Forest Service, the Bureau of Reclamation, and the U.S. Fish and Wildlife Service. Its budget was administered by the California Department of Forestry and the University of California Cooperative Extension Program. The group received subsidies that helped it obtain equipment and software that would be very expensive to purchase, including donations of free software from ESRI, a major GIS software company.

Other collaborative efforts have looked for organizations with complementary interests and sought funding and other resources through partnership arrangements. With neither the resources nor the legal authority to influence land development practices beyond the Rocky Mountain National Park's boundary, park land-use specialist Larry Gamble works closely with the Rocky Mountain National Park Associates, a nonprofit "friends of the park" group. The group provided money to hire a consultant to help a large landowner adjacent to the park prepare a master plan to guide development of the area in a manner that protects park resources. A new land trust in the area was approached to provide funding to acquire a conservation easement on the property.

Human Power

Many collaborative efforts recognize that people who care about a resource often are willing to contribute their time and energy to help out. As described in chapter 2, the San Gorgonio Volunteer Association provides critical labor for the Forest Service in managing the San Gorgonio wilderness area. Nestled high in the beautiful San Bernardino mountains but within an hour's drive of more than 7.5 million people, the forest is a favorite destination of Southern Californians eager to escape urban living for the weekend. As a result, the San Gorgonio is one of the most visited wilderness areas in the nation and was being "loved to death," with certain popular areas being trampled into dustbowls.

Recognizing limits on its staff resources, the Forest Service solicited volunteer assistance for backcountry patrols in the early 1980s, and many wilderness enthusiasts signed up. Within a couple of years, those volunteers decided to form their own organization, and the San Gorgonio Volunteer Association was born. Alice Krueper, one of the founders of the SGVA, explains, "The San Gorgonio is so important to many of us, such a part of our lives." The strong connection that the volunteers have with the wilderness area provides a powerful motivation for them to invest significant energy in helping steward the area. For example, the group donated more than nine thousand person-hours of volunteer time to the San Bernardino National Forest in 1992 and made more than seventeen thousand visitor contacts during volunteer wilderness patrols. Forest Service interpretive specialist Barb Ward says, "I keep being surprised. If you just ask people to do stuff, it's amazing what people will do for you. I think, 'No, I can't ask anyone to do that,' but then I do, and they just jump right in and do it."

Accessing Expertise and Ideas

Natural resource management requires a considerable amount of scientific and technical information, and groups seek expertise and ideas from many sources. Sometimes collaborative efforts look for expertise to build understanding of the issues of concern, thereby guiding problem solving and, at the same time, making the efforts more credible beyond the group. At other times, they look for management ideas that others have tested and evaluated. Groups also look for help in managing their process of interaction by soliciting third-party assistance with facilitation. By reaching out, they magnify the power of their partnership considerably. On-the-ground management is enhanced in ways that could not be achieved by relying on the skills and expertise of the partnership members alone.

Acquiring Scientific and Technical Expertise

Representatives of many collaborative groups emphasize the importance of aggressively involving experts. George Hirchenberger, BLM representative to Montana's Blackfoot Challenge, suggests, "It is critical to seek out professionals, whether or not they are specifically working on a watershed project. There are always biologists, state range conservationists, or others with the expertise. The last thing you want to do is to do a project that you are eventually going to have to redo. If for some reason they cannot help you to make the decisions, they have the resources to find someone else who can." TNC representative to the Nanticoke Watershed Alliance Mark Zankel emphasizes, "It is not reasonable to expect watershed group staff to be science experts in every area that you need it, so the key is to get people with expertise to be the technical resources for the group—whether that is regular involvement or collaborative research projects or just being able to come when there is an issue being discussed and they can provide some technical expertise and be a backboard for people to ask questions. Bring those people into the process."

Lisa Jo Frech, executive director of the Nanticoke effort, notes that accessing external expertise involves outreach and networking: "We are always asking people to come and to make presentations or to critique other presentations. It is like a spider web that is always growing. We are always evolving; we are always looking to catch somebody else in our net. We ask, 'Here is what we are handling now—who should we attract to handle this?' Or, 'Here is an issue that we are not planning on having to handle—who do we need to work on that issue?' It is my job to know who is out there doing what and who we can call on. We are not working in a vacuum here. If we do not have the people we need, then we go get them. If I do not know who they are, I know somebody who does."

Clearly, a wide range of possible sources of expertise exists. Teri Devlin, TNC representative to the Darby Partnership in Ohio, says, "Understand that there are agencies available to get that science done. Do not ignore colleges and universities. Welcome in those experts and be clear in what your needs are. Don't just say, 'Can you become a partner?' Say, 'We need GIS mapping; we need to know about X.'"

One obvious source of expertise is state and federal agencies. The Upper Stony Creek watershed effort in Northern California has stretched its limited resources by relying on outside agency personnel for specialized expertise. For instance, the project has "borrowed" staff time of a local Forest Service archaeologist to conduct required cultural resource assessments on project sites. Forest Service personnel and the California State Department of Forestry and Fire Protection handle the group's prescribed burns. A local staff member from the California Department of Fish and Game participates in the group's wildlife protection projects, including fencing riparian corridors and ponds. In addition, the group uses local University of California cooperative extension farm advisors to teach a watershed education program for local landowners.

University researchers provide another significant source of expertise. For example, the Nanticoke Watershed Alliance relies on experts from Salisbury State University. In developing the Huron River Adopt-a-Stream program, director Joan Martin found that her relationship with a faculty member of the University of Michigan's School of Natural Resources and Environment was particularly beneficial. To broaden her own understanding of stream systems, Martin, a biologist by training, sat in on Professor Mike Wiley's aquatic ecosystems course. While attending the class, she talked to him, she says, "about giving us a bit of advice and a hand, and that's grown into a very helpful relationship." That scientific expertise helped make Adopt-a-Stream a credible and successful program. Martin comments that Professor Wiley was "really the key, I think, to our developing a program that's quite respectable and thorough."

Getting Ideas from Others

To effectively address an issue does not mean that one must inevitably invent a new strategy or process. At times it simply takes seeking ideas, advice, or models from others who have confronted and grappled with a similar issue or situation. For example, the successful negotiation over forest plan appeals on Utah's Manti-LaSal National Forest was prompted by new forest supervisor George Morris's observation of similar multiparty interactions on his former forest in California. Joan Martin modeled the Huron River Adopt-a-Stream program after the Adopt-a-Stream program of Maryland's Save Our Shores, a project that began more than two decades ago. Under Martin's leadership, the Huron River program eventually shifted from the Maryland program's emphasis on cleanups to more of a focus on volunteers conducting scientific studies of creeks in the watershed, an activity more suited to the emerging needs of the Huron River.

Looking outward for what has worked in similar situations uncovered a unique opportunity for Forest Service management of Roan Mountain in

North Carolina and Tennessee. As described in chapters 5 and 7, the grassy, treeless meadows known as balds that characterize the area provide habitat for numerous threatened, endangered, and sensitive species. Managers and interest groups wanted to maintain the Roan Highlands in their current state of "baldness" but were not sure how to do so. Toecane District Ranger Paul Bradley heard about a joint project that the Kika de la Garza National Goat Research Center at Langston University in Langston, Oklahoma, and the Forest Service were doing on national forest land in Arkansas, using goats to prepare sites for replanting after clearcuts. He wondered if goats could help manage the Roan balds. He decided it was worth a try and contacted the goat research center. Eventually, a Challenge Cost-Share agreement with Langston University was drawn up, and the project was underway, jointly managed and monitored by the Forest Service and its multi-interest Mt. Roan Advisory Group.

Assistance with the Process of Collaboration

For many groups, the collaborative process is a new way of interacting, and they need help managing the process. To get that help, they often reach out to third-party facilitators. In the East Fork Quinn River case, Dave Torrell was asked to facilitate because he was skilled at process management and was known and trusted by the parties who needed to work together. The Applegate Partnership relied on the skills of John Lange, a communications professor at Southern Oregon State College. When Forest Supervisor George Morris convened a two-day negotiation in his office to try to resolve appeals on the Manti-LaSal National Forest plan, he hired two independent facilitators, Peter Fogg and John Kennedy, to manage the communication process. Participants included three individuals from the Forest Service and four representatives of the appellants. Morris recognized the lack of trust that had developed between the parties and realized the benefit of turning to independent facilitators to help begin discussions.

Building Public and Political Support

Sometimes what is needed to promote the activities of a collaborative group is not others' expertise or resources; it is others' ability to build the public or political support that will enable the collaborative effort to proceed. As discussed in chapter 3, many insititutional structures and attitudes impede efforts to collaborate. Agencies in successful collaborative processes often seek the help of others in fostering public and political support in order to overcome inertia, skepticism, or attempts to politically "fix" a situation in ways counter to the agreements reached through the collaborative process. Drawing from her experience coordinating the Toledo Oak Openings Working Group,

Michelle Grigore emphasizes that "a strong core of citizen support is really important"—it often provides the pressure that in turn encourages agencies to embrace a partnership's efforts. Oak Openings volunteers form an important constituency that pressures local governments and agencies to support restoration.

Working with Interest Groups and the Media

In the Beartree Challenge, Seth Diamond solicited the endorsement of environmental and other organizations to help the project achieve "wide-based support." Diamond recalls, "I got a fair amount of bad press in the proposal planning stage, mainly from wilderness groups skeptical about any logging on the district. . . . There was distrust of the Forest Service, distrust of the Forest Service–timber company alliance, distrust of our use of the media—people thought it was just a PR move." Diamond overcame that skepticism by "directly confronting it—not like typical bureaucrats who say nothing," he says. "I let them know what we were doing." He notes that it was also critical to have the support of environmental groups such as Defenders of Wildlife and The Nature Conservancy that could help educate and allay the concerns of other environmental groups. "It's helpful to use other groups as go-betweens," he says.

Groups frequently reach out to the media to build public support for their efforts. An aggressive media campaign was the means by which Seth Diamond promoted the Beartree Challenge. When faced with early opposition, he put together an all-out effort that used all types of media—television, magazines, newspapers, and video. He estimates that about one hundred articles were written on the project over a four-year period and says, "We marketed the program aggressively, not so much to say that this was the answer, but to show people what we were doing." Some forty to fifty presentations were made in Montana and in Washington, D.C., to educate a wide array of people, from congressional members to schoolchildren.

Working with Elected Officials

Some collaborative partnerships build support for their efforts by working political channels to educate and influence key elected officials. Such an approach was critical to the success of the Negrito ecosystem management project's efforts to acquire funding. The Negrito project's early years were characterized by "fits and starts" due to a "frustrating" lack of funding, according to Forest Service District Ranger Gary McCaleb. It finally received funding through a line item included in a congressional appropriations bill that earmarked funds for the new "ecosystem management" project. This special attention from Congress was the result of efforts by Senator Jeff Bingaman (D-NM), who met with the coordinating group about the Negrito project after personal lobbying by one of the conservationists involved with the project. The result was $2.2 million given to the Forest Service Albuquerque regional office to be apportioned among the ten southwestern forests for ecosystem management activities. Project proponents were delighted with the decision to earmark $96,000 of that fund specifically for the Negrito. Much of the funding was used to support an extensive terrestrial ecosystem survey designed to set a baseline for assessing future management activities.

Development of a state park within the Ozark National Forest also benefited from explicit attention to building political support for the effort. When the Arkansas State Park Service and the Forest Service collaborated with the U.S. Fish and Wildlife Service, the Arkansas Game and Fish Commission, and several state and regional conservation organizations to explore potential redevelopment of an old lodge site on Mt. Magazine, they knew that their objectives would never be achieved without the support of key constituent groups and state elected officials. To build that support, an Environmental Review Committee (ERC) was established with broad representation of a diverse set of interested groups, and a memorandum of understanding was signed that was designed to "strengthen cooperative efforts to preserve, protect and enhance the ecological and cultural resources of Mt. Magazine, while promoting recreational use." The planning process overseen by the committee appears to have been effective at working with group concerns, and the resultant plan was not appealed by any group. Indeed, the project is viewed by many as a model in environmental sensitivity, with less than twenty acres (1 percent of the mountaintop) affected by construction. Additionally, over thirty important environmental mitigation measures governing construction were incorporated into the plans, including new areas set aside for previously unprotected species.

Throughout the planning process, federal and state legislators and Governor Bill Clinton were kept informed about the workings of the ERC. According to Forest Service team leader Rob Kopack, "All elected officials were kept abreast of progress by communications at key points in the process" in order to build their understanding and support for the project when it was needed. The transparency and forthrightness of the process kept politicians up to date on information and assumptions behind the decision-making process. Elected officials were then invited to share their thoughts and concerns. In Kopack's view, this "fishbowl approach to planning" took some of the pressure off the Forest Service, Arkansas State Parks, and the elected officials because, he says, "Anyone could look in and see what we were doing, all viewpoints and opinions were considered, and anyone that was interested was kept informed." The involvement of the elected officials was a major factor in the overall success of the project. When the Arkansas legislature was initially hesitant to fund the project, Kopack contacted some of the politicians who had been kept informed throughout the project's development. Their political support was crucial in getting approximately $1 million in state funds appropriated.

Getting Help by Giving Help

As indicated in chapters 1 and 2, collaboration is not an end; it is simply one means of achieving the broader goal of sound and acceptable management of natural resources. By not losing sight of that fundamental objective, some agency officials have recognized the importance of giving help to others, not just getting help for themselves. They have developed collaborative initiatives that assisted adjacent communities and in so doing enhanced the planning and management of public and private resources. They have facilitated community planning efforts by linking communities in need to available public resources. They have also provided critical expertise and advice to communities and developers, which promoted sound management of broader ecosystems. Ultimately, by helping others, they have helped themselves.

Linking Resources to Community Needs

In Adams County, Idaho, Forest Service District Ranger David Spann improved the situation facing the national forest by helping those outside its borders. He helped local communities access funding and expertise so that they could undertake community development projects. Since the community was heavily dependent on the Forest Service and local sawmills as primary employers, and forest resources could no longer be sustained at historic levels, Spann perceived an agency interest and responsibility to help those communities. With a population of three thousand located three hours away from Boise, Adams County is somewhat isolated from the state's economic centers. In 1990, Spann helped organize the Adams County Development Corporation to explore community needs and ways to diversify the economy. He was president of the corporation for two years and a long-time board member. Peter Johnson, district ranger from Adams County's other forest district, was also a member of the board.

Under the auspices of the corporation, a recycling center was created and a county-wide recycling program put into place. David Spann facilitated planning meetings. The Forest Service also provided flip charts and pens for these meetings, which, according to Spann, "may not sound like a lot, but it's meaningful for a small group that has no funding." The district's office computer was used in writing up the plan. The corporation also helped develop a senior citizens center in the town of New Meadows. Spann used his knowledge of the government offices in Boise to link the building committee with the state commerce department, a filter organization for HUD grants. The strategic plan produced by the corporation was also used when the sawmill in the town of Council closed. It served as the basis for the community's "developing a stronger economic development plan and outreach for businesses and getting three new businesses to locate in town," according to Spann.

Spann played "the role of networking facilitator—looking for who the major game players were who were not linking together." Because his office was in Boise, he knew the local community as well as the government and was well positioned to link the two. "Boise does not want to approach the community like 'big brother,' and the community members feel they don't know who to talk to," he said at one point. The skills and perspectives of Forest Service personnel contributed in ways beyond facilitation. According to Spann, "In the case of a small community like Adams County, the professionalism that the Forest Service brought to the table, in supporting people and helping them with their plans [was helpful]. And helping them understand that they needed to identify a need for action and then alternatives. And then going about bringing together people that might help. I think all of those things have been very important." By helping the community diversify its economy, Spann helped the Forest Service reduce demand for timber supplied from the national forests. In doing that, he also facilitated the transition by the forest and the community to a more sustainable course.

Providing Expertise and Advice

Gary Earney, a planner on the San Bernardino National Forest, recognized the value to the national forest inherent in giving help to adjacent communities. The San Bernardino National Forest is located just fifty miles from downtown Los Angeles, in one of the fastest-growing suburban areas in the United States. Due to rapid, uncontrolled population growth, the forest in recent years has been threatened by residential and commercial developments near its border. "There are seven cities that touch up to the forest on just this one district," explains Cajon District Ranger Elliott Graham. The entire San Bernardino National Forest is bounded by twenty-six different cities (five are within the forest boundary) and numerous smaller, unincorporated bedroom communities. "We're not in a sleepy little town in Colorado. We're talking [development projects that include] fifteen hundred homes at a whack," says Graham. Such developments are particularly detrimental to the forest because of the topography and ecology of the area. The forest and the surrounding towns are located in extremely steep, unstable, and fire-prone chaparral canyons. Poorly planned development near the forest border can encourage fires, erosion, flooding, and overuse of recreation facilities, all of which ultimately degrade the fragile and rare chaparral ecosystem within the forest.

In the mid-1980s, Earney, the Cajon District's lands and recreation officer, decided that the best way to encourage responsible development in the area, and thereby protect national forest resources, was to get involved in local government planning. A good example of the effect of his interaction with local planners and developers is the Hunter's Ridge development, several hundred multimillion-dollar homes proposed to be built in a riparian canyon in the city of Fontana and adjacent to the national forest. The Forest Service was concerned that the development was not "fireproof." Fires had come through that canyon on a fairly regular eighteen-year cycle, and without adequate measures the next fire might wipe out the development entirely. In addition, the development proposal included equestrian trails that led right up to the forest and into an area that had been set aside in the forest plan for wildlife and biodiversity preservation. Equestrian use was not compatible with the forest's planned use. Finally, the plan called for the removal of a road that led into the forest and was needed for fire-fighting equipment access; unfortunately, the Forest Service did not have a right-of-way to the road.

During a three-month period, numerous meetings were held between the Forest Service, the developer, and city planners. At those meetings, Earney made several suggestions for how to improve the development. He explained the problems with the proposed equestrian trails and the access road and suggested the developer hire a wildfire consultant who could make specific recommendations on how to fireproof the neighborhood. Earney promoted win-win solutions. He suggested alternate routes for the equestrian trails that would link them to a huge regional trail system instead of into the forest. He persuaded the developer to use the improvements to his advantage and sell his development as a "fireproof community" with the latest in technology and layout design to minimize the threat of fire damage.

From the Forest Service's perspective, the most obvious benefit of becoming involved in local planning is minimizing development impacts on national forest resources. The Hunter's Ridge development is now less of a fire hazard to the forest than it would have been. Earney reports: "In the spring of 1988 all environmental and design work was completed on the Hunter's Ridge project. That fall a major fire occurred that swept over that area, before construction began, repeating to the date, day of the week, time of day, and location the last major fire that burned that area exactly eighteen years previously (the Meyers Fire of 1970). The value of the negotiated fire mitigation measures was dramatically displayed for all."

Earney's local planning efforts are directed at land management activities beyond the national forest boundary. Furthermore, "the great majority of it," he comments, is done "after hours, on my own time." He emphasizes, however, that it is time well spent: "In many cases, agreements are made that actually improve the quality of natural resource management on the lands of all involved, make the on-the-ground jobs of our field personnel easier, and improve the quality of our forest visitors' experience." District Ranger Graham goes one step further when he concludes, "This is the most critical thing we can do to protect the forest."

Successful partnerships mobilize resources, access expertise and ideas outside their organizations, and build political support that enables them to proceed. Many have recognized the win-win potential of activities that assist others. They get help by giving it to others. All of these strategies are grounded in the relative richness and diversity of information and human resources in the United States. Collaborative groups recognize this abundance of talents and understand that they do not have to go it alone. Others are there to help. Indeed, in the process of helping, a broader set of individuals and groups develop an understanding of the objectives of the collaborative group and develop ownership in the effort. By working together, these groups and individuals build bridges that provide essential pathways to a sustainable future.

Part III

Getting Started

Chapter 12

A Primer for Agencies

Previous chapters have identified and discussed the many creative steps taken by participants in collaborative processes that enabled their efforts to succeed. But what enabled those individuals to take those steps? Individual initiative and perseverance are important, but a reliance on those factors will take an agency only so far. It is not sufficient for agencies to wait and hope that their employees will take the collaborative ball and run with it. Nor is it enough for agencies to say to their employees, "Read this book and do what it says."

Public agency leadership is essential to the success and spread of collaborative efforts. While state and federal agencies are the first to come under attack by a disgruntled public in conflict situations, they also are the first source looked to for leadership out of the impasse. Agencies are the only parties to a collaborative effort that have explicit authorities and responsibilities assigned to them under law, and they are often major landowners within the area of concern. They must recognize their unique and central role in guiding collaborative initiatives. What form should that leadership take?

This chapter is designed as a primer for agencies that want to encourage the development of collaborative initiatives that bridge boundaries. According to the dictionary, a primer is "a textbook that gives the first principles of any subject." We propose five simple principles for enhancing public agency leadership in promoting and supporting collaborative resource management processes:

1. Help your employees *imagine* the possibilities of collaboration in carrying out important work, building necessary relationships, and generating better decisions.

2. *Enable* your employees to develop and use collaborative arrangements by such means as enhancing employee capabilities and providing resources and flexibility to those who are already motivated to collaborate.

3. *Encourage* your employees to experiment with collaborative approaches to resource management by influencing the attitudes of staff and supervisors and providing incentives to employees and groups outside the agency to be involved in collaborative initiatives.

4. *Evaluate* the effectiveness of differing approaches to promoting and undertaking collaborative arrangements in the agency and how they might be modified.

5. *Be committed* to the process and follow through with your agency's agreements and responsibilities.

These five principles provide a basic conceptual framework to help agencies consider ways to begin reinventing their organizational procedures. This chapter illustrates many different ways that an agency can act on each of these principles.

Imagining Collaborative Possibilities

One way to expand the use of collaborative approaches is to increase people's awareness that such arrangements are possible, take various forms, and can yield numerous benefits. There is no one right way to build productive relationships and efforts to expand the development of collaborative approaches need to recognize that reality. The success stories documented in this book are very diverse in elements such as who initiated the collaborative processes, how they were structured, how long they lasted, whether agency funds were invested in them, and how staffing was arranged. Most facilitators of meetings and formal negotiations understand that while there are overall guidelines and frameworks that can be established to organize a process, there is never a single approach that works at all times.

Sparking the imagination of agency employees is not best achieved through new mandates or explicit procedures that frame and constrain employee actions to a narrow set of predetermined activities. Rather, helping people imagine the possibilities of collaborative processes and supporting their efforts can help promote their development in locally appropriate ways. As discussed in the preface, stories told in a variety of accessible and nonthreatening ways, by and to a number of different agency and nonagency audiences, are a particularly effective way to provide images of what has been done and to stimulate the imagination of others about what they might do.

Convey Images in Many Ways

Tap existing as well as new avenues for conveying images of success. Existing agency or professional society newsletters can be used to relate stories about effective linkages, including contact information for individuals participating in them. Similarly, guidebooks or manuals can be developed on the topic of collaboration or on a subset of topics, such as partnerships or dispute resolution. Such documents should include examples of ongoing relationships and a discussion of how individuals can deal with specific policy issues, such as federal contracting and advisory committee requirements. As illustrated by the diversity of cases presented in this book, there is no dearth of stories to be told that convey lessons from collaborative experiences in the public realm. The topics covered in this book should provide a good basis for constructing "how-to" manuals, and the cases presented here and elsewhere provide a rich set of ongoing examples.

Explore the full range of technology transfer mechanisms available to expose employees to examples of successful collaborative processes and key concepts of making linkages work. Such mechanisms might include videotaped examples of successful collaborative processes carried out in different geographic locations and that deal with various issues and organizations. Agency staff and nongovernmental participants could tell their own stories in videos, and agencies could easily facilitate exchange of those tapes within and beyond their organizations. For several of the success stories we documented, videotapes have already been developed by participants. Good examples are the videos developed by the Applegate Partnership, the Blackfoot Challenge, and the Cameron County Coexistence Committee, in which diverse participants reflect on what they have done and why it has worked. Agencies simply have to communicate the availability of this information and facilitate exchange between units.

Provide opportunities for interactive information exchange. For example, electronic computer files accessible via agency Web sites or intra-net systems can be created that would include examples of successful collaborative partnerships, indexed by such factors as location, activity, and issue type, so that individuals contemplating such arrangements could scan others' experience with them. If possible, those files could be updated interactively, so that employees who want to share their experiences could do so in a fairly painless way, and others could easily access their wisdom. These Web sites could be structured in numerous interactive formats, linking to other sites and cases as well as allowing individuals to ask questions, pose situation-specific dilemmas, make suggestions, and begin building relationships with others. The ongoing accumulation of stories and the comments of those who participated can help agency analysts and decision makers distill overall lessons about collaboration and accumulate a record for use with external audiences such as Congress.

Provide Opportunities for Participants to Tell Their Own Stories

Provide a means for engaging individuals who have successfully created collaborative initiatives to tell their own stories. These pioneers are conduits of good ideas and could travel for brief periods to other agency units to personally describe what they did and confer on the situations facing other units.

Create networks of individuals to facilitate the transfer of ideas and experiences about collaboration and provide direct support for those who seek to experiment with such arrangements. These networks could be created through a variety of means, including computer conferencing or simply distributing lists of contacts. The most effective exchange of ideas and advancement of understanding and confidence come from people talking and working together face to face, not simply reading about or observing others from a distance. Networks can facilitate cross-agency exchange of ideas and problems and can diffuse innovation across the vast geographic spaces typically involved in environmental and natural resource management.

Shine "spotlights" on individuals, units, or projects that have been involved in innovative collaborative efforts. Spotlighted activities and individuals will get the attention of employees at the same time that they provide recognition to those who were involved. The specific topic of rewarding performance will be discussed below, but one of the first steps in promoting the use of imagery and getting people to imagine the possibilities inherent in collaboration is to get their attention. By recognizing and rewarding innovative collaborative relationships, agency leaders have the potential to highlight collaboration as an important and sanctioned activity. Creating "heros"—individuals who model effective and appropriate behavior in a way that others want to emulate—is one mechanism for capturing the attention of employees and sanctioning changes in their behavior.

Capitalize on Existing Meeting and Conference Opportunities

Include collaboration as a topic in meetings or conferences about other resource management issues. Numerous venues already exist in which the topic of collaboration can be discussed. Hence, collaboration should not be partitioned into something that is done by one individual or one group; rather, it is a tool that should be employed by many types of agency employees. Viewing collaboration as a tool of relevance to wildlife biologists, timber sale planners, land management planners, recreation managers, and range staff, among others, means that the topic of building collaborative relationships should be explored at meetings and workshops on those specific resource-related topics. Perhaps the best way to promote the creation of collaborative partnerships is to place them within the context of more traditional work activities.

Spark the Attention and Ideas of Those Beyond Agency Walls

Communicate the possibilities inherent in enhanced collaboration to non-agency individuals and groups, including community groups, local and state governments, and other federal agencies. It is just as important to attract the attention and stimulate the imagination of individuals and organizations beyond the agency's boundaries. Many of the successes mentioned in this book arose out of the initiative of people who simply cared about the issues or resources managed by a public agency and were willing to do something to help address them. Bridges link agencies with individuals in the external world, and hence the ideas underlying relationships often can and should come from outside the agencies.

Tie into existing community-based opportunities by having agency staff go to town meetings and meetings of organized groups to describe ongoing issues, management priorities, and new initiatives of the agency. Staff members can highlight the potential for forming a variety of linkages and provide illustrations of how others have built effective relationships in similar contexts. Agency officials should understand and use existing social networks (including church and social service groups, environmental and user groups, and chambers of commerce) as a point of entry into adjacent communities. Asking for assistance and ideas is neither a sign of weakness or dereliction of duty, nor a panacea. But in many places it may open the possibility of new working relationships between agencies and neighbors.

Develop materials for local and regional media describing ongoing issues and the potential for joining forces to work on common problems. For example, the highly effective media campaign aimed at forest fire prevention could be supplemented by public service spots describing the management of common property resources like national forest or wildlife refuge resources. Such spots could be constructed in collaboration with existing partners and highlight ongoing successes. They would provide both a sense of recognition for existing bridges and imagery about what could be done for those who might get involved in a comparable arrangement.

Prepare and distribute a "wish list" through media outlets and other channels that describes several high-priority areas for collaborative initiatives. Such a list would represent the agency's interests and not necessarily those of others in the community, but by flagging critical needs from the agency's perspective, potential collaborators might be found. Alternatively, the agency's ideas might serve as the starting point for a discussion about other common problems or areas for collaboration.

Enabling Employees to Be Effective at Collaboration

While images of effective collaboration can help employees understand how they can use such bridges in public resource management, agencies can carry out a number of specific actions that will enable motivated staff members to more effectively build relationships with the outside world. Ask whether your employees have the human power, skills, and resources needed to build bridges and the administrative and procedural flexibility to use them. Develop staff capabilities through training and hiring and by instituting personnel policies that reinforce external relationships.

Train Individuals and Teams

Enhance the skills and abilities of employees through grounded training of individuals and teams. At a minimum, a training program would include a several-day short course, a videotaped skill-oriented presentation, a set of self-paced guidebooks, and tutoring by individuals skilled in collaborative processes. Topics might include communications, interpersonal dynamics, meeting facilitation, administrative and policy guidelines for partnerships, negotiation, conflict management, team building, and group problem solving. Training should focus on "people" skills, such as how to interact with different individuals or groups in various situations, and "process" skills, such as how to structure and facilitate collaborative problem-solving processes. Topics such as effective facilitation might require more lengthy training and be targeted at a smaller set of individuals, while topics such as a basic overview of different collaborative processes might be conveyed in a half-day, on-site presentation and discussion.

Most topics are best covered through multiple exposures that allow individuals to incorporate lessons into their day-to-day job experiences. An analysis of Forest Service training programs in conflict management in the early 1980s suggests that while a four-day short course was very helpful to participants, additional opportunities for training were needed and desired.[1] Single, short exposures to new material allow individuals to gain an appreciation for the topic but are ineffective at building skills.

Focus training both on skill development and on understanding how to transfer the skills to "real world" situations. One of the concerns raised in our survey of participants in the Forest Service conflict management training program was that participants had more difficulty in applying the skills from the program on the job than understanding the nature or importance of the skills themselves. Problems became evident as theory was converted to practice and as staff members who had received the training ran into ambivalent or resistant coworkers or superiors. Training materials on collaboration and related skills should address these implementation topics explicitly, including how to obtain the support of individuals who are skeptical about collaborative relationships.

Train whole management teams simultaneously. Since some of the problems in implementing collaborative skills and understanding lie in a lack of support from coworkers, implementing a training program that involves multiple members of a single unit can mitigate resistance and promote discussion about opportunities for collaboration on the unit. It provides a rich opportunity to develop teams that better understand how to work together and work with others beyond the agency's boundary. A traveling training program that would move from unit to unit could minimize the travel costs of participants and place the ideas and skills involved firmly within the local context. Indeed, on some topics, such as conflict management, involving nonagency individuals in training may be productive and provide a good foundation for additional agency-nonagency relationships.

Use stories of experiences within your own agency as examples in the training materials to keep the training as grounded as possible. Sometimes training programs do not succeed because the content is abstract for participants, or the anecdotes used by trainers are too far removed from the participants' experiences. If the content is not integrated into the cognitive structures that employees use to carry out everyday work, they can conclude, "That approach worked there, but it could never work here." Drawing examples from relevant activity areas that are subject to the same kinds of administrative constraints and guidelines can help overcome the "not here" phenomenon.

Have coaches or mentors available within the agency to assist those who have participated in training programs and are now trying to apply what they have learned to real situations. The first and major hurdle to capitalizing on the potential benefits of training is taking that first step once back in the field. Having someone readily available to discuss issues can encourage action or simply provide a shoulder to lean on and increase the value of the training investment to the agency.

Enhance Workforce Composition

Seek "people" and "process" skills across the agency's workforce. Collaboration is a critical part of many agency professionals' jobs. It is not an activity limited to public affairs officers, volunteer coordinators, or rural development specialists, nor should it be seen as such. Indeed, only a handful of public affairs officers were involved in the cases documented in this book. Most of these cases were carried out by a wide array of staff members and line officers. Consequently, collaborative capacity can be enhanced by promoting staff members with people and process skills and by hiring new staff members.

To obtain the skills that are needed, it might be appropriate for agencies to influence the training of relevant professionals, so that new hires come versed in communication, problem-solving, and negotiation skills. These are not traditional skills for resource and environmental professionals and may conflict with the motives of many who seek such careers. To the extent that agencies can send clear signals to educational institutions and potential employees about the skills they seek, individuals will be better prepared to make a positive contribution in the future.

Hire designated "linkers," including facilitators and mediators, partnership coordinators, and rural development specialists. While collaboration is a part of many staff members' jobs, individuals with high levels of knowledge and specific skills are needed to foster a rich array of agency-nonagency relationships. Creating such positions also will send a message about the importance of these kinds of roles within the agency, particularly if it is done in a way that does not imply that the positions will "take care of" partnerships on their own. Individuals with skills such as mediation can be used as circuit riders who travel within a region and apply their skills where most needed. They can also serve as tutors and advisors to others in the agency. Other positions, such as partnership coordinators and rural development specialists, function most effectively by developing relationships with outside groups over the long term. These individuals need to stay in place.

Provide Resources

Provide flexibility that facilitates cross-unit, interagency, and multiyear budgeting. One commonly cited barrier to cross-boundary collaboration is a budgeting system that emphasizes activities that are predictable, measurable, and organized by narrow line items. Yet collaboration often takes time, requires the help and assistance of others, and involves expenses that are not always foreseen and do not fit into narrow line items. Budget categories that focus on broader ecosystem-level outcomes might facilitate efforts that require cross-boundary activities. Another problem in funding partnerships and other collaborative arrangements lies in the inability to forecast appropriate levels of activity for more than one year. Many people involved in ongoing collaborative processes complain about delays in securing funding as units waited for the year's budget to be established. While budget procedures may not be under agency control, perhaps portions of the budget could be assumed as fixed commitments on a two-year basis, with other activities at greater risk of cuts, depending on the final size of the budget.

Provide a start-up fund for collaborative activities. A number of agency staff members involved in the cases in this book complained about the "hurry up, wait, and hurry up" phenomenon involved in initiating new activities. That is, they are pressured to get an activity going, then have to wait a long time for approvals and funding, then have little time left to actually carry out the work. For groups outside the agencies, delays in receiving funding can be particularly damaging since they often have low levels of other operating funds to pay expenses. As a result, many potential partners are reluctant to get involved. Creating a start-up fund that would allow small-scale partnerships and other linkages to get going would help offset some of the problems and overcome some of the hesitancy of potential partners. There may be a low-level risk involved in creating such a fund, in that some of the activities or expenditures may ultimately not be approved. But rarely are the delays due to uncertain approval; rather, people are waiting because of lengthy bureaucratic procedures.

Create a discretionary fund in appropriate agency offices for small expenses connected with collaborative initiatives, such as coffee at meetings. Many bridge-building entrepreneurs in public agencies complain about having to cover the costs of simple "hosting" expenses such as coffee and donuts out of their own pockets, because agency funds are not available or not worth the paperwork involved in securing them.

Increase Flexibility

Cut the red tape that constrains collaboration. Both agency and nonagency partners involved in collaborative arrangements complain of too much paperwork involved in small-scale tasks. Because collaborative processes work best when tailored to the people, contexts, and issues at hand, it is not surprising that flexibility is needed in order to enable employees to build productive bridges. Provide more discretion at the local level to run with ideas. Many agency participants, particularly at the local district level, complain of being micro-managed, most often on activities seen as innovative. Make it clear where flexibility lies for staff and line officers to pursue a collaborative initiative at the local level, and let them exercise judgment accordingly. Of course, flexibility needs to be balanced by measures ensuring accountability, and those are discussed in chapter 13.

Develop the use of flex time for employees, so that they can participate in collaborative processes that often are conducted in the evenings or on weekends. Many members of the public who would be interested in interacting with the agency cannot do so during normal working hours, consequently agency staff have to go to town meetings or set up weekend information tables in supermarkets on their own time. Simple changes in standard operating procedures that would allow more flexibility in scheduling work time would facilitate the development of relationships with nonagency groups.

Temper the conservatism of financial and legal officers. Collaborative processes are by definition innovative and experimental. Since such efforts can take a multitude of forms and potential collaborators and partners are highly diverse, they often are viewed as "problems" by financial and legal officers in public agencies. That is, they do not fit exactly into prescribed operating procedures. The response has been delayed approvals or a lot of burdensome constraints. Agency leaders should work to clarify appropriate collaborative activities in a way that is flexible and relies on local discretion. Building standard operating procedures that take these factors into account may help offset the fears of middle managers as they face proposals for new collaborative initiatives. Doing so may also cut down delays in getting approvals.

Create Formal Links with Other Agencies

Public environmental and natural resource agencies have many activities and requirements in common. One relatively straightforward way to build relationships that enhance coordination across a spectrum of issues is simply to begin working together on shared tasks. Look at what you do and have in common with others and connect those things in a symbiotic fashion that makes the whole greater than the individual parts.

Explore the possibility of shared computer networks that would establish links between agencies and groups. At a minimum, incompatibilities between data systems in federal agencies should be resolved so that multi-agency monitoring and research can be carried out. Computer-based communications links can also facilitate interaction between individuals located across the considerable distances inherent in resource management. For example, electronic conferences about plans and issues on a forest unit could provide an additional mode of interaction between agencies and interest groups. Shared use of a geographic information system could also allow interested individuals to formulate common images and try out alternative scenarios.

Institute multi-agency shared visioning and/or planning processes that capture a physical (or even "issue") landscape in common terms and goals. For example, the National Environmental Policy Act's requirements for assessments and environmental impact statements could be a shared task, improving the quality, focus, and scope of the environmental analysis at the same time that it links the agencies involved.[2] Many agencies require unit-level planning. Conducting planning through a multi-agency team could offset some of the fragmentation seen in traditional agency-by-agency planning.

Encouraging the Development of Collaborative Relationships

Agencies should actively encourage employees and nonagency groups to begin collaborating when problem solving would be improved by interaction. While providing imagery, resources, and flexibility can enable individuals to

take action, influencing their attitudes and rewarding their efforts can motivate them to move forward. Current attitudes about collaboration range from
enthusiasm and mild support to skepticism and outright hostility. If the connection of collaborative processes to agency mission and objectives is made
clear, perceptions and attitudes about the appropriate role of collaboration in
resource management will be enhanced. If people feel their efforts are supported and believe that agency leaders are behind them, they will be much
more willing to pursue new initiatives.

Influence Perceptions and Attitudes

For many individuals motivated to build cross-boundary relationships, the current level of uncertainty about objectives and methods in public environmental
and resource management is confusing and defeating. An era of confusion and
uncertainty along with fear of personnel reductions has tended to make people
retrench into what they know best. To the extent that agency leadership can
build a stronger and clearer statement of current direction and back it up, some
individuals will be more likely to try out innovative activities. If people remain
confused about appropriate direction, they will be unsure about steps they
should be taking to get to this uncertain end. If their organizational compass
has two or more points, they will not know which way to proceed.

Incorporate a clearer understanding of how collaborative processes fit into
updated notions of resource management. As agencies pursue initiatives such
as ecosystem management that require improved coordination and collaboration, it is vitally important that a more robust model of environmental and
natural resource management legitimize collaborative approaches. Such an
updated vision of management also would place agencies in a more proactive
mode, so that employees who are now feeling attacked from all sides and
alienated from both the public and agency leaders would feel better about
their role.

Provide Incentives

While implementing these recommendations will remove some of the disin-
centives that currently exist for individuals and groups to be involved in collaborative processes, it is also important to focus on creating positive
incentives for collaborative initiatives. The types of incentives that are effective
vary. For some employees, commendations and recognition may be important. For others, bonuses and an influence on promotion may be needed. For
groups outside the agency, having the agency make a conscious effort to build
a relationship with them might be enough incentive, while others would
respond to small grant funds and publicity for their groups. At times, simple
low-cost actions that recognize the contributions of nongovernmental participants through letters, notices to local newspapers, patches on caps, and the

like go a long way to making people feel valued and their efforts worthwhile. Annual awards and commendations for innovative and/or notable collaborative initiatives can help provide a positive incentive. Such recognition should be made of both agency and nonagency groups.

Maintain government-administered incentive programs. It is important to maintain and expand inducements for potential partners in cooperative endeavors. As noted in earlier chapters, federal programs that support collaboration (such as the Forest Service cost-share matching funds program) are important catalysts for action. Agency programs that provide start-up funds for collaborative efforts, reimburse some of the costs for nonagency participants, and cover the costs of facilitation and initial meetings are needed. Gearing incentive programs to activities that achieve ecosystem objectives, rather than administrative ones, may be appropriate. Hence, designating a fund for planning or management action within the Elkhorn Mountains or the San Pedro River ecosystem, for example, and opening it to competitive proposals from a variety of parties might result in multiparty activity at the right geographic scale.

Make collaboration a part of many employees' jobs and recognize the time involved in dealing effectively with nonagency partners. A move "back to basics" should not oversimplify the task of effective resource management. Building cooperative arrangements should be viewed as a task equal to prepping a timber sale or building a diverse workforce. If collaboration is valued by agency leaders, such value must be reflected in job descriptions and expectations. If it remains something that is done out of the goodness of the individual employee's heart, then the opportunities inherent in such arrangements will not be achieved.

Broaden personnel performance criteria to include collaborative activities. Performance evaluation sends very clear signals to employees as to what is important to the agency's leaders. Employees should be evaluated both on the efforts they put into agency-nonagency collaboration and on how successful those efforts become. Well-intended and thoughtfully designed efforts to build bridges that did not work out should not be penalized but rather evaluated and learned from. Similarly, to help ensure broader agency commitment it is important to extend this element of personal evaluations up the line. Supervisors need to support the concept of collaboration and encourage their employees. Having agency leaders communicate the importance of collaboration and including collaboration in personnel evaluations of managers are strategies to make this happen.

Evaluating the Experience with Collaboration

An agency's long-term capacity for collaboration requires ongoing experimentation and an explicit process of learning from the experiments. This book is an attempt to examine successful collaborative processes and draw lessons from collaboration pioneers. Agencies need to carry on this work by evaluating the effectiveness of collaborative approaches in pursuing their missions. What worked, what did not work, and why? What has been accomplished? This kind of evaluation can be included in unit-level planning and evaluations. Outcome measures can be constructed to assess the accomplishments and value of different collaborative initiatives. Units can construct short sets of collaboration objectives annually and evaluate progress made. Feedback from nonagency partners and collaborators should be incorporated, so that a broader set of information about unit performance is received than just complaints and appeals of decisions.

Learn from failures, not just successes. Recognize that collaboration is not always going to work, and do not take it personally or penalize those who tried when it doesn't. Expect that even the most thoughtfully designed attempts to build bridges may fail. For example, sometimes groups in a negotiation determine that they can more effectively accomplish their objectives outside the process. Groups involved in a management partnership may find that their objectives for a project are inconsistent. Or the personalities in organizations may simply be too difficult. Many of these kinds of variables are not under the control of agency staff, and they can doom even the best-intentioned effort to build a bridge. Regardless, it is important to try to learn why a specific situation failed and move on without abandoning the attempt to bridge the agency's boundary. It is also important to recognize benefits that accrue to the well-intentioned failures. Even in situations that break down, benefits often result from the attempt: heightened understanding of the parties' concerns, contacts and relationships between groups, and recognition of the value of having tried to work together, for example.

Evaluate the effectiveness of training, incentives, and other approaches for enabling and encouraging employees. Evaluations of training programs should assess what helped, what did not, and what else participants feel they need. Surveys of participants in collaborative arrangements should be conducted periodically to determine their motivations and needs. It also is important to analyze situations where collaborative approaches never arose or failed. Assess what other factors seem to constrain or promote collaboration in the agency and modify strategies for encouraging collaboration accordingly.

Committing to the Process and Products of Collaboration

While agencies can do many things to help employees develop cross-boundary bridges, few of those measures will succeed if they do not have a foundation of agency commitment to the collaborative approach. Many cases highlighted in this book were examined over time. In some, productive working relationships were maintained and extended to other problems and issues. Others withered and died, and still others left a legacy of distrust, anger, and betrayal among participants. One key factor distinguished the collaborative processes that led to these different outcomes: agency commitment. When agency leaders understood and supported the collaborative effort and upheld the agency's agreements, relationships were strong and remained intact. When agency leaders were not committed in that way, the bridges between the agency and nonagency world crumbled and often made a bad situation worse.[3]

One of the most straightforward measures of organizational commitment comes from the responsiveness of agency higher-ups: having the "boss" support the efforts of bridge-building pioneers and do what he or she can to help make the collaboration work. We have discussed the barriers to collaboration imposed by a lack of agency commitment in chapter 3 and how some agencies effectively ensure and demonstrate commitment in chapter 8. We once again highlight the importance of agency commitment to the promise of collaborative resource management. Without it, collaboration is a risky venture and will be resisted.

Use Consistent Measures in Employee Performance Evaluations

Evaluate the success and effectiveness of collaborative processes using measures developed specifically for that purpose. In those situations where agency officials have recognized the need to employ new standards for guiding and judging the collaborative approach, bridges are strong and thriving. In situations where old standards for review and evaluation were applied to the new endeavors, the collaborative initiatives were undercut. Providing clear direction to employees about the objectives for a collaborative process and how progress toward achieving those objectives will be measured is the first step in establishing and demonstrating commitment. It is important to make those agency expectations explicit and known to all participants at the outset of a collaborative process.

Maintain Continuity within Agency Collaborative Relationships

Effective collaboration occurs within a context of relationships, and transferring staff members often breaks up those relationships. Commitment is demonstrated by maintaining continuity, and personnel transfers damage continuity unless they are managed carefully. While transfers are often initiated for good organizational reasons, they can be a barrier to the development and maintenance of productive relationships with individuals and groups outside the agency. From the standpoint of outside groups, transfers diminish institutional memory, and relationships and contacts become uncertain. It is disheartening for an outside group to work to get to know a district ranger, establish a working relationship with him or her and develop a shared understanding of priorities and objectives, and then have that individual transferred five states away. There are ways to achieve the benefits of transferring personnel without moving people so much.

The ideal prescription for maintaining continuity is to keep the same key individuals in place. However, the reality is that keeping people in place is not always preferable or possible from an individual or an organizational perspective. In the normal course of an organization's life, individuals retire, move to new jobs, and are transferred within the agency or organization. There are ways to mitigate the effects of such changes on a collaborative initiative, however.

Many situations are sustained when the individuals who retired, left, or were transferred are replaced by like-minded individuals who see value in the collaborative activities and choose to continue in a similar mode. Key individuals must be replaced quickly before relationships begin to fade and in a manner that promotes continuity. Often there is overlap in the staff member's time on the job, or a team exists into which the replacement can step and be more easily acclimated to the situation. Some people make a point to keep clear files, brief their replacements, and introduce them to key individuals in the community.

In contrast, in the situations where bridges are not sustained, key individuals are often simply not replaced, a consequence of downsizing in an agency. Even when key staff members are replaced, it is often after a significant lag time, in a less than permanent manner, or with a different set of priorities and direction from above.

Follow Through with Your Commitments

Respect and support the decisions of collaborative groups involving your agency. Commitment includes not just initiating collaborative processes, but also supporting actions that result from them. Agency leaders must be committed to following through on agreements reached or make an honest effort to explain why an agreement has become problematic and must be revisited. While the agency will always possess the statutory responsibility to make final decisions and agency officials need to follow administrative procedures, by participating as a full partner in these processes, agencies can ensure that group decisions are technically and legally valid and thereby supportable by the agency. One of the worst outcomes is for an agency that initiated a collaborative arrangement to fail to implement the resulting agreements.

Believe in the Potential of Collaboration

Collaborate for the right reasons. While a collaborative approach does not fit all situations, being clear on agency needs and objectives will help leaders and staff recognize when collaboration may be promising and ensure commitment to the process. Agency participation must be sincere from start to finish, and that sincerity can be rooted only in a firm belief that collaboration is an appropriate way to proceed in a given situation. If collaboration is viewed as a public relations activity, an effort to placate an angry constituency, or a task to fulfill procedural mandates, the results may be more damaging than doing nothing at all.

By imagining collaborative possibilities, enabling and encouraging employees, evaluating efforts at building bridges, and being committed, agency leaders can provide a foundation for more effective relationships with the world around them. Each of these elements needs to be adapted to an agency's specific management situation. Implementation strategies may well vary from our examples, and efforts to promote collaboration should take place as integral components of other strategies to update and reinvent agency management. While the full range of suggested activities may seem daunting, changing even some small items can help. By all accounts, those agencies that have tried to foster greater levels of cross-boundary interaction have been rewarded by their efforts.

Chapter 13

Ensuring Accountability

Collaborative resource management is not without its critics. Legitimate concerns have been raised that highlight the underlying issue of accountability. Many of these concerns have been heightened by events involving the Quincy Library Group.[1] The debate has become quite emotional and polarized. Some argue the virtues of civic discourse, community building, and locally based solutions. Others argue that national interests must be protected, environmental concerns should not be overshadowed by local economic concerns, and decisions reached through collaborative processes must be scientifically defensible. Both sides of this debate are correct. Collaboration holds great promise but must be bounded by mechanisms to ensure accountability of the process and those involved in it to existing laws and the rights of others not sitting at the table.

What ensures that public choices are not "captured" by private interests? What ensures that local interests do not subsume national interests? Are collaborative partnerships simply a Y2K version of the Y1.9K problem of private interests appropriating natural resources for their own good? Proponents of collaboration must address these questions at a policy level, and each collaborative effort must develop answers that are effective in their particular context.

At the same time, it is important to recognize that collaborative initiatives that affect public resources exist within an institutional structure that creates incentives and provides at least some level of accountability. It is wrong to assume that these efforts are unbounded free-for-alls in which participants establish direction in an unconstrained way. It is also wrong to structure them in an unbounded way, ignoring relevant laws and procedures. Ultimately, each participant is influenced by a set of incentives established by law, policies, politics, and institutional norms. Those incentive structures must be designed to simultaneously promote good-faith collaboration and adherence to broader public policy objectives. It is a balancing act that is challenging yet essential to secure the benefits of collaboration while ensuring accountability.

The Critics' Concerns

Critics have raised three primary and fundamental concerns about collaborative groups. First, they argue that the authority invested by Congress in federal agencies to implement laws and regulation should not devolve to a collaborative group. They emphasize that agencies cannot abdicate their legal responsibilities and authorities and bestow them on an unelected, unrepresentative group. Second, they insist that groups who have not participated in a collaborative process should not be completely shut out of a decision-making process when public resources are at stake. Such groups should have an opportunity to air their concerns and be assured that they will be considered in agency decision making. Third, critics fear that collaborative groups lack the scientific and technical expertise possessed by government agencies and that the agreements they produce will not be scientifically sound.

Sierra Club chairman Michael McCloskey is the most often cited critic in this debate. He has referred to collaboration as a "new dogma" that proposes that cooperation among stakeholders is preferred to "normal governmental processes." He asks "whether these collaborators are acting in an advisory role with respect to public resources or whether they are being given power." He argues: "Instead of hammering out national rules to reflect majority rule in the nation, transferring power to a local venue implies decision-making by a very different majority—in a much smaller population. But it gets worse. By then adopting a consensus rule for that decision-making, small local minorities are given an effective veto over positive action. Thus, the process has the effect of disempowering both national as well as local majorities. Those not represented by any organized interest in a community may be totally disempowered, and if the status quo is environmentally unacceptable, this process gives small minorities a death grip over reform. Any recalcitrant stakeholder can paralyze the process and defy the popular will. Only lowest common denominator ideas survive the process."[2]

Legal scholar George Cameron Coggins has similarly written that collaborative groups transfer "authority to make public resource decisions from the federal land management agencies to local citizens. Power, thus, is 'devolved' upon localities." To Coggins, the question is whether land management agencies should be allowed to delegate their authority to a collaborative group. He concludes, "Blind belief in·discussion and consensus is just a phoney substitute for a real system of decision-making."[3]

While our experience examining close to two hundred collaborative processes over the past decade suggests that these fears have been realized on only a handful of occasions, we nonetheless fully agree with the cautions raised by McCloskey, Coggins, and others. Blind endorsement of a collaborative process is foolhardy, as is blind criticism. Defiance of Coggins's "real system of decision making" or McCloskey's "normal governmental processes" is also foolhardy and will lead to the certain demise of a collaborative venture because it will lack the legitimacy and credibility necessary for success.

We share the view of other scholars who argue that collaborative processes should be held to the same standards of judgment applicable to any public decision-making process, including traditional administrative, judicial, and legislative processes.[4] Any public decision-making process must be able to demonstrate that it is legitimate, fair, and wise. By doing so, it becomes credible and accountable to the broader public interest. To be more specific, any process should be able to meet the following tests:

- *Is it legitimate?* Is it tied to existing law and regulation through the direct involvement of responsible officials? Does it provide for normal public review and comment opportunities for those who care about the issues but are either unable or uninterested in participating directly?

- *Is it fair?* Does it involve credible representatives of those who will be affected by its decisions and recommendations? Is it open, accessible, and transparent so that no individual is excluded except by his or her own choice, and no decision is imposed without agreement? Are decisions made in a manner that encourages consensus not capitulation?

- *Is it wise?* Does the process encourage participants to focus on the problems needing to be solved? Does it promote creativity and flexibility to allow effective management direction to be framed? Are decisions well rooted in current scientific understanding? Are there direct links between participants in the process and the appropriate sources of knowledge, expertise, and information that will enable those at the table to understand and act consistent with this current understanding? Moreover, does the process ensure that decision making is consistent with scientific knowledge or highlight where it is not? Does it recognize areas of uncertainty and provide credible opportunities for learning and adaptation?

All three criteria go beyond the issues that critics of collaboration have raised. Legitimacy includes the critics' concerns about the devolution of agency power. Fairness ensures that all parties have a chance to have their concerns heard by decision makers. Wisdom includes scientific grounding as well as a focus on the effectiveness of agreements. Indeed, one of the major problems associated with mechanisms that have been used to ensure accountability in the past is that they produced inflexible, formulaic procedures that constrain creative solutions. (The next section of this chapter describes the traditional solutions to the problem of accountability and the problems that they in turn have produced.) All of these issues need to be addressed when framing a collaborative approach.

The balance of this chapter describes how this can be done and the role of participants and policy makers in ensuring that it is done. As was true in most of the cases highlighted in this book, collaborative processes should be developed as adjuncts to normal administrative processes. Government agencies cannot and should not devolve their decision-making authority to collaborative groups. Norms of good process design should be followed, and procedures for appeal and review should be maintained to allow any group— in or out of the process—to raise concerns. Opportunities for independent scientific review should be expanded, and scientifically based performance standards should be adopted where they are appropriate. Monitoring and post-decision evaluation should be used as an extension of collaborative processes to test the scientific viability of adopted strategies and suggest necessary changes.

At the same time, policy makers must recognize that traditional mechanisms for ensuring accountability that constrain flexibility and creativity need to be changed. Provisions in the Federal Advisory Committee Act (FACA) need to change, and agency implementation of administrative procedures under NEPA needs to be less formulaic. The goal of these reforms is to promote better on-the-ground resource management through decision making that is scientifically sound, is in accordance with statutory goals, and deals with the concerns of affected parties. Ways must be found to simultaneously promote effective collaboration while ensuring the accountability of collaborative processes. We believe this can be done.

The Issue of Accountability

The problem of ensuring that public decisions are accountable to societal standards has been with us for as long as there has been civil society, and various solutions have been devised. Accountability is a particular issue in natural resource management because managing natural resources and environmental quality involves a public trust: That is, private actions and those of public-sector guardians involve obligations to the broader public interest. Those obligations are defined by laws such as the Endangered Species Act and the Clean Water Act and norms such as those implied by being a neighbor and part of a community.

The traditional concern in resource management was that individuals or corporations would violate the public trust either by securing a larger than equitable share of the benefits of the resources or by leaving others with significant uncompensated external costs. Indeed, the Progressive Conservation movement of the early 1900s responded to massive exploitation of public lands by developers and speculators.[5] Fraud, collusion between government agents and speculators, and a basic lack of control accompanied the transfer of public resources into private hands at a mind-boggling rate and led to ecological damage. Those events led to the establishment of many of the precursors of today's natural resource agencies. The larger public good would be protected, it was thought, because someone would be "minding the store." Individuals in those agencies would be held accountable to the public interest through constraints imposed by new laws and policies.

This movement was an outgrowth of the broader turn-of-the-century Progressive movement, which fought the concentrated power of the big business trusts. The trusts or combines controlled prices, regulated supply, and suppressed competition. While they created wealth for numerous Carnegies and the like, other interests were suppressed. Those other interests had no ability to influence decision making because they lacked political power or economic might. The Progressives' critique was that corporations were too close to each other, and big business was too close to government. Their solution was to fragment power by breaking up the trusts and regulating the relationship between businesses and government. As described in chapter 1, government agencies were to make resource management decisions on technical grounds divorced from the corrupting influence of politics.

Agencies established in that period were concerned by the potential for their employees to become too close to their constituents. That concern was particularly significant in the case of an agency like the Forest Service, where dispersed employees lived in local communities that were dependent on adjacent national forest resources. Their kids went to school with the children of loggers; their neighbors worked for contractors who depended on national forest timber. Over time, it became difficult for agency employees to balance the competing interests of their neighbors and their employers. Close ties undercut the ability of agency leaders to control personnel and keep them accountable to the larger public interest as defined by law, agency procedures, and the interests of leaders. Indeed, the worst fear of the Progressive Conservationists and agency leaders was that agency employees would become "captured" by regulated parties.

By all accounts, the critique was accurate at the beginning and throughout the first two-thirds of the twentieth century. Examples from many areas of government regulation, like oversight of the trucking industry by the Interstate Commerce Commission, demonstrated collusion between regulated party and regulator.[6] Narrow interests often dominated cooperative management institutions and advisory boards such as grazing boards and fisheries councils.[7]

The Traditional Response

The standard response to the problem of unaccountable agencies and corporations was to develop laws, agency rules, norms, and procedures that emphasized control. The idea was that if we cannot trust people to act in the right way, we must prescribe and enforce appropriate behavior. For example, annual timber sale quotas were identified for each national forest unit and became targets enforced through personnel and unit evaluation. The means of achieving ends—such as the size of clearcuts or the type of safety equipment to wear when building a trail—were similarly dictated.

Processes of interacting with the public were decreed through laws such as the Federal Advisory Committee Act[8] and the National Environmental Policy Act. FACA was born out of a concern that the federal advisory committees of the 1940s and 1950s were captured by narrow, private interests who had undue influence on federal agency decision making, and were expensive and wasteful as well. Some of those concerns related to antitrust problems inherent in the close collaboration of industry groups and regulatory agencies. According to legal analyst Michelle Nuszkiewicz, "FACA was a legislative effort to cure specific ills, above all the wasteful expenditure of public funds for worthless committee meetings and biased proposals. . . . In addition to monitoring the number and cost of advisory committees, FACA was designed to ensure public access to and notice of advisory committee meetings. Some in Congress found it ironic that prior to FACA's enactment the interested public often couldn't even find out about the activities of a committee supposedly representing their views to the federal government."[9]

To carry out those objectives, FACA established a series of administrative procedures. Advisory boards have to include a full balanced set of stakeholders, have a clearly defined purpose, and be deemed official by an elaborate chartering process. To apply for a charter, an agency must (among other duties) list all members of the committee, describe the committee's duties and the length of time it will function, and estimate the number and frequency of meetings and annual operating costs. Since only individuals listed in the application can formally participate in meetings, in practical terms, that requirement means that applicants are forced to list anyone who might possibly be involved over the life of the group. Notice of the establishment of a new group must be published in the *Federal Register,* and the committee cannot meet or take action until a charter is issued.

Meetings of advisory committees are regulated. Each meeting must be open to the public, and detailed minutes must be kept. The records, minutes, drafts, and other documents used by a committee have to be available for public inspection and copying. Timely notice has to be provided of each meeting through publication in the *Federal Register* and other means. Compensation for committee members and other expenses of the committees are guided by government-set controls. Each advisory group terminates within two years after a charter is filed, unless action is taken to renew the group, which includes filing a new charter.

Besides legal instruments such as FACA, a broad set of organizational procedures also was instituted to control behavior. For example, the policy of frequently transferring staff members helped ensure the allegiance of the workforce to the agency by making the agency the primary source of identity for its employees. According to Herbert Kaufman, writing in his classic 1960 work, *The Forest Ranger*, "The impact of rapid transfer is more profound than training alone; it also builds identification with the Forest Service as a whole. For during each man's early years, he never has time to sink roots in the communities in which he sojourns so briefly. He gets to know the local people who do the manual work in the woods, but not very well in the short time he spends with them. He barely becomes familiar with an area before he is moved again. Only one thing gives any continuity, any structure, to his otherwise fluid world: the Service."[10] Writing more than twenty years later, Michael Frome noted the same dynamic: "Transfers, particularly in early career years, tend to give the forester one primary reference group, his own organization; unless he strives hard to prevent it, the individual, despite involvement in local communities and far-flung assignments, becomes internalized."[11] By encouraging employees to identify primarily with the agency, the likelihood of agency officials becoming "captured" by local interests was reduced.

The clear message of these and other mechanisms aimed at controlling the interaction of agency employees with the public was that such interaction was suspect and potentially corrupting. It called to mind the definition of collaboration listed second in dictionaries: a collaborator was someone who helped the enemy.

The Balance between Control and Flexibility

Many of these policies were well intended and important changes in their day, and elements of them remain relevant to current resource management. But their emphasis on control is problematic. The policies are inherently inflexible, prescribing some behaviors and constraining others. Flexibility is not necessary when on-the-ground conditions do not vary from those conceived in the policy, full information is available to frame the prescription, innovation or cost-cutting is undesirable, and the objectives of the policy are unlikely to evolve. But those conditions do not describe the state of natural resource and environmental management today.

FACA provides a good example. The burdensome procedures contained in

FACA might be effective in some regulatory settings but are unduly binding to the kind of ad hoc, informal work groups desirable in resource management. Formal charters bind the group to a set of specific tasks and members at the start but collaborative groups often evolve as interests and issues become clear and individuals seek to join or drop out. FACA's chartering process makes that sort of evolution difficult. FACA constrains agencies from listening to just one interest but makes it difficult to work with many. Also, natural resource and environmental problems are ongoing and evolving in nature, not conforming to FACA's image of issues that can be identified, analyzed, and resolved in two years or less.

In a number of national forest advisory groups, FACA's lack of flexibility and red tape have limited creativity and frustrated group members. Since many of those individuals are contributing their time and energy out of a desire to help agencies achieve better management, having to deal with nonproductive red tape is tremendously discouraging and leads some individuals to opt out. The result has been less effective access as outside groups turn away from interacting with federal agencies. For agency employees trying to convene groups, having to "go through the motions" to satisfy procedures whose benefits are unclear is burdensome.

Similarly, while NEPA has changed federal project evaluation in important and fundamental ways, it inadvertently has tended to lock agencies into one model of participation. As commonly interpreted, NEPA involves people very early and very late in the decision-making process. Because the scoping of issues and concerns is required at the earliest stages of a project idea and comments on draft impact statements are required late in the process, outside groups miss out on opportunities to understand decision-making constraints, share information interactively, and provide creative solutions. A recent study of the experience with public involvement in habitat conservation planning indicated that NEPA was very ineffective as a public involvement process because of the mismatch in the timing of the NEPA process with the decisions made in ongoing HCP negotiations.[12] A 1989 study of planning on thirteen national forests found "little public involvement during the middle stages of planning when the alternatives were being developed and evaluated." "This was unfortunate because many of the key decisions were made during the middle stages of planning," according to the study.[13] As Jim Matthew, representative of the Yakama Indian Nation in the Plum Creek HCP notes, "Once you get to the draft EIS, they have already cut the deal. At that stage, you can't really do too much to the document."

An emphasis on control also tends to disempower and demotivate people. It implies a lack of trust. Constraining people's ability to be creative limits their interest in innovation. At times, it can result in people following rules even when those rules obviously are mismatched to the situation at hand. In arguing for government that is less rule bound, *Reinventing Government* authors Osborne and Gaebler observe, "We embrace our rules and red tape to prevent bad things from happening, of course. But those same rules prevent good things from happening. They slow government to a snail's pace. They make it impossible to respond to rapidly changing environments. They build wasted time and effort into the very fabric of the organization."[14] The authors connect the situation back to its historical context: "To control the 5 percent who were dishonest, the Progressives created the red tape that so frustrates the other 95 percent."[15]

The current situation also is mismatched to the current context of resource management as described in chapter 1. Shifting values, diverse interests, a need for more information, and access to additional resources all require managers to be able to interact flexibly and creatively with the world around them. Accountability mechanisms that isolate agencies from other groups doom the agencies to ineffectiveness.

Promoting Accountable Collaboration

If a control-oriented structure is problematic, how can accountability be assured while collaboration goes forward? If collaboration proves a promising approach to making better decisions, how can the flexibility it needs be provided while accountability is ensured? Collaborative efforts are decision-making processes that operate within a set of incentives and standards. The challenge is to create an institutional and cultural context that provides incentives to promote good-faith collaboration while simultaneously ensuring adherence to larger policy objectives. How can this be done?

Process-Derived Accountability

The first and most obvious answer is that collaborative processes should be developed as adjuncts to normal decision-making processes. Writing over a decade ago, MIT Professor Lawrence Susskind noted that collaborative "approaches must be treated as supplements—and not alternatives—to conventional decision making." "Officials with statutory power must retain their authority in order to ensure accountability," he argued.[16] Hence, decisions produced through multiparty negotiation still need to pass muster under legally derived administrative procedures. For an agency like the Forest Service, collaborative decisions still need to move through procedures with opportunities for agency evaluation and public comment and challenge. In essence, the accountability of a collaborative process can be ensured by its connection to McCloskey's "normal governmental processes."

Furthermore, we have observed that collaborative processes often go beyond the accountability provided by administrative procedures. Indeed, an effective process ensures a different and often broader form of accountability. By having many eyes at the table, more interests are aware of decision-making considerations. Since each participant is accountable to its constituents, and all are accountable to the rules of the process, the resulting decision is often held to a higher standard than traditional rule-making procedures that focus only on procedural steps. Fairness, the likelihood of solving a problem, and even scientific legitimacy may be better protected through a well-designed multiparty process than through a closed-door agency process.

To achieve this higher level of accountability, two process prerequisites must be met: affected groups need to be able and willing to participate, and norms of good process management need to be followed. As described in chapter 1, changing patterns of political power in the United States have helped greatly in making it more likely that a full range of interests will be represented at the table. Whereas once only a narrow set of economic interests was organized to affect resource management decisions, today there is a remarkable diversity of action-oriented interest groups organized at the local, regional, and national levels. The reported rise of the "New West," defined by the diversification of economic and political interests in western communities, and other changes in American society, such as the rise of retirees as a political force, will tend to further weaken the traditional power of resource-extraction interests and promote this diversification of political forces. The national environmental organizations may not control these interests at the local level in a way that assures their dominance, but most of the resource-dependent communities that we examined had vocal environmentalists, many of whom were at least as strident as the national groups.[17]

Collaborative processes must be carried out in accordance with norms of good collaborative decision making, as described in chapter 6. The processes should be inclusive of all who care about the issues on the table, not just those with formal authority or political power. In most of the collaborative processes examined in this book, participants were vigilant about seeking a diverse array of perspectives at the table to ensure the credibility of the process and that they would be able to address all aspects of the issues of concern. Processes should be open, accessible, and transparent so that nonparticipants can observe or learn about discussions and decisions of the group and become involved if they choose. To promote full exploration of issues and open-minded and creative problem solving, collaborative processes should employ decision rules that encourage consensus. They should have mechanisms in place that enable participants to learn about the scientific and technical dimensions of the issues to be addressed and have access to outside expertise that will enable them to make informed decisions.

Guidelines capturing these norms have been written into regulations, as is the case with the current BLM resource advisory council process and the new National Forest Management Act planning rules.[18] Ultimately, however, the burden for achieving a representative, inclusive, productive, and credible process is shared by the parties to the process.

Opportunity for Appeal and Independent Scientific Review

Another way to ensure accountability is through mechanisms that allow decisions to be reviewed by independent sources. Resource management decision making clearly has benefited from the extension of citizen suit and other appeals processes established in federal law. Better, more scientifically grounded decisions have resulted, and agencies have improved the quality of their technical analysis considerably in response to the need to report it in impact statements, forest plans, and the like. Indeed, one of the reasons "capture" is no longer the problem it was fifty years ago, is that an extensive set of laws now governs behavior and provides opportunities for people outside agencies to know about and challenge proposed actions. The structure of this legal framework combined with expansion of the number and skills of groups interested in natural resource management makes it more likely that provisions will be enforced and political pressure brought to bear in support of them.

If collaboration is institutionalized as a decision-making mechanism, opportunities for appeal need to be provided to ensure technical validity and representativeness of the opinions expressed in the agreement of the group. If the process is structured and implemented in a sound and representative manner, then appeals should be the exception. The concerns of likely appellants should be dealt with through the process, if only by helping appellants to understand why their interests cannot be met. In addition, good-quality scientific information should be brought to bear on the problem at hand. The opportunity to challenge the direction suggested by collaborative groups provides an important check on the quality of their agreements, and a valuable incentive to the group to proceed through a credible and legitimate process.

One way to help check the technical validity of decisions is to institute mechanisms for independent scientific review. As discussed in chapter 7, collaborative groups often use independent scientific experts as a means of fact-finding and bounding uncertainty. Independent review can provide useful information to decision makers; it can also provide the group with a greater incentive to get help in order to make sure that the science underlying its agreements is sound. While some agency officials may resent independent review or view it as an intrusion on their bureaucratic turf, others may view it as preferable to tightly defined standards that constrain their flexibility in seeking desired ends.[19] Technical staff often do not fear independent review because they believe that they will do things right and that any review will simply confirm that fact.

Performance Standards

It is important to maintain regulatory "bottom lines" where they make sense—that is, where outcomes can be defined in a way that captures the intent of policy objectives. The ESA's requirement that federal actions cannot consciously destroy critical habitat of a listed species, NFMA's viability regulations, and ambient water-quality standards are good examples. As measures of ecosystem "health" and "integrity" are developed, comparable standards should be put into place even if they are targeted on rates of change rather than absolute outcomes (e.g., moving toward a natural hydrological flow regime or reestablishment of natural disturbance patterns).[20]

While some view (and others fear) collaborative decision making as a replacement for traditional standard setting, it is used best as a complement to traditional regulatory approaches. That is, top-down, legislated standards of behavior can be meshed with bottom-up collaborative efforts to flexibly and creatively move in the direction of the standards. In preaching the benefits of "civic environmentalism," his term for collaborative decision making, political scientist DeWitt John notes, "What the country needs (and is building) is a dual environmental system: one with strong centralized standard-setting and oversight alongside pragmatic, bottom-up decision making. Environmental protection is a paradox: It requires national standards together with discretion for particular communities, particular factories, and particular industries."[21] He also says, "Civic environmentalism is not a replacement for traditional regulatory policies; it is rather a complement to those policies."[22]

Standard setting can create incentives for groups to seek collaborative solutions to meet the standards. For example, the Endangered Species Act has its most significant impact on behavior in creating a set of incentives that encourages affected groups to respond. Many times, cooperative efforts for endangered species protection have been undertaken because of the fear of putative action under the ESA regulations. Actions taken toward the protection of salmon stocks, the marbled murrelet, the Coachella Valley fringe-toed lizard, and the whooping crane have occurred because stakeholders feared the potential chaos of regulatory actions.[23] These actions were cooperative, in that the stakeholders voluntarily committed to a process of dispute resolution that would protect the endangered species and their own interests, not the least of which was maintaining control over the direction of the situation. But those actions were also induced by a regulatory scheme that generated significant incentives for action.

Few of the places that developed habitat conservation plans, including the successful effort in Clark County, Nevada, would have undertaken their projects without the incentives provided by the ESA. Those include the positive incentive of enhanced development certainty granted to landowners with an approved plan and the negative incentive of the ESA's prohibitions on harming endangered species on private lands. Similarly, the long-standing Kirtland's warbler partnership was motivated by federal and state laws. The Forest Service and the FWS are motivated by the federal ESA. The Michigan DNR operates under the mandate of a state endangered species act. All parties have incentives to work together to fulfill their similar mandates.

Regulatory standards and guidelines can play an important role in bounding the decision space of a collaborative effort: giving participants a credible target and occasionally providing an absolute bottom line. It is important to specify outcomes as clearly as possible. Where that cannot be done at an aggregate level, processes can be developed to create locally relevant standards. As standards are created, however, it is important that they provide flexibility that can yield creative solutions. Hence, where at all possible, standards should specify ends and not the means to achieve those ends. As General George Patton once said, "Never tell people how to do things. Tell them what you want them to achieve, and they will surprise you with their ingenuity."[24] That has been our experience with collaborative groups. When they have been able to agree on a goal, either because it was mandated externally or because they identified it as a result of their process, often those groups have been remarkably creative in finding ways to cooperatively meet that goal.

Monitoring and Evaluation

One of the reasons performance standards have been less useful in the past is that so little monitoring is undertaken after decisions are made. Hence, traditionally little accountability has been apparent in spite of what is provided by theory. If agencies do not know the effects of their management approaches, it is hard to criticize their behavior. If stakeholders do not know the results of agency decisions, they cannot push for changes. If elected officials are uninformed as to what happened, it is hard to believe that the accountability granted through a statute is being realized. Ignorance is not bliss when problems occur because of it.

Agreements reached through collaborative processes need to include provisions for monitoring the effectiveness of strategies and do so in a way that reinforces the collaboration. Monitoring of key performance indicators is necessary. Periodic evaluation conducted by the collaborative group, or in a process sanctioned by the group, is needed to assess performance and adapt as needed. Monitoring conducted at the ecosystem level is essential. By requiring unit-level reports, making agency information more accessible to nonagency groups, involving a host of interests in decision making, and giving these groups the means to challenge decisions in a timely fashion, an effective accountability system can be created.

Because most of the collaborative processes examined for this book are either ongoing or occurred over an extended period of time, multiple opportunities arose for those involved to field-test ideas and determine their effects. Many groups conducted small-scale experimental projects and assessed their impacts before extending the prescription to other areas. Most incorporated monitoring in a very direct and deliberate manner because those involved recognized the higher standard to which their actions would be held. Their effectiveness was firmly rooted in their credibility, and consequently those processes evidenced far more monitoring and evaluation than that seen traditionally in government agency resource management.

Federal Advisory Committee Act

While it is important to ensure that collaborative processes are accountable, it is also important to provide adequate flexibility so that decision making can be well matched to the situation at hand. As described above, FACA and the way that NEPA has been implemented have been problematic and need to be modified to promote effective decision making.

There is no doubt that FACA has had salutary effects in some areas of federal policy by limiting some of the worst effects of unbalanced and closed-door advisory groups. As the late Senator John Heinz once exclaimed, "Federal advisory committees have come a long way since their closed-door past, and Federal policy making today wouldn't be the same without the input of their members."[25] FACA was a necessary response to historical problems with advisory boards. It was a reactive, regulatory program that focused primarily on minimizing the problems evident in advisory boards.

However, the FACA system was not structured to foster true democratic participation; it was explicitly structured to impede *un*democratic participation. The two objectives are quite different. While no doubt FACA has promoted inclusiveness by default, it is not effective at doing so given today's political, legal, and organizational environment. It does not provide a proactive structure and a set of incentives to encourage the open exchange of information and collaborative decision making needed in today's pluralistic society. Indeed, its mechanisms stand in the way of a number of needed innovations in federal administration.

In our judgment, collaborative resource management processes should be exempt from FACA. Precedent exists for an exemption. Recovery planning under the ESA is exempted by a provision of the law, as are the fishery councils established under the Magnuson-Stevens Act.[26] In the cases we examined, there was no benefit to groups moving through the burdensome FACA-chartering process, yet there were considerable costs in time and flexibility. As FACA-chartered committees, such groups often were perceived as more legitimate but ironically were less accountable to the need to be broadly representative. Through the chartering process, the individuals chosen to represent specific interests were not always supported by affected groups, and elected officials influenced the composition of the committees for political reasons. In other situations, federal officials undermined the effectiveness of multiparty working groups by not participating because the groups were not FACA-chartered. While FACA's overall effectiveness needs careful study, the act has limited usefulness in resource management and is burdensome. An exemption is one way around the problem.

The National Environmental Policy Act

The environmental impact statement process created under NEPA is an important vehicle for agency disclosure and appeal by nonfederal parties. It was never intended to be an overarching structure for public involvement but has become the basic template for agency actions in many cases. NEPA's requirements for scoping and comments on draft impact statements provide a useful opportunity for public input early and late in the review process, but NEPA's full potential as a mechanism for effective public agency dialogue has not been realized. At a minimum, additional trigger points need to be incorporated for soliciting public input at points in the middle of the NEPA process when real decision making is occurring. As described above, by the time a draft EIS is produced, much of the agency decision making has occurred, and the time spent by the public on comments is wasted and ultimately frustrating.

Ideally, ways can be found to marry the NEPA process with more interactive collaborative approaches so that the product of a collaborative group is both a well-tested and publicly reviewed set of ideas and an agency-produced assessment capable of satisfying the draft EIS requirement (which would then be subjected to public comment and agency revision into a final EIS). While in some cases of collaborative management NEPA has seemed superfluous, it appears reasonable to use NEPA as a means of ensuring accountability of the collaborative process if it can be reinvented in an efficient and effective manner. Sherri Barrett, FWS representative to the Clark County HCP process, comments on the valuable link between NEPA review and collaborative group accountability: "It's important to let the larger public know what is occurring, and NEPA can serve as a check of a steering committee's representativeness."

Responsibility for Ensuring Accountability

Who should shoulder the burden of ensuring the accountability of a collaborative process? At one level, all participants in the process have an obligation and considerable incentive to do so. As detailed in the cases in this book, participants in these processes are investing considerable time and energy in trying to solve problems and resolve disputes. They can achieve their own ends and receive benefits from the effort they have invested only if the process is ultimately deemed acceptable to other participants and agency decision makers, as well as to those who would challenge the process's agreements. Hence, each participant has a considerable incentive to make sure that the group's decisions are credible and legitimate. Otherwise, they have wasted a lot of their own time.

At the same time, government agencies and institutions have a unique role and responsibility in these processes. While they should be capitalizing on opportunities to collaborate, they must recognize that they—and only they—are the final decision makers. Some argue that the role of agency participants in collaborative processes is solely as a facilitator of other participants' interactions. However, based on our review of successful collaborative processes, it is clear that where a group succeeded and was held in high regard by the broader community, the agency did not step back into a purely facilitative role. Rather, it provided essential leadership that guided the group while simultaneously representing its own interests within the process. It ensured that the sideboards provided by existing law and regulation were in place and understood, and that those individuals present recognized that implementation of decisions could occur only through established administrative processes, including procedures for public review and comment. It took on the responsibility of ensuring the accountability of the process while still promoting collaborative interaction among multiple participants.

In our judgment, most of the cases highlighted in this book were both successful and accountable. We examined numerous cases as they evolved over a three- to five-year period, and in those few instances where a lack of accountability was evident, groups inside or outside the process pointed that out. Those cases then struggled to shift course or simply disbanded. A process that is proceeding in a manner that is nonrepresentative, contrary to current scientific understanding, or counter to mechanisms that ensure accountability is sure to draw public attention and criticism. The Quincy Library Group is an excellent case in point.[27]

All in all, we believe that issues of accountability can be addressed while still promoting collaboration. While policy changes can foster collaboration and ensure accountability, many improvements can happen within the authority provided by existing law. Indeed, most of the success stories profiled within this book occurred within existing policy structures. Some of the purported policy obstacles, including the Freedom of Information Act and the Sherman Antitrust Act, never appeared as significant hurdles. And with the notable exception of the Quincy Library Group, most cases were lauded by diverse organizations and individuals, elected officials, and the press, all of whom marveled at their accomplishments in comparison to the previous state of impasse.

To the staunchest critics of collaboration, we urge care in the baseline used for comparisons. The current regime of rules and regulations has yielded over-exploited resources, ineffective decision making, inadequate enforcement, constrained resources, and limited monitoring while consuming great amounts of organizational resources and producing impasses and frustration. Will a regime that relies on collaboration result in better outcomes for critical resources such as endangered species? At an abstract level, the answer should be no. If the FWS and the National Marine Fisheries Service enforced the law fully, the species would be better off without the negotiations that lead to HCPs. But this presumes full information, unlimited enforcement resources, and political will that far exceeds anything the agencies have been able to muster. As seen in many of the cases described in this book, information, resources, and political support are often more readily available when multiple parties work together to collaboratively solve complex problems.

We want to reiterate that there are times when multiparty collaboration is inappropriate.[28] In many situations, however, collaboration is a more promising approach to addressing resource management issues and can be undertaken in a manner that is effective and accountable to public trust responsibilities. Our belief is that the multiple opportunities for public review and comment that collaborative processes provide ensure at least equal if not greater accountability than we have seen in agencies acting in isolation. Indeed, by using a broad set of approaches to promote accountability, including appropriate performance standards, rights of appeal and review, and the checks and balances provided by "many eyes at the table," collaborative management efforts may ultimately be more accountable than traditional decision-making processes have been in practice.

Chapter 14

A Message to Individuals

*I*f we had to set down a recipe for success in resource management, it would be something like the following:

1. Get good quality information.

2. Mobilize and develop capable people from a spectrum of interests at an appropriate geographic scale.

3. Provide them with opportunities for interaction and exploration, and incentives to find creative solutions to problems.

4. Enable them to implement solutions in a way that mobilizes resources, shares ownership, and moves adaptively to a future that will be characterized by changes in values and knowledge.

5. Mix thoroughly, provide adequate resources, and stand out of the way.

Collaborative processes and partnerships can help with all of these tasks. They are one of many strategies needed to accomplish effective natural resource management in the future. The concept of building an interactive network of ideas, information, and capabilities must be integrated into the way that other tasks are approached and structured. It is part of a way of thinking about ecosystem-scale management that cannot be held in isolation from other resource management tasks.

At the same time, it is important to keep in mind that the objective of collaboration is better resource management and not collaboration for its own sake. Collaboration is not the answer to all problems, but it can be helpful in many situations. So it is important to evaluate each situation as a candidate for a collaborative process and not to blindly advocate or oppose collaboration. For example, Steve Hinchman, director of the Western Slope Environmental Resource Council in Colorado, has been a member of a collaborative advisory group for a grazing allotment that overlaps the West Elk Wilderness. He says, "My overall goal in this process is not to advance the agenda of the environmental movement. My overall goal is to improve the environmental conditions in the lower Gunnison Basin." The group has achieved improvements in elk habitat, cattle forage, and riparian health over the last two years. Neighboring ranchers now want to use the same process on their allotments. "Regardless of what's happening in Washington, D.C., positive changes are happening here," says Hinchman. "We resolve conflicts with our neighbors. . . . The Gunnison sage grouse that lives nearby is going to become an endangered species, and now we have the relationships in place to deal with it without it becoming a war zone."

While collaboration is primarily a tool for achieving effective resource management, it does speak to core values and needs in individuals, agencies, and communities. Most people want to be neighborly, solve common problems, have face-to-face relationships with others that are pleasant and affirmative, take pride in their organizations and communities, and take ownership in the directions set by public decision-making processes. Democratic norms emphasize the importance of civic discourse as a means of knitting together the diverse set of interests inherent in a pluralistic society. It is hard to view the high levels of conflict, disassociation, and impasses produced by many of our administrative, legislative, and judicial processes as the best we can do.

Collaborative approaches can help realize many of these core needs. Indeed, some argue that the emergence of collaborative processes represents a return to time-honored ways through which communities historically dealt with their problems. As Jim Allen, hunting outfitter and participant in the Three-Quarter Circle Ranch collaborative resource management group in Wyoming, comments: "It's funny that our society has come to this; all we have done is come full circle. In history it seems there has always been some sort of a tribal council or village gathering. But look, now we spend an hour and a half on e-mail a day. That's about as cold and impersonal as it gets. We as a society don't get together nearly as much as we used to. And so collaborative resource management is nothing more than an old-time tribal council gathering." Environmentalist Jack Shipley, cofounder of the Applegate Partnership, agrees: "What we are talking about here really isn't very sophisticated. It's not high tech. It's old common sense stuff that probably the pioneers had to rely on or not survive."

The balance of this chapter presents a summary of our advice to individuals considering a collaborative approach to environmental problem solving or resource management.

Summary Advice

To individuals seeking to build expanded relationships with groups outside an agency, our advice may sound much like a Nike "Just Do It" advertisement:

1. Numerous opportunities currently exist to build an expanded network of relationships among agencies and other groups involved in and affected by resource management. We suggest you start by capitalizing on prevailing opportunities. At the same time, initiating contact with outside groups, not just responding to their concerns, is important. Sometimes even small steps can yield considerable benefits. Picking up the telephone and starting a conversation with a manager in another agency or an interest group can be an important first step and less overwhelming than you might think.

2. There are many different types of collaborative relationships, and there is no one right way to build bridges that promote collaboration. We suggest an adaptive management approach: Try something and learn from it. Experiment, evaluate, and revise direction accordingly. This approach may seem like a process of "stumbling along," but the reality is that personal commitment and perseverance is what enabled many collaborative partnerships to succeed.

3. Attempts at collaboration are not always going to work. Don't take it personally. Due to diverse interests and perspectives, conflict will be inevitable in such interactions. We suggest working through the conflict by listening, being open-minded, and focusing on how to creatively pursue resource management objectives, not on carrying out a certain way to achieve those objectives. At the same time, don't lose sight of your own interests and concerns. When necessary and appropriate, pursue other strategies for meeting your interests if collaboration is proving ineffective.

4. Many useful skills are involved in a collaboration, but the key skills are not rocket science. Humility, honesty, sincerity, being down to earth, creativity, understanding your own group's interests, and having the ability to listen and understand others' points of view are all important components of the relationships that underlie collaborative efforts. The individuals who have been involved in successful collaborative initiatives are not superhuman. Rather, they are individuals who tried doing something, stuck with it, and were willing to put a fair amount of energy into the endeavor.

5. Build your capacity to initiate, guide, or participate in a collaborative process. As noted in chapter 3, Su Rolle, USFS-BLM liaison to the

Applegate Partnership, refers to collaboration as "a kind of awkward dance that none of us knows the steps to." We believe "dancing lessons" can help. Several collaborative efforts arranged for weekend workshops or evening training sessions that helped the group as a whole build understanding and skills in collaboration, communication, and group problem solving that enabled them to work together more effectively.

A Guide to Getting Started

For individuals who are interested in exploring the potential of collaboration or who are designing ways to collaborate, we offer a set of questions that summarize the major themes of the book. Ask yourself the following as a means of triggering ideas and thinking of ways to structure the collaboration so that it is more likely to succeed:

1. *Can collaboration help me achieve my objectives?* Is your objective to access information, solve site-level problems, mobilize expertise or resources to help get work done, or influence people's behavior across a fragmented landscape? In such cases, a collaborative approach may work. Is your objective to set precedent or advance a specific policy objective across a range of sites? If so, action in a different decision-making arena such as the courts or a legislature may be more appropriate.

2. *Is the situation amenable to a collaborative solution?* Is it characterized by such fundamental value differences that collaboration is likely to provide little room for agreement? Do the different groups who should be involved have the incentive to engage in an effective way, or can incentives be structured to encourage their participation?

3. *Are there ways to build on common ground?* Are there shared goals, problems, concerns, or sense of place that can be used to focus groups' attention or develop a common vision? Can solutions be imagined that would allow different goals to be achieved simultaneously?

4. *Can new opportunities for interaction be imagined?* Can establishing new lines of communication among agencies or groups help? Will a program of outreach provide needed information or mobilize others to get involved? Can a new structure such as a coordinator position or advisory board enable collaboration?

5. *Can the process of interaction be improved or structured to be meaningful, effective, and enduring?* Can mechanisms be provided to ensure early, often, and ongoing involvement by affected interests? How can you

ensure that affected interests are represented in the process? Can consensus be established as a decision-making norm? How should the process be facilitated and the meetings managed so that people's time is used effectively? Should the process be institutionalized in a way that ensures its credibility and effectiveness over the long term?

6. *Can the involved individuals be guided to focus on the problem in a new way, so that prior positions or traditional conceptions of agency roles do not constrain them?* Will it help to expand the definition of the problem or area of concern to encompass a more holistic vision? Can processes be created that enable participants to learn together and bound their discussions with credible information?

7. *How can a sense of responsibility and commitment be fostered, so that groups take ownership of the problem, the process, and the agreements?* Can groups' perception of interdependence be developed and used to promote a common vision? Can the discussions be guided so that people focus on the problem and not on who was to blame? Can agency commitment to the problem and process be enhanced so that agencies and other groups live up to their agreements and maintain support of the collaborative effort?

8. *How can the process of interaction take into account the personalities of participants?* Can you find ways to shatter misperceptions and foster understanding of the true concerns of the involved parties? Can relationships be built by fostering trust and respect of each other's interests and need to be involved? Can transitions in relationships be managed so that they do not undermine the collaborative effort? Can you find ways to motivate people to be involved by demonstrating success through small steps, or by making activities fun or hands-on? What cultural elements need to be considered when designing processes or dealing with people?

9. *How can you establish a proactive and entrepreneurial sense to the effort?* Are there energetic individuals who can be encouraged to dedicate their time and energies to promoting the collaborative initiative? Can existing opportunities such as government programs be used to catalyze activity? Can the effort demonstrate success or be cast as an innovation to motivate others to be involved or contribute resources to the effort? How can you encourage people to persist in the face of difficulties?

10. *What kind of help does a potential partnership need?* Among the diversity of interests in a community, who might offer that help? Is there expertise, ideas, or funding that can be mobilized to help the collaboration succeed? Can public or political support be built? Can the effort's goals be achieved by helping others?

The number of questions to be asked and the fact that few of these questions have "right answers" suggest that effective collaboration requires a great deal of work. Many individuals have found it difficult and at times exhausting yet simultaneously very rewarding for themselves and their organizations. They are proud of their efforts and convinced that they have accomplished on-the-ground action, often in spite of agency bureaucracies or the incentives provided by traditional decision-making processes. Indeed, we have often been astounded by the ebullience of participants' comments when the processes are going well and their level of commitment when they face difficulties. Many have found the process of collaboration a transforming experience for themselves. As Su Rolle puts it: "I feel like I can never really go back. I can't go back to seeing neighbors and community in the same way. I can't go back and see the agencies that are across the boundary from us as somebody separate that we shouldn't work with in a totally different way."

Notes

Preface

1. Steven L. Yaffee, *Prohibitive Policy: Implementing the Federal Endangered Species Act* (Cambridge, MA: MIT Press, 1982).
2. Julia M. Wondolleck, *Public Lands Conflict and Resolution: Managing National Forest Disputes* (New York: Plenum Publishers, 1988).
3. Steven L. Yaffee, *The Wisdom of the Spotted Owl: Policy Lessons for a New Century* (Washington, DC: Island Press, 1994).
4. Julia M. Wondolleck and Steven L. Yaffee, *Building Bridges Across Agency Boundaries: In Search of Excellence in the U.S. Forest Service* (Ann Arbor: University of Michigan, 1994), a research report to the USDA–Forest Service, Pacific Northwest Research Station.
5. Barbara Gray, "Conditions Facilitating Interorganizational Collaboration," *Human Relations* 38 (1985):912.
6. Julia M. Wondolleck and Steven L. Yaffee, *Sustaining the Success of Collaborative Partnerships: Revisiting the Building Bridges Cases* (Ann Arbor: School of Natural Resources and Environment, University of Michigan, 1997), a research report submitted to the USDA–Forest Service, Pacific Northwest Research Station.
7. Julia M. Wondolleck and Steven L. Yaffee, "The Long-Term Consequences of Using Negotiation to Resolve National Forest Planning Disputes," Sixth International Symposium on Society and Resource Management, Pennsylvania State University, State College, May 22, 1996.
8. Steven L. Yaffee and Julia M. Wondolleck, *Negotiating Survival: An Assessment of the Potential Use of Alternative Dispute Resolution Techniques for Resolving Conflicts Between Endangered Species and Development* (Ann Arbor: School of Natural Resources and Environment, University of Michigan, 1994), a research report to the Administrative Conference of the United States.
9. Jeremy Anderson and Steven Yaffee, *Balancing Public Trust and Private Interest: Public Participation in Habitat Conservation Planning, A Summary Report* (Ann Arbor: School of Natural Resources and Environment, University of Michigan, 1998), a research report commissioned by the National Wildlife Federation.
10. Steven L. Yaffee, Ali F. Phillips, Irene C. Frentz, Paul W. Hardy, Sussanne M. Maleki, and Barbara E. Thorpe, *Ecosystem Management in the United States: An Assessment of Current Experience* (Washington, DC: Island Press, 1996).
11. Christine Coughlin, Merrick Hoben, Dirk Manskopf, Shannon Quesada, and Julia Wondolleck, *The Controversy Over Collaboration: An Assessment of Collaborative Resource Management Partnerships* (Ann Arbor: School of Natural Resources and Environment, University of Michigan, 1999).
12. For example, in an experiment where participants were asked to explain the motion of two randomly moving dots on a computer screen, they almost always did so with a story. See Theodore R. Sarbin, *Narrative Psychology: The Storied Nature of Human Conduct* (New York: Praeger Publishers, 1986).
13. Suzanne Hidi and William Baird, "Interestingness: A Neglected Variable in Discourse Processing," *Cognitive Science* 10 (1986):179–194.

14. Richard E. Neustadt and Ernest R. May, *Thinking in Time: The Uses of History for Decision-Makers* (New York: Free Press, 1986).

15. U.S. Department of Agriculture, "National Forest System Land and Resource Management Planning: Proposed Rule," 64 *Federal Register* 54073–54112, October 5, 1999.

16. For example, the World Wildlife Fund's ecoregional assessment process and The Nature Conservancy's ecoregional planning process both place an emphasis on partnerships and cross-landscape collaboration. See Taylor H. Ricketts, Eric Dinerstein, David M. Olson, Colby J. Loucks, William Eichbaum, Kevin Kavanagh, Prashant Hedao, Patrick T. Hurley, Karen M. Carney, Robin Abell, and Steven Walters, *Terrestrial Ecoregions of North America: A Conservation Assessment* (Washington, DC: Island Press, 1999), and The Nature Conservancy, *Designing a Geography of Hope: Guidelines for Ecoregion-Based Conservation in The Nature Conservancy* (Arlington, VA: The Nature Conservancy, 1997).

Chapter 1

1. Steven L. Yaffee, "Why Environmental Policy Nightmares Recur," *Conservation Biology* 11 (April 1997):328–337.

2. Yaffee, *The Wisdom of the Spotted Owl.*

3. For example, studies by the University of Michigan's Center for Political Studies indicate that in 1964 some 63 percent of adults said they could trust the government most of the time. By 1988, that figure had dropped to 37 percent. In 1964, some 70 percent said government was run for the benefit of all. By 1988, some 67 percent said government was run for the benefit of a few special interest groups.

4. For example, the Gallup poll reported declining confidence in the U.S. Congress, from 42 percent of respondents in 1973 to 32 percent in 1989 to 22 percent in 1997. George Gallup, Jr., *The Gallup Poll: Public Opinion 1997* (Wilmington, DE: Scholarly Resources, 1998), 131–132.

5. For example, in the 1960 presidential election, approximately two-thirds of those eligible to vote did so. By 1988, that number had dropped to roughly half of eligible voters. Only a third of eligible voters vote in congressional elections, and the percentages of young people who vote is even worse. For an interesting discussion of American voting behavior, see David Broder, "Not Voting and Proud of It," *Washington Post*, October 10, 1999, B8.

6. Robert D. Putnam, "Bowling Alone: America's Declining Social Capital," *Journal of Democracy* 6 (January 1995):65–78.

7. Indeed, columnist Robert Samuelson argues that the public blames these institutions even when all objective measures suggest they have been spectacularly successful in the post-war period. Robert J. Samuelson, *The Good Life and Its Discontents: The American Dream in the Age of Entitlement 1945–1995* (New York: Times Books, 1995).

8. David S. Broder, "Civil Life and Civility," *Washington Post*, January 1, 1995, C-7.

9. David S. Broder, "The Widening Search for Civility," *Washington Post*, January 3, 1996, A-15.

10. Mark O. Hatfield, "Consensus in the Upper Klamath Basin," *Consensus* (newsletter of the MIT-Harvard Public Disputes Program) 29 (January 1996), 12.

11. Yaffee, *The Wisdom of the Spotted Owl*, 305–309.

12. EPA's Office of Sustainable Ecosystems and Communities promotes the use of Community-Based Environmental Protection through training, grants, and tech-

nical assistance. See, e.g., U.S. Environmental Protection Agency, *Community-Based Environmental Protection: A Resource Book for Protecting Ecosystems and Communities*, September 1997, Ref. No. EPA-230-B-96-003.

13. Susan Hill MacKenzie, "Ecosystem Management in the Great Lakes: Some Observations from Three RAP Sites," *Journal of Great Lakes Research* 19 (1993):136–144.

14. Peter Aengst, Jeremy Anderson, Jay Chamberlin, Christopher Grunewald, Susan Loucks, Elizabeth Wheatley, and Steven Yaffee, "Introduction to Habitat Conservation Planning," *Endangered Species Update* 14 (July/August 1997):5–9.

15. Oregon has eighty-eight watershed councils recognized by the Governor's Watershed Enhancement Board. See their Web site at: www.4sos.org/homepage/whoweare/gweb_wscs.html, March 19, 1999.

16. Steven L. Yaffee, "Three Faces of Ecosystem Management," *Conservation Biology* 13 (August 1999):713–725.

17. Samuel P. Hays, *Conservation and the Gospel of Efficiency: The Progressive Conservation Movement 1890–1920* (New York: Atheneum, 1975).

18. Gifford Pinchot, *Breaking New Ground* (New York: Harcourt Brace, 1947).

19. Samuel T. Dana and Sally K. Fairfax, *Forest and Range Policy*, 2nd edition (New York: McGraw-Hill, 1980).

20. Herbert Kaufman, *The Forest Ranger: A Study in Administrative Behavior* (Baltimore: Johns Hopkins University Press, 1960).

21. Committee of Scientists (K. Norman Johnson et al.), *Sustaining the People's Lands: Recommendations for Stewardship of the National Forests and Grasslands into the Next Century* (Washington, DC: U.S. Department of Agriculture, 1999), xiv–xv.

22. Bruce Babbitt, "Managing Biodiversity," *Nature Conservancy* 44 (January/February 1994): 17–18.

23. R. Edward Grumbine, "What Is Ecosystem Management?" *Conservation Biology* 8 (1994):1–12; N.L. Christensen, A.M. Bartuska, J.H. Brown, S. Carpenter, C. D'Antonio, R. Francis, J.F. Franklin, J.A. MacMahon, R.F. Noss, D.J. Parsons, C.H. Peterson, M.G. Turner, and R.G. Woodmansee, "The Report of the Ecological Society of America Committee on the Scientific Basis for Ecosystem Management," *Ecological Applications* 6 (1996):665–691; K.A. Kohm and J.F. Franklin, "Introduction," in *Creating a Forestry for the 21st Century: The Science of Ecosystem Management* (Washington, DC: Island Press, 1997), 1–5.

24. Margaret A. Moote, Sabrina Burke, Hanna J. Cortner, and Mary G. Wallace, *Principles of Ecosystem Management* (Tucson: Water Resources Research Center, University of Arizona, 1994).

25. B.A. Stein et al., "Significance of Federal Lands for Endangered Species," in E.T. LaRoe, *Our Living Resources: A Report on the Distribution, Abundance and Health of U.S. Plants, Animals and Ecosystems* (Washington, DC: National Biological Service, 1995), 398–401.

26. U.S. General Accounting Office, *Endangered Species Act: Information on Species Protection on Non-Federal Lands* (Washington, DC: Government Printing Office, 1994), 8.

27. Kathryn A. Kohm and Jerry F. Franklin, "Introduction," in Kathryn A. Kohm and Jerry F. Franklin, eds., *Creating a Forestry for the 21st Century: The Science of Ecosystem Management* (Washington, DC: Island Press, 1997), 3.

28. C.S. Holling, "What Barriers? What Bridges?" in Lance H. Gunderson, C.S.

Holling, and Stephen S. Light, eds., *Barriers and Bridges to the Renewal of Ecosystems and Institutions* (New York: Columbia University Press, 1995), 14.

29. C.S. Holling, *Adaptive Environmental Assessment and Management* (New York: John Wiley, 1978), 1.

30. Kai N. Lee, *Compass and Gyroscope: Integrating Science and Politics for the Environment* (Washington, DC: Island Press, 1993).

31. Jeff Sirmon, William E. Shands, and Chris Liggett, "Communities of Interests and Open Decisionmaking," *Journal of Forestry* 91(July 1993):17.

32. R.A. Heifetz and R.M. Sinder, "Political Leadership: Managing the Public's Problem Solving," in Robert Reich, ed., *The Power of Public Ideas* (Cambridge, MA: Harvard University Press, 1990), 179–203.

33. Timothy P. Duane, "Community Participation in Ecosystem Management," *Ecology Law Quarterly* 24 (1997):771–797.

34. Robert Putnam, *Making Democracy Work: Civic Traditions in Italy* (Princeton, NJ: Princeton University Press, 1993).

35. See, e.g., Judith E. Innes, "Planning through Consensus Building: A New View of the Comprehensive Planning Ideal," *Journal of the American Planning Association* 62 (1996):460; Lawrence E. Susskind and Jeffrey Cruikshank, *Breaking the Impasse: Consensual Approaches to Resolving Public Disputes* (New York: Basic Books, 1987).

36. See, e.g., James Q. Wilson, ed., *The Politics of Regulation* (New York: Basic Books, 1980).

37. DeWitt John, *Civic Environmentalism: Alternatives to Regulation in States and Communities* (Washington, DC: CQ Press, 1994), 10.

38. DeWitt John and Marian Mlay, "Community-Based Environmental Protection: Encouraging Civic Environmentalism," in Ken Sexton, Alfred A. Marcus, K. William Easter, and Timothy D. Burkhardt, eds., *Better Environmental Decisions: Strategies for Governments, Businesses and Communities* (Washington, DC: Island Press, 1999), 355.

39. See note 12, this chapter.

40. David Osborne and Ted Gaebler, *Reinventing Government: How the Entrepreneurial Spirit Is Transforming the Public Sector* (New York: Plume/Penguin, 1992), 250.

41. Osborne and Gaebler, *Reinventing Government*, 251–252.

42. Steven L. Yaffee and Julia M. Wondolleck, "Building Bridges Across Agency Boundaries," in Kohm and Franklin, *Creating a Forestry for the 21st Century*, 381–396.

Chapter 2

1. J. Michael Scott, Blair Csuti, Kent Smith, J.E. Estes, and Steve Caicco, "Gap Analysis of Species Richness and Vegetation Cover: An Integrated Biodiversity Conservation Strategy," in Kathryn A. Kohm, ed., *Balancing on the Brink of Extinction: The Endangered Species Act and Lessons for the Future* (Washington, DC: Island Press, 1991), 282–297.

2. Thomas J. Peters and Robert. H. Waterman, Jr., *In Search of Excellence: Lessons from America's Best-Run Companies* (New York: Warner Books, 1982), 224–234.

3. Southern Appalachian Man and the Biosphere (SAMAB). *The Southern Appalachian Assessment Summary Report*, report #R8-TP25 (Atlanta: USDA–Forest Service, Southern Region, 1996).

4. Connie P. Ozawa, *Recasting Science: Consensual Procedures in Public Policy Making* (Boulder, CO: Westview, 1991), 62.

5. Clare M. Ryan, *Leadership in Regulatory Negotiations at the Environmental Protection Agency: An Analysis of Roles*, unpublished PhD dissertation (Ann Arbor: University of Michigan, 1996), 52.

6. Wondolleck and Yaffee, "The Long-Term Consequences of Using Negotiation to Resolve National Forest Planning Disputes;" Gail Bingham, *Resolving Environmental Disputes: A Decade of Experience* (Washington, DC: Conservation Foundation, 1986).

7. Peter Aengst, Jeremy Anderson, Jay Chamberlin, Christopher Grunewald, Susan Loucks, Elizabeth Wheatley, and Steven Yaffee, *Balancing Public Trust and Private Interest: An Investigation of Public Participation in Habitat Conservation Planning* (Ann Arbor: School of Natural Resources and Environment, University of Michigan, 1998), xiv.

8. Clearly, there are drawbacks to cooperative working arrangements. They can result in work of varying quality. Where volunteers are used to perform needed activities, staffing arrangements may be less stable. For example, volunteers may not show up on a rainy day even if work is scheduled. Agency employees needed to supervise and train cooperators may have to do so during evenings and weekends. Agency control over the direction and methods of a project is less, and while work may be accomplished, it may not take the form agency officials would like. Since there is a competition for people's time, the tasks most needed and doable by less skilled workers, such as routine maintenance work, may not motivate the involvement of partners. See, e.g., Steven L. Yaffee, "Using Nonprofit Organizations to Manage Public Lands," *Transactions, North American Wildlife and Natural Resources Conference* 48 (1983):413–422.

9. Management Institute for Environment and Business, *Conservation Partnerships: A Field Guide to Public-Private Partnering for Natural Resource Conservation* (Washington, DC: National Fish and Wildlife Foundation, 1993), 10.

10. *Chicago Tribune*, December 27, 1990.

11. Kaufman, *The Forest Ranger*.

Chapter 3

1. Christopher Moore, *The Mediation Process: Practical Strategies for Managing Conflict* (San Francisco: Jossey-Bass, 1996); Barbara Gray, *Collaborating: Finding Common Ground for Multiparty Problems* (San Francisco: Jossey-Bass, 1989), 255–256.

2. Gray, *Collaborating*, 250.

3. Bingham, *Resolving Environmental Disputes*, 66.

4. See, e.g., David A. Lax and James K. Sebenius, *The Manager as Negotiator: Bargaining for Cooperation and Competitive Gain* (New York: Free Press, 1986).

5. Garrett Hardin, "The Tragedy of the Commons," *Science* 162 (1968):1244.

6. Aristotle, *Politics, Book II*, ch. 3.

7. Hardin, "The Tragedy of the Commons," 1244.

8. Garrett Hardin, "Political Requirements for Preserving Our Common Heritage," in H.P. Brokaw, ed., *Wildlife and America* (Washington, DC: U.S. Council on Environmental Quality, 1978), 314.

9. R.J. Smith, "Resolving the Tragedy of the Commons by Creating Private Property Rights in Wildlife," *CATO Journal* (1981):465–467.

10. D.R. Luce and H. Raiffa, *Games and Decisions: Introduction and Critical Survey* (New York: Wiley, 1957), 94–95.

11. Indeed, a 1975 review of the literature indicated that more than two thousand papers had been devoted to the prisoner's dilemma game. See B. Grofman and J. Pool, "Bayesian Models for Iterated Prisoner's Dilemma Games," *General Systems* 20 (1975):185–194.

12. Max H. Bazerman, *Judgment in Managerial Decision Making* (New York: Wiley, 1986), 128–131.

13. Jean Pasquero, "Supraorganizational Collaboration: The Canadian Environmental Experiment," *Journal of Applied Behavioral Science* (March 1991):42.

14. Rosabeth Moss Kanter, "Collaborative Advantage: The Art of Alliances," *Harvard Business Review* (July/August 1994):97.

15. Andrew Inkpen, "Creating Knowledge Through Collaboration," *California Management Review* (Fall 1996):136–137.

16. Dale Blahna and Susan Yonts-Shepard, "Public Involvement in Resource Planning: Toward Bridging the Gap Between Policy and Implementation," *Society and Natural Resources* 2 (1989):222.

17. Blahna and Yonts-Shepard, "Public Involvement in Resource Planning," 223.

18. Blahna and Yonts-Shepard, "Public Involvement in Resource Planning," 223.

19. Quoted in Jon Christensen, "In Arizona Desert, a Bird Oasis in Peril," *New York Times,* May 4, 1999, F5.

20. Kathleen Shea Abrams, Hugh Gladwin, Mary Jean Matthews, and Barbara C. McCabe, "The East Everglades Planning Study," in Douglas R. Porter and David A. Salvesen, *Collaborative Planning for Wetlands and Wildlife* (Washington, DC: Island Press, 1995), 243.

21. Steve Selin and Deborah Chavez, "Developing a Collaborative Model for Environmental Planning and Management," *Environmental Management* 19 (1995):189–195.

22. Kanter, "Collaborative Advantage, 107.

23. William A. Wall, Potlach Corporation, personal communication, April 1, 1996.

24. Wondolleck and Yaffee, Sustaining the Success of Collaborative Partnerships.

25. Wall, personal communication.

26. Porter and Salvesen, *Collaborative Planning for Wetlands and Wildlife,* 277.

27. Peter Lorange and Johan Roos, "Why Some Strategic Alliances Succeed and Others Fail," *Journal of Business Strategy* (January/February 1991):25–30.

28. Wall, personal communication.

29. Stephen Kaplan and Rachel Kaplan, *Cognition and Environment: Functioning in an Uncertain World* (Ann Arbor, MI: Ulrich's, 1982).

30. Kanter, "Collaborative Advantage, 105.

31. Janet A. Weiss, "The Powers of Problem Definition: The Case of Government Paperwork," *Policy Science* 22 (1989):97–121; Donald Schön, *The Reflective Practitioner: How Professionals Think in Action* (New York: Basic Books, 1983).

32. Tim W. Clark and Richard P. Reading, "A Professional Perspective: Improving Problem Solving, Communication and Effectiveness," in Tim W. Clark, Richard P. Reading, and Alice L. Clarke, eds., *Endangered Species Recovery: Finding the Lessons, Improving the Process* (Washington, DC: Island Press, 1994), 359.

33. Selin and Chavez, "Developing a Collaborative Model," 193.

34. Yaffee, *The Wisdom of the Spotted Owl.*

35. Selin and Chavez, "Developing a Collaborative Model," 193.

36. Ben W. Twight, *Organizational Values and Political Power: The Forest Service versus the Olympic National Park* (University Park: Pennsylvania State University Press, 1983).

37. Tim W. Clark and Ann H. Harvey, "Implementing Endangered Species Recovery Policy: Learning As We Go?" *Endangered Species Update* 5 (1988):35–42.

38. Richard P. Reading and Brian J. Miller, "The Black-Footed Ferret Recovery Program: Unmasking Professional and Organizational Weaknesses," in Clark, Reading, and Clarke, *Endangered Species Recovery*, 84–85.

39. Selin and Chavez, "Developing a Collaborative Model," 193.

40. Gray, *Collaborating*, 248.

41. Michael McCloskey, "The Skeptic: Collaboration Has Its Limits," *High Country News*, May 13, 1996, 7.

42. Wondolleck, *Public Lands Conflict and Resolution*.

43. Gray, *Collaborating*, 265.

44. Gray, *Collaborating*, 166–176.

45. Selin and Chavez, "Developing a Collaborative Model," 189.

46. Rosabeth Moss Kanter, *When Giants Learn to Dance: Mastering the Challenge of Strategy, Management, and Careers in the 1990s* (New York: Simon and Schuster, 1989), 142.

47. Nancy Roberts and Raymond Bradley, "Stakeholder Collaboration and Innovation: A Study of Public Policy Initiation at the State Level," *Journal of Applied Behavioral Science* (June 1991):221.

48. Robert Axelrod, *The Evolution of Cooperation* (New York: Basic Books, 1984), 5–6.

49. For examples of successful common pool resource institutions, see Elinor Ostrom, *Governing the Commons: The Evolution of Institutions for Collective Action* (Cambridge, UK: Cambridge University Press, 1990).

50. Axelrod, *The Evolution of Cooperation*, 73–87.

51. Axelrod, *The Evolution of Cooperation*.

52. Axelrod, *The Evolution of Cooperation*, 126.

53. Axelrod, *The Evolution of Cooperation*, 130.

54. Axelrod, *The Evolution of Cooperation*, 135.

Chapter 4

1. Michael Jackson, "Letter to the Editor," *Feather River Bulletin*, September 1989.

2. See chapter 13, note 1.

3. In discussing the concept of an environmental sense of place, Professor Charles H.W. Foster notes that while we often think of place and space as synonymous, a sense of place is not purely a physical location (nor is it always delimited by geography). According to Foster, "Places are considered to be physical locations imbued with human meaning [that] display three primary characteristics: a landscape setting, a set of associated activities, and a significance to people. Thus, place involves both humans and nature, not the presence of one to the exclusion of the other." Charles H.W. Foster, *The Environmental Sense of Place: Precepts for the Environmental Practitioner* (Needham, MA: New England Natural Resources Center, June 1995), 2.

4. Richard L. Knight and Peter B. Landres, eds., *Stewardship Across Boundaries* (Washington, DC: Island Press, 1998).

5. Barbara Gray, "Conditions Facilitating Interorganizational Collaboration," *Human Relations* 38 (1985):930–931.

6. Gray, "Conditions Facilitating Interorganizational Collaboration," 930.

7. Charles H.W. Foster, "What Makes Regional Organizations Succeed or Fail?" Paper delivered at the Joint Symposium of the American and Canadian Water Resources Associations, Toronto, Ontario, April 2, 1990, 6.

8. The negotiation literature indicates that people are more risk-taking when faced with potential losses than when faced with potential benefits. Having a common threat draws on this psychological dynamic to foster cooperative action in response to a potential loss. See Bazerman, *Judgment in Managerial Decision Making*.

9. Beryl R. Collins and Emily Russell, *Protecting the New Jersey Pinelands* (New Brunswick, NJ: Rutgers University Press, 1988), 1.

10. Yaffee et al., *Ecosystem Management in the United States*, 250.

11. Lawrence S. Bacow and Michael Wheeler, *Environmental Dispute Resolution* (New York: Plenum, 1984), 46–50.

12. M. Sherif, "Superordinate Goals in the Reduction of Intergroup Conflicts," *American Journal of Sociology* 63 (1958):349–358.

13. Barbara Gray describes a number of strategies by which parties in conflict can identify common goals through "joint information searches," including group visioning processes to develop and evaluate future scenarios (Gray, "Conditions Facilitating Interorganizational Collaboration," 926). Similarly, the organizational management literature highlights the usefulness of creating a mission statement as a way of focusing a unit on its ultimate objectives. For example, organizational behavior scholar Ron Westrum notes the importance of multiparty groups developing a "common vision" of what is to be achieved in describing successful endangered species recovery efforts. Ron Westrum, "An Organizational Perspective," in Clark, Reading, and Clarke, *Endangered Species Recovery*, 331.

14. Kenneth Reardon, "Enhancing the Capacity of Community-Based Organizations in East St. Louis," *Journal of Planning and Research* 17 (1998):323–333.

15. Lax and Sebenius, *The Manager as Negotiator*.

16. Lax and Sebenius, *The Manager as Negotiator*.

Chapter 5

1. Much of the conflict over forest planning in the 1970s and early 1980s can be attributed to "a lack of opportunity for different groups to jointly determine where and how timber resources are available and with what consequences" (Wondolleck, *Public Lands Conflict and Resolution*, 200).

2. Warren Bennis and Patricia Ward Biederman, *Organizing Genius: The Secrets of Creative Collaboration* (Reading, MA: Addison-Wesley, 1997), 212.

3. Quoted in P. Sherlock, "Idaho Learns to Share Two Rivers," *High Country News*, May 13, 1996, 9–10.

4. Quoted in Sherlock, *High Country News*, 9–10.

5. 43 *Code of Federal Regulations* 1784.6-1.

6. 16 *U.S. Code* 1852 (1999).

7. Luther Propst, William F. Paleck, and Liz Rosan, "Partnerships across Park Boundaries: The Rincon Institute and Saguaro National Park," in Knight and Landres, *Stewardship Across Boundaries*, 257–278.

Chapter 6

1. Gray, *Collaborating*, 15; Wondolleck, *Public Lands Conflict and Resolution.*
2. The literature on effective ways to structure a collaborative process is extensive. See, e.g., Susan L. Carpenter and W.J.D. Kennedy, *Managing Public Disputes: A Practical Guide for Handling Conflict and Reaching Agreements* (San Francisco: Jossey-Bass, 1988); Moore, *The Mediation Process;* and Lawrence Susskind, Sarah McKearnan, and Jennifer Thomas-Larmer, eds., *The Consensus Building Handbook: A Comprehensive Guide to Reaching Agreement* (Thousand Oaks, CA: Sage, 1999).
3. Aengst et al., *Balancing Public Trust and Private Interest.*
4. The academic literature on collaboration agrees with this observation. University of California at Berkeley scholar Judy Innes argues for processes that are "communicatively rational." According to Innes, "A decision is 'communicatively rational' to the degree that it is reached consensually through deliberations involving all stakeholders, where all are equally empowered and fully informed, and where the conditions of ideal speech are met. . . . Communicatively rational decisions, then, are those that come about because there are good reasons for them rather than because of the political or economic power of particular stakeholders" (Innes, "Planning through Consensus Building," 461).
5. Clare M. Ryan, *Leadership in Regulatory Negotiations at the Environmental Protection Agency: An Analysis of Roles,* unpublished PhD dissertation (Ann Arbor: University of Michigan, 1996), 52.
6. Carpenter and Kennedy, *Managing Public Disputes.*
7. Gray, "Conditions Facilitating Interorganizational Collaboration," 924.
8. See, e.g., Michael Doyle and David Straus, *How to Make Meetings Work* (New York: Jove Books, 1976).
9. Barbara Gray views this process of establishing ground rules as "an essential step in assuring that the parties accept responsibility for the process" (Gray, *Collaborating*, 266–267).
10. Quoted in Frank Clifford, *Los Angeles Times,* November 15, 1995.

Chapter 7

1. See references listed in chapter 1, note 23.
2. Many academic and popular books describe the dimensions of such an approach. Most emphasize a multiphased problem-solving process. For example, Pennsylvania State University professor Barbara Gray identifies three overall stages of problem solving: problem setting, direction setting, and implementation. She writes that the "inability to achieve the appropriate conditions during each phase may be the best source of explanations to date for why collaborative efforts fail. For example, premature efforts to structure collaborations can render them ineffective because the appropriate mix of stakeholders has not been identified or because those participating have not yet agreed on a common direction" (Gray, "Conditions Facilitating Interorganizational Collaboration," 932). Krannich, Carroll, Daniels, and Walker advocate a process they term "collaborative learning" for effectively involving stakeholders in complex natural resource conflicts and promoting collaborative sharing of information and ideas. According to

these authors, "Collaborative learning redefines the conflict or problem as a 'situation.' Rather than trying to find 'the solution,' parties are encouraged to develop improvements over the status quo situation. Results are measured as 'progress' rather than by some absolute standard of 'success'" (Richard Krannich, Matthew Carroll, Steven Daniels, and Greg Walker, *Incorporating Social Assessment and Public Involvement into Ecosystem-Based Resource Management: Applications to the East Side Ecosystem Management Project,* report prepared for USDA Eastside Ecosystem Management Project, under order no. 43-OEOO-4-9111, 1994, 112).

3. Barbara Gray emphasizes that "it is important that parties know up front the scope of the effort to which they are proceeding, since differing expectations can derail the proceedings." At times, reaching an appropriate problem definition will involve expanding the issues on the table to address the interests of a critical stakeholder. In other cases, the process of defining the problem should narrow the issue to make the collaboration more manageable and focused (Gray, *Collaborating,* 57).

4. Roy J. Lewicki, Joseph A. Litterer, John W. Minton, and David M. Saunders, *Negotiation,* 2nd edition (Burr Ridge, IL: Irwin, 1994), 83.

5. Richard L. Wallace and Tim W. Clark, "Solving Problems in Endangered Species Conservation: An Introduction to Problem Orientation," *Endangered Species Update* 16 (March/April 1999):28–34.

6. Linda L. Putnam and Majia Holmer, "Framing, Reframing, and Issue Development," in Linda L. Putnam and Michael E. Roloff, eds., *Communication and Negotiation* (Thousand Oaks, CA: Sage, 1992), 128–155.

7. Chris Argyris and Donald A. Schön, *Theory in Practice: Increasing Professional Effectiveness* (San Francisco: Jossey-Bass, 1974).

8. Roger Fisher, William Ury, and Bruce Patton, *Getting to Yes: Negotiating Agreement Without Giving In,* 2nd edition (New York: Penguin, 1991).

9. Lewicki et al., *Negotiation,* 85.

10. Quoted in Hank Fischer, *Wolf Wars* (Helena, MT: Falcon, 1995), 58.

11. Osborne and Gaebler, *Reinventing Government,* 108–137.

12. Julia M. Wondolleck and Clare M. Ryan, "What Hat Do I Wear Now? An Examination of Agency Roles in Collaborative Processes," *Negotiation Journal* 15 (April 1999):107.

13. The importance of effective information sharing to the success of collaborative groups is corroborated by other studies of collaboration. For example, Bennis and Biederman's study of six collaborative efforts that the authors termed Great Groups found, "All Great Groups share information effectively" (Bennis and Biederman, *Organizing Genius,* 212). Krannich and coauthors propose the following three-step process of collaborative learning: In the first step, parties emphasize "common understanding" of a situation by exchanging information, discussing best- and worst-case futures, and using maps or other techniques to visually represent the situation. In the second step, participants brainstorm possible improvements to the status quo situation that would address specific interests and concerns. In the final stage, participants discuss and evaluate the suggestions for improvements. These authors argue that following such a process "encourages people to learn actively, to think systemically, and to gain knowledge from one another about a particular problem situation" (Krannich et al. *Incorporating Social Assessment and Public Involvement,* 113–114).

14. John Stuart Mill, *Principles of Political Economy*, 5th edition (New York: D. Appleton, 1897).

15. For example, Fisher, Ury, and Patton emphasize the importance of considering multiple options to encourage participants to recognize the trade-offs inherent in the different options and to help generate a solution that promotes the interests of multiple parties (Fisher, Ury, and Patton, *Getting to Yes*, 56–80).

16. Fisher, Ury, and Patton, *Getting to Yes*, 60–65.

Chapter 8

1. Some quotations in this section are from Applegate Partnership, "Working Beyond Conflict Towards Solutons," (CPO Box 277, Applegate, OR 97530), Video, n.d.

2. Gray, "Conditions Facilitating Interorganizational Collaboration," 921.

3. Harold P. Simonson, *Beyond the Frontier: Writers, Western Regionalism, and a Sense of Place* (Fort Worth: Texas Christian University Press, 1989), 145.

4. Unfortunately, agency commitment to the Blue Mountains Natural Resources Institute faltered when the institutes's budget was eliminated in January 2000.

5. Fisher, Ury, and Patton, Getting to Yes, 81–94.

6. Barry G. Rabe, *Beyond NIMBY: Hazardous Waste Siting in Canada and the United States* (Washington, DC: Brookings Institution, 1994), 80.

7. Rabe, *Beyond NIMBY*, 74.

Chapter 9

1. Kanter, *When Giants Learn to Dance*, 158.

2. Caleb Solomon, "Clearing the Air," *Wall Street Journal*, March 29, 1993, A1.

3. Michael Schrage, *Shared Minds: The New Technologies of Collaboration* (New York: Random House, 1990), 153.

4. Kanter, "Collaborative Advantage," 105.

Chapter 10

1. Selin and Chavez, "Developing a Collaborative Model," 191.

2. In the policy literature, these individuals have been called "fixers" (Eugene Bardach, *The Implementation Game: What Happens After a Bill Becomes a Law* [Cambridge, MA: MIT Press, 1977]). The organizational management literature refers to them as "maestros" and highlights their importance to successful innovation (Westrum, "An Organizational Perspective," 343–345). A study commissioned by Texas Instruments found that of seventy new product introductions, those that succeeded were generally those that had a "volunteer champion" to lead them. Those without such a champion typically failed (Tom Peters, "The Rational Model Has Led Us Astray," *Planning Review* [March 1982]:16–22).

3. Bennis and Biederman, *Organizing Genius*, 199–200.

4. For example, the literature on business alliances recommends that organizations charge specific individuals with the responsibility of taking a leadership role in managing their collaborative relationships. "Companies seeking to build and sustain interorganizational alliances need to recognize and implement the roles of corporate 'statesmen,' 'diplomats,' and 'peace observers' who not only seek out and build peace treaties and alliances . . . but also, on an ongoing basis, guard against misunderstandings, misinterpretations, and perceived or real betrayals

that may lead to the disintegration of the relationship. The partners in the alliance need to recognize that peace is often fragile, and once the initial euphoria of reaching the treaty (alliance) has faded, the statesmen and diplomats (relationship/boundary managers) will need to be continuously vigilant in anticipating conflict and nurture the alliance by managing these risks proactively" (Kuldeep Kumar and Hans G. Van Dissel, "Sustainable Collaboration: Managing Conflict and Cooperation in Interorganizational Systems," *MIS Quarterly* [September 1996]:279-300).

5. Applegate Partnership, "Working Beyond Conflict Toward Solutions."

6. Kanter, "Collaborative Advantage," 103. Also, Charles Foster recommends that regional collaborative efforts start with "issues that are visible, tangible, and most important, doable" (Charles H.W. Foster, "What Makes Regional Organizations Succeed or Fail?" paper delivered at the Joint Symposium of the American and Canadian Water Resources Associations, Toronto, Ontario, April 2, 1990, 6).

Chapter 12

1. Julia M. Wondolleck, "The Role of Training in Providing Opportunities for Environmental and Natural Resource Dispute Resolution," *Environmental Impact Assessment Review* 8 (Fall 1988):233–248.

2. We are grateful to Professor Margaret Shannon, State University of New York at Buffalo, for this insight.

3. What are the consequences of a lack of broader agency commitment to collaborative efforts in an agency? Our studies have shown that the result, more often than not, is that bad situations are made worse. Time and again, when agency commitment lapsed, we heard comments such as: "I no longer work with the Forest Service on any issues in any kind of collaborative process. . . . While I also have grave doubts about the efficacy of the legal process, lawsuits seem to be the only way to change anything." Another individual expressed, "I now feel negotiation with the agency is almost always fruitless. There are exceptions, but they are rare." Yet another concluded, "These approaches would have worked in Region [X] if the Forest Service operated in good faith. Because they have not, there is a systematic lack of trust of the Forest Service. This will be a tough hurdle for the agency to get over." Even a Forest Service planner commented, "I am disappointed, to say the least, if not less, in the Forest Service's commitment to consensus building and trust building. . . . Much has been lost by broken promises." In short, rather than building the bridges necessary for effective resource management, critical bridges were burned when agency commitment flagged.

Chapter 13

1. The Quincy Library Group (QLG) is an interesting anomaly in collaborative resource management. As described in chapter 4, it began as many collaborative initiatives begin: in the energies and willingness of traditional adversaries in a community to see the problems they faced as shared problems that they all had a responsibility to do something about. Most aspects of the QLG's development mirror the patterns of other community-based collaborative groups. However, several unique events shifted this collaborative process into a category of its own. The lack of direct involvement (for whatever reason) of Forest Service officials responsible for the three national forests affected by the QLG's plan meant that the process was not fully representative or tied to existing law and regulation. Out

of frustration with seemingly unresponsive federal land managers, the group took its plan to an enthusiastic congressional delegation, who embraced it and ushered it through the legislative arena. Eventually, Congress enacted a modified QLG plan and forced its implementation on the Forest Service.

Those events have been troublesome for QLG participants, the Forest Service, Congress, national environmental organizations, and, indeed, those of us who view collaboration as an appropriate and effective process for enhancing environmental and natural resource management. There have been many accusations and counteraccusations about what is "to blame" for the manner in which this process spun off in a new direction. Some argue that it was the Forest Service's reluctance to participate as a full partner; others that it was the QLG's failure to fully include those federal land managers. Still others blame the decision to oppose the group's efforts by the national environmental community, while others attribute it to the failure of the QLG to include those interests. Still others cite the overzealousness of elected officials who raised the banner of a community success story and thereby politicized it in ways that tarnished its cooperative beginnings.

Rather than a model collaborative effort, the QLG suddenly became the focus of an acrimonious debate. Its original consensus agreement has been transformed into a congressionally imposed solution. It has been strategically lauded and denounced by supporters and detractors, portrayed by the media in positive as well as negative terms, and is confusing to onlookers who do not know what to make of either the QLG or the notion of collaboration in natural resource management. From our perspective, the QLG story contains many important lessons about how to structure and manage a collaborative resource management process and how to ensure that it is credible, legitimate, and accountable to the broader public interest.

2. McCloskey, "The Skeptic: Collaboration Has Its Limits."

3. George Cameron Coggins, "Of Californicators, Quiblings and Crazies: Some Perils of Devolved Collaboration," *Chronicle of Community* 2 (Winter 1998): 27–31.

4. See, e.g., Susskind and Cruikshank, *Breaking the Impasse*, 21–33; Judith E. Innes, "Evaluating Consensus Building," in Susskind, McKearnan, and Thomas-Larmer, *The Consensus Building Handbook*, 631–675.

5. Hays, *Conservation and the Gospel of Efficiency.*

6. Hays, *Conservation and the Gospel of Efficiency.*

7. Paul J. Culhane, *Public Lands Politics: Interest Group Influence on the Forest Service and the Bureau of Land Management* (Baltimore: Johns Hopkins University Press, 1981).

8. 5 *U.S.Code* app. 1-15 (1988 & Supp. I 1989).

9. Michelle Nuszkiewicz, "Twenty Years of the Federal Advisory Committee Act: It's Time for Some Changes," *Southern California Law Review* 65 (1992): 966–967.

10. Kaufman, *The Forest Ranger,* 177–178.

11. Michael Frome, *The Forest Service,* 2nd edition (Boulder, CO: Westview, 1984), 54.

12. Aengst et al., *Balancing Public Trust and Private Interest.*

13. Blahna and Yonts-Shepard, "Public Involvement in Resource Planning," 216.

14. Osborne and Gaebler, *Reinventing Government,* 111.

15. Osborne and Gaebler, *Reinventing Government,* 111.

16. Susskind and Cruikshank, *Breaking the Impasse*, 11. See also Lawrence E. Susskind, "Environmental Mediation and the Accountability Problem," *Vermont Law Review* 6 (1981):40–47.

17. In a diversity of political forces lie the checks and balances that the country's founders put in place and that guard against undue exploitation by any one interest. Diversity may cause other problems, but it is less likely to result in the capture of government institutions by narrow interests. Political scientist Paul Culhane commented in 1981 that changes in political organization in the 1970s enabled the Forest Service and BLM to change their approach to controlling capture: "The agency's more balanced clientele eliminated the capture threat. One district manager noted that both the Forest Service and BLM 'have a unique opportunity among federal agencies to avoid capture by their users because they have multiple users'" (Culhane, *Public Lands Politics*, 227).

18. U.S. Department of Agriculture, "National Forest System Land and Resource Management Planning: Proposed Rule," 64 *Federal Register* 54073-54112, October 5, 1999; 43 *Code of Federal Regulations* 1784.6-1.

19. The recent USDA Committee of Scientists that convened to review national forest management found that most land managers were willing to accept independent review if it meant more on-the-ground flexibility (Committee of Scientists, *Sustaining the People's Lands*, xxx–xxxi).

20. See, e.g., Reed F. Noss, Michael A. O'Connell, and Dennis D. Murphy, *The Science of Conservation Planning: Habitat Conservation Under the Endangered Species Act* (Washington, DC: Island Press, 1997), 111–136; and Richard Margoluis and Nick Salafsky, *Measures of Success: Designing, Managing and Monitoring Conservation and Development Projects* (Washington, DC: Island Press, 1998).

21. John and Mlay, "Community-Based Environmental Protection," 354.

22. John, *Civic Environmentalism*, 14.

23. Yaffee and Wondolleck, *Negotiating Survival*.

24. Quoted in Osborne and Gaebler, *Reinventing Government*, 108. This advice is consistent with Osborne and Gaebler's *Reinventing Government* prescription that government be "mission-driven." See pages 108–137.

25. Quoted in Nuszkiewicz, "Twenty Years of the Federal Advisory Committee Act," 966–967.

26. Regional fishery councils are exempted from FACA compliance under the Magnuson-Stevens Act at 16 *U.S. Code* 1852i(1)(1999). ESA Recovery teams are exempt from FACA at 16 *U.S. Code* 1533(f)(2)(1999). National Marine Sanctuary advisory councils are exempt from FACA at 16 *U.S. Code* 1445a(1999).

27. See note 1, this chapter.

28. See discussion at the beginning of chapter 3.

Index

Accountability, ensuring, 229
  accountability, the issue of, 232–33
  controlling behavior, agencies', 234–35
  critics' concerns, the, 230–32
  Federal Advisory Committee Act, 242–43
  flexibility and control, the balance between, 235–37
  monitoring and evaluation, 241–42
  National Environmental Policy Act, 243
  performance standards, 240–41
  process-derived accountability, 237–39
  promoting accountable collaboration, 237–45
  responsibility for, 244–45
  review, opportunity for appeal and independent scientific, 239–40
Acknowledging and rewarding efforts, 171
Adams County (ID), 206–7
Adaptive management approach, 136–37
Administrative Conference of the United States, xiv
Adversarial decision-making processes, xii, 7, 122–23
  see also Them to us, transforming
Advice, providing expertise and, 207–9
Advisory committees, 95–96, 234–35
Agencies developing capacity to deal with resource management challenges:
  attitudes, influence perceptions and, 223
  committing to the process and products of collaboration, 225–28
  communities, developing, 44–45
  continuity within agency collaborative relationships, 226–27
  enabling employees to be effective at collaboration, 218–22
  encouraging development of collaborative relationships, 222–24
  enhancing agency leadership, five principles for, 213–14
  evaluating the experience with collaboration, 224–26
  flexibility, 221–22
  imagining collaborative possibilities, 214–17
  incentives, 223–24
  interest groups, 30–31, 238
  multi-agency shared visioning /planning processes, 222
  public service, collaborative relationships forming basis for, 42–43
  resources, provide, 220–21
  support for collaboration, building, 150–51
  traditional response, the, 234–35
  train individuals and teams, 218–19
  updating skills of workforce, 41, 43–44
  workforce composition, enhance, 219–20
  see also Organizational listings; individual subject headings/agencies
Agriculture, United States Department of (USDA), 14
  see also Forest Service, U.S.
Alaska recreation plan:
  cultural differences, 172
  flexibility, 131
  framing problems appropriately, 127–28
  funding, 107
  overworking the public, 114
  ownership of the process, 148
  patient, being, 192
  see also Tongass National Forest
Alberta Province (Canada), 154–55
American firms and pioneering metaphor of the individualistic entrepreneur, 51
Amoco, 163
Amtrak, 28–29
Anacostia River:
  coordinating efforts, 37–38
  geographic integration, landscape-scale, 125
  innovation, using the symbolic power of, 189–90
  organizational structure, an efficient, 112–13
  success, installing hope by demonstrating, 169–70
Animas River, 153

Applegate Partnership, 4
  adversarial conflict, 7
  communication, 151–52
  responsibility/commitment, fostering a
    sense of, 139–42
  trust and respect, fostering, 59, 163, 165
  videos used to convey images of suc-
    cess, 215
Arkansas State Park Service, 205
Army Corps of Engineers, U.S., 35, 38
AT&T, 90
Attitudes and perceptions, barriers due
  to:
  agencies developing capacity to deal
    with resource management chal-
    lenges, 223
  group attitudes about each other, 59–60
  mistrust, 58–59
  organizational norms and culture,
    60–62
  support for collaboration, lack of,
    62–63
Audubon Society, 39, 83

Barataria-Terrebonne NEP, 95
Barriers to collaboration, 48–49, 66–68
  see also Attitudes and perceptions, bar-
    riers due to; Institutional/structural
    barriers
Beartree Challenge:
  communication, working at outreach
    through, 90–91
  energetic/dedicated individuals, 175–77
  fact-finding, joint, 132–33
  identity, creating a strong project, 75
  New Perspectives Program, 184
  risk, willing to take a, 182
  seams in the bureaucratic wall, ex-
    ploiting, 184
  support, building public and political,
    204
Biases in human judgment, xi, 50–51
Blackfoot Challenge:
  established relationships, capitalizing
    on, 163
  Fish and Wildlife Service, U.S., 130
  history behind, 97
  small, the value of starting, 188
  social networks, using community-
    based, 185
  videos used to convey images of suc-
    cess, 215
Blue Mountains Natural Resources Institute (BMNRI), 153

Bob Marshall Wilderness Complex, 175
Boundary-spanning forces, traditional, 6
"Bowling Alone: America's Declining So-
  cial Capital" (Putnam), 7
Bowling Green State University, 79
Bridges to a sustainable future, building:
  guide to making collaboration work,
    19–21
  innovation, reasons behind, 5–11
  Kiowa National Grasslands, 3–4
  management, a new style of resource, 3,
    11–18
  uses and mechanisms of collaboration,
    18–19
"Building Bridges across Agency Bound-
  aries: In Search of Excellence in the U.S.
  Forest Service," xii
Bureau of Land Management (BLM):
  Coordinated Resource Management
    process, 183
  Elkhorn Mountains, 87–88
  Resource Advisory Councils, 95, 239
  resource constraints, 9
  San Pedro River, 52
Bureau of Reclamation, 199
Business, reliance on big, 10
Butterflies:
  burning areas to create habitats for, 123
  Karner blue, 79, 114, 135
  Oregon silverspot, 38, 132, 178–79

California Coastal Conservancy, 199
California's Natural Communities Conservation Planning process, 183
California State Water Board, 199
Cameron County Coexistence Committee (TX):
  crisis, seeing opportunities in, 186
  misperceptions and fostering under-
    standing, shattering, 159, 162
  nurturing/honoring/respecting   rela-
    tionships, 166–67
  problem-focused approach, 120–22
  social networks, using community-
    based, 186
  success begets success, 190–91
  videos used to convey images of suc-
    cess, 215
Canada, 154–55
Chicago Tribune, 40
Chicago Wilderness project, 4
Circle A Ranch, 196
Civic engagement, decline in, 7–9
Civic environmentalism, 17, 240

Clark County (NV):
  Endangered Species Act, 241
  facilitation, 109
  meetings, well-managed, 111–12
  public involvement, 102–4, 107
  small, the value of starting, 187
  steering committees, 113
  technical advisory committee, 135
Clifton-Choctaw Tribe, 45, 148, 172–73
Coalition for Unified Recreation in the Eastern Sierra (CURES):
  facilitation, 109
  fun as a motivator for involvement, 169
  interdependence, recognizing, 143–44
  interests, community of, 128
  leading by example, 144–45
  processes, crafting meaningful/effective/enduring, 100–101
  purpose, a sense of ongoing, 116
  small, the value of starting, 188
  visioning process, 81
Collaboration, the challenge of, 47
  advice, summary, 249–50
  attitudes and perceptions, barriers due to, 58–63
  barriers, overcoming, 66–68
  broadening traditional notion of collaboration, xiii
  defining, xiii
  dilemma, the basic, 48–51
  evaluating the experience of collaboration, 224–25
  guide to getting started, 250–52
  institutional and structural barriers, 51–57
  process of collaboration, problems with the, 63–66
  see also individual subject headings
Collaboration, why, 23
  agencies/organizations/communities, developing, 41–45
  decisions, support for and making wise, 30–35
  getting work done, 36–41
  understanding, building, 24–30
  see also individual subject headings
Color, the Forest Service recruiting people of, 43–44
Commitment to the collaborative approach, 63, 148–53, 225–28
  see also Responsibility/commitment, fostering a sense of
Common ground, building on:

compatible interests, 82–85
fears/problems, shared, 76–78
goals/interests, shared, 78–82
place or community, a sense of, 73–76
Quincy Library Group, 71–73
Commons, tragedy of the, 49
Communication:
  Applegate Partnership, 151–52
  computers, 222
  Negrito ecosystem, 152
  outreach through, 89–92
  spark attention and ideas of those beyond agency walls, 217
  understanding, building, 25
Communities:
  agencies and, relationships between, 42, 44–45
  events and field trips, community, 73–75
  interests, acknowledge and make sense of the community, 16
  place or community, a sense of, 73–76
  resources linked to community needs, 206–7
  social networks, using community-based, 185–86
  values/attitudes/norms vary between, 171–73
Compatible interests, 82–85
Competition and cooperation, managing tension between, 5, 48–49
Computer-based communications, 222
Concurrence and support, building, 34–35
Conferences, collaboration as the topic in, 216–17
Consensus decision making, 105–6, 109
Consumption of natural resources, 26
Continuity within agency collaborative relationships, 226–27
Coordinating efforts, 37–38, 93–94
Costs, shared, 154–55
Creating a Forestry for the 21st Century: The Science of Ecosystem Management (Kohm & Franklin), 15
Creative thinking, 133–34
Credible information, bounding the problem with, 134–37
Crisis, seeing opportunities in, 186
Cultural differences, 171–73
Culture/norms, organizational, 60–62

Darby Partnership, 26–27, 107, 108, 113, 133

Decentralized decision making, 16–17
Decision-making processes:
    adversarial, xii, 7, 122–23
    biased and ineffective, xi–xii
    changes in the processes through which
        choices are made, 31
    concurrence and support, building,
        34–35
    consensus, 105–6, 109
    decentralized, 16–17
    dispute resolution, 33–34
    habitat conservation plans, 102
    legitimate/fair/wise, 231
    organizational boundaries, building re-
        lationships across, 31
    process-derived accountability, 237–39
    recrafting resource management, 32
    solving common problems, 32
    traditional, 60, 101–2
    value-based choices, 30
    see also Problem-focused approach
Deerlodge National Forest, 33
Defense Department, U.S., 52
Differences, cultural and community,
    171–73
Dispute resolution, 33–34
Diversification process, 6
Double-loop learning, 127
Ducks Unlimited, xiii
Dunes, preserving, see Guadalupe-Nipomo
    Dunes Preserve

Earth Day, 12
East Fork Quinn River, 195–97
East St. Louis (IL), 82
Ecosystem-based approach to resource
    management, 14–16, 183
Educating the public, 28–29
Eel River, 27, 122, 180–81, 199
Elected officials, working with, 204–6
Elkhorn Mountains, 9, 87–89, 126, 132,
    142–43, 151
Energetic/dedicated individuals:
    Beartree Challenge, 175–77
    extraordinary effort, 179–80
    individual leaders, 177–79
    local champions, 179
Entrepreneurial and proactive approach:
    Beartree Challenge, 175–77
    energetic/dedicated individuals, 176–80
    help, getting and giving, 200
    innovation, 10–11
    opportunities, taking advantage of ex-
        isting, 183–86

persistence, 191–93
    proactive vs. reactive, 180–83
    success, nothing succeeds like, 186–91
Environmental assessments (EAs), 129
Environmental groups, 62
    see also individual group
Environmental impact statement (EIS),
    102
Environmentalism, civic, 17, 240
Environmental   Protection   Agency
    (EPA):
    Amoco, 163
    Community-Based   Environmental
        Protection, 17
    dispute resolution, 33
    funds to enable groups to participate,
        107
    Great Lakes National Program, 115
    institutionalizing collaboration, 115
    National Estuary and Remedial Action
        Planning programs, 10, 95, 183
    outside stakeholders, involvement of, 35
    pesticides, 119
    wetlands, 40
    wood-burning stoves, 30
Environmental   Review   Committee
    (ERC), 205
Equipment, 198–99
ESL Action Research Project (ESLARP),
    82
ESRI, 199
Evaluating the experience with collabora-
    tion, 224–26, 241–42, 248
Expertise, the democratization of, 25, 36,
    200–203

Facilitation, 108–10, 203
Facilities, new, 97–98
Fact-finding,   managing   uncertainty
    through, 29–30, 132–33
Failures, learning from, 192–93
Fairness, 153–55, 231
Falcon, Aplomado, 119–20, 170–71
Fears/problems, shared, 76–78
Feather River, 93–94, 105–6, 168
Feather River Bulletin, 71
Field trips and community events, 73–75
Fire and butterfly habitats, 123
Fire mitigation measures, 208
Firewood sales, 146
Fish and Wildlife Service, U.S. (FWS):
    Blackfoot Challenge, 130
    butterflies, 123
    Endangered Species Act, xi, 241

funding, 199
Habitat Conservation Planning program, 10
Huron-Manistee National Forest, 37
negative perception of, 159–60
outside stakeholders, involvement of, 35
Ozark National Forest, 205
Partners for Wildlife Program, 183
public involvement, 13
resource constraints, 9
Warbler, Kirtland's, 29
wetlands, 39
Flexibility in attitudes/procedures, 53–56, 123–24, 131, 221–22, 235–37
Florida Department of Environmental Regulation (FDER), 53
Forest Ranger, The (Kaufman), 235
Forest Service, U.S.:
    Amtrak, 28–29
    anger and frustration focused at, 13
    Beartree Challenge, 90–91
    "Building Bridges across Agency Boundaries: In Search of Excellence in the U.S. Forest Service," xii
    butterfly, Oregon silverspot, 132
    Challenge Cost-Share programs, 10, 183
    Clifton-Choctaw Tribe, 45
    Coalition for Unified Recreation in the Eastern Sierra, 144–45
    color, recruiting people of, 43–44
    Deerlodge National Forest, 33
    distrust of, 58
    East Fork Quinn River, 195–97
    Elkhorn Mountains, 87–88
    Endangered Species Act, 241
    facilitation, 203
    fact-finding, joint, 132
    firewood sales, 146
    flexibility in policies/procedures, 54, 131
    funds to enable groups to participate, 107, 199
    goats, 136
    Huron-Manistee National Forest, 37
    implementation of national forest planning, xi
    Kika de la Garza National Goat Research Center, 203
    Kiowa National Grasslands, 3
    Mill Creek Canyon Management Partnership, 39–40
    New Perspectives program, 183, 184
    Ozark National Forest, 205
    public involvement, 104–5
    resource constraints, 9, 36

    resources linked to community needs, 206–7
    Roan Mountains, 95, 202–3
    San Bernardino National Forest, 208
    technical planning process, 52
    Tongass National Forest, 28, 91
    traditional roles, going beyond, 130–31
    training individuals and teams, 218–19
    Upper Stony Creek initiative, 202
    Warbler, Kirtland's, 29
    wood fiber, industrial-sized production of, 11–12
Fragmentation of interests/power/authority, 6, 52
Framing problems appropriately, 127–28
Fun as a motivator for involvement, 168–69
Functional activities on a single piece of ground, integration of, 125–26
Funds to enable groups to participate, 107, 199–200, 204–5, 221
Future, sustainable, see Bridges to a sustainable future, building

Geographic information system (GIS), 141
Geographic integration, landscape-scale, 15, 125
Georgia Pacific (GP), 43, 59, 83–84, 191, 193
Gila River, 74, 131
Goals:
    conflicting missions and, 52–53
    shared interests and, 78–82
    unifying visions and, 142–43
Goats, 136, 203
Government, reliance on big, 10
    see also Agencies developing capacity to deal with resource management challenges; Legislation; Trust in government and each other
Great Lakes National Program, 115
Green Mountain National Forest, 110–11, 145, 161, 169
Grizzly bears, 175
    see also Beartree Challenge
Group attitudes about each other, 59–60
Guadalupe-Nipomo Dunes Preserve, 84–85, 90–92, 144, 157–59, 172

Habitat conservation plans (HCPs):
    butterfly, Karner blue, 114, 135
    decision-making processes, 102
    Endangered Species Act, 183, 240–41

Habitat conservation plans (*continued*)
  facilitation, 109
  Fish and Wildlife Service, U.S., 10
  National Environmental Policy Act,
    236
  Orange County, 107, 116, 133
  Plum Creek, 104
  salamander, Red Hills, 135–36
  San Diego County, 112
  see also Clark County (NV)
Help, getting and giving:
  advice, providing expertise and, 207–9
  East Fork Quinn River, 195–97
  expertise and ideas, accessing, 200–203
  resource mobilization, 198–200
  resources linked to community needs,
    206–7
  support, building public and political,
    203–6
Henry's Fork Watershed Council, 92–93
High Country News, 93
Holistic perspective, 124–26
Hope, demonstrating success to instill,
  169–70
Humboldt National Forest, 195–97
Huron-Manistee National Forest, 37, 93
Huron River:
  expertise, acquiring, 202
  field trips, 73–74
  fun as a motivator for involvement, 169
  ownership of the problem, 147
  science and management, 135
  self-sustaining processes, 116–17

Identity, creating a strong project, 74–75
Imagery, positive, 17–18, 214–17
Impasse, the costs of, 6–7, 13, 25
Importance and need, a sense of, 116
Incentives, 51–52, 223–24
Inclusive and representative efforts, 106–7
Individual effort and success of the
  group, 177–79
Individuals *vs.* organizations, focusing
  on, 161–62
Informal relationships, 92–93, 160–61
Information, bounding the problem with
  credible, 134–37
Information, democratization of, 13,
  24–27, 215
Innovation, 5
  entrepreneurs at work, 10–11
  impasse, the costs of, 6–7
  mistrust and a declining sense of re-
    sponsibility, 7–9

no other way to get things done, 9–10
  symbolic power of, 189–90
Institutionalizing collaboration, 115–16
Institutional/structural barriers:
  goals/missions, conflicting, 52–53
  inflexible policies/procedures, 53–56
  opportunity or incentives, lack of, 51–52
  resource constraints, 56–57
Integrative perspective, 124–26
Interaction opportunities, see Opportunities for interaction, creating new
Interdependence, recognizing, 143–44
Interests, community of:
  acknowledge and make some sense of,
    16
  agency decisions, challenging, 30–31
  compatible interests, 82–85
  diversity of action-oriented interest
    groups at local/regional/national
    levels, 238
  fragmentation of interests, 6, 52
  problem-focused approach, 128
  shared interests/goals, 78–82
  support, building public and political,
    204
International Paper, 135–36
Internet, the, 215
Interstate Commerce Commission (ICC),
  233

Japanese firms, 51
Jargon, using, 134

Kika de la Garza National Goat Research
  Center, 203
Kiowa National Grasslands, 3–4, 37, 124,
  182, 188
Kisatchie National Forest, 45

Laguna Atascosa National Wildlife Refuge,
  119–21, 170–71
Langston University, 203
Leadership, 144–45, 177–80
  see also Agencies developing capacity to
    deal with resource management chal-
    lenges
Learning:
  double-loop, 127
  failure, learning from, 192–93
  mutual, committing to a process of,
    132–34
  public, learning from the, 27–28

Legislation:
Clean Water Act, 11, 95, 152, 196, 232
Endangered Species Act (ESA), xi, 10–11, 102, 123, 183, 232, 240–41
Federal Advisory Committee Act (FACA), 56, 232, 234–36, 242–43
Freedom of Information Act (FOIA), 56, 245
Magnuson-Stevens Act, 95, 243
National Environmental Policy Act (NEPA), 6, 129, 222, 234, 236, 243
National Forest Management Act (NFMA), 6, 11, 239, 240
Sherman Antitrust Act, 245
Legitimacy of public decision making process, 231
Lewis and Clark National Forest, 175
see also Beartree Challenge
Lizard, Coachella Valley fringe-toed, 240
Local champions, 179
Local focus, a, 75–76
Logging, 28, 182–83, 198–99

Malpai Borderlands Group, 4, 32
Management practices/policies:
adaptive management approach, 136–37
anecdotes and metaphors, xv
broadening traditional notion of collaborative relationships, xiii
complexity/uncertainty/change, dealing with, 15–16
decentralized decision making, 16–17
decision-making processes, biased/ineffective, xi–xii
evolution of, 11–14
geographic/temporal scales, using, 14–15
implications for agencies/individuals seeking to build bridges, xvi
interests, acknowledge and make sense of community, 16
positive imagery, 17–18
revolutionary approach, 5
sharing management responsibility, 38–39
storytelling, xv
successful, xii–xiv
time, issue of change over, xiv
see also individual subject headings
Manti-LaSal National Forest, 109, 185, 202, 203
Maryland's Save Our Shores, 202
McKenzie Watershed Council, 111–12
Media, working with the, 204, 217

Meetings, well-managed, 110–12, 216–17
Memorandum of understanding (MOU), 34–35, 87–89, 94–95, 151
Metaphors, xv
Michigan Department of Natural Resources (MDNR), 29, 37, 39, 241
Mill Creek Canyon Management Partnership, 34–35, 39–40, 78–79, 123–24, 128–29
Minority population recruited by Forest Service, 43–44
Misperceptions and fostering understanding, shattering, 159–60, 162
Mission statements, 80–82
Molokai (HI), 76
Monitoring and evaluation, 241–42
Mono Basin National Forest, 57, 81
Mono Lake, 99
Motivating involvement:
acknowledging and rewarding efforts, 171
fun, 168–69
Laguna Atascosa National Wildlife Refuge, 170–71
Oak Openings project, 170
success, instilling hope by demonstrating, 169–70
Mt. Magazine, 205
Mt. Roan advisory committee, 95–96, 136
Multi-agency shared visioning /planning processes, 222

Nanticoke Watershed Alliance, 111, 162, 164, 165, 202
National Association of Conservation Districts, 39
National Estuary Programs (NEPs), 95, 183
National Fish and Wildlife Foundation (NFWF), 39
National Park Service, 37, 168
National Wildlife Federation (NWF), 33–34
National Wild Turkey Federation (NWTF), 43, 59, 83–84, 193
Natural Areas Stewardship, Inc. (NASI), 96
Natural Resource Conservation Service (NRCS), 3, 80
Natural Resources Defense Council, 12
Nature Conservancy, The (TNC):
butterfly, Oregon silverspot, 38, 123, 132, 178–79
ecoregional planning efforts, 183

Nature Conservancy (*continued*)
fact-finding, joint, 132
geographic integration, landscape-scale, 125
Guadalupe-Nipomo Dunes Preserve, 84–85, 90, 144, 157–59
institutionalizing collaboration, 115
Molokai (HI), 76
San Pedro River, 52
Negrito ecosystem:
communication, 152
consensus decision making, 105–6
elected officials, working with, 204–5
Forest Service, U.S., 130
identifying with a place, 74
integrating different elements of a problem, 126
ownership of the process, 148
persistence pays off, 191
NEP, *see* National Estuary Programs
Nipomo Dunes, *see* Guadalupe-Nipomo Dunes Preserve
NJ Ranches, 196
Noncombative approach to discussions, 122–23
Nongovernmental organizations, xvi, 24
agencies reinforcing their own tough decisions, 35
inflexibility, procedural, 54
opportunities for interaction, creating new, 96–97
resource constraints, 57
see also specific organizations
Norms/culture, organizational, 60–62
Northeast Delta Resource Conservation & Development District, 76
North Klamath Bioregional Group, 145–46
Nurturing/honoring/respecting relationships, 166–67

Oak Openings project:
inclusive and representative efforts, 106
institutionalizing collaboration, 115
mission statements, 81–82
motivating involvement, 170
nongovernmental organizations, 96
ownership of the problem, 147
patient, being, 192
shared goals, 79
support, building public/political, 203–4
Olympic National Park, 61
Opportunities for interaction, creating new:
advisory committees, 95–96

communication, working at outreach through, 89–92
coordinators, 93–94
crisis, seeing opportunities in, 186
Elkhorn Mountains, 87–89
entrepreneurial and proactive approach, 183–86
facilities, new, 97–98
informal relationships, 92–93
institutional barriers, 51–52
memorandums of understanding, 94–95
nongovernmental organizations, 96–97
stories, provide opportunities for participants to tell their own, 216
Orange County (CA), 107, 116, 133
Oregon Watershed Enhancement program, 10
Organizational boundaries, building relationships across, 31
Organizational capacity, 41–42
Organizational norms and culture, 60–62
Organizational structure, an efficient, 112–15
Owl, spotted, xi, 60
Owl Mountain Partnership, 106, 109–10
Ownership of the problem and the process, 146–48
Ozark National Forest, 205

Patient, being, 191–92
People skills, 218
Perceptions, see Attitudes and perceptions, barriers due to
Performance standards, 240–41
Persistence, the importance of, 191–93
Personnel policies, 55
Pesticides, 119
Pioneering metaphor of the individualistic entrepreneur, 51
Pisgah National Forest, 136–37
Place-based approach of civic environmentalism, 17
Place or community, a sense of, 73–76
Plumas County (CA), 71–73, 93–94
Plum Creek, 102, 104
Policies/procedures, inflexible, 53–56
Political culture, changes in, 6, 31, 238
Political support, building, 204–6
Positive attitudes/imagery, 17–18, 123–24
Potlach Corporation, 54
Prisoner's dilemma, 49–50
Proactive approach, 180–83
see also Entrepreneurial and proactive approach

Problem-focused approach:
credible information, bounding the problem with, 134–37
framing problems appropriately, 127–28
holistic perspective, 124–26
interests, focus on, 128
Laguna Atascosa National Wildlife Refuge, 119–21
learning together, 132–34
new approaches, a willingness to try, 121–24
ownership of the problem, 147
procedural constraints, rising above, 128–30
solution vs. problem oriented, 127
team-based, 113–14
them to us, transforming, 145–46
traditional conceptions of agency roles, not bound by, 130–32
Problems/fears, shared, 76–78
Procedural constraints, rising above, 128–30
Processes, crafting meaningful/effective/enduring:
accountability, process-derived, 237–39
consensus decision making, 105–6
early/often/ongoing involvement, 103–4
facilitation, 108–10
importance and need, a sense of, 116
inclusive and representative, 106–7
institutionalizing collaboration, 115–16
meetings, well-managed, 110–12
organizational structure, an efficient, 112–15
ownership of the problem, 147–48
problems with the process of collaboration, 63–66
real/substantive involvement, 104–5
self-sustaining processes, 116–17
Sierra, Eastern, 99–101
traditional decision-making approaches, moving away from, 101–2
training individuals and teams, 218
Progressive Conservation movement, 233
Property rights movement, 130
Public involvement:
Clark County (NV), 102–4, 107
early/often/ongoing, 103–4
educating the public, 28–29
Fish and Wildlife Service, U.S., 35
learning from the public, 27–28
local focus, a, 75–76
motivating, 168–71
1970s, rallying call for agencies in the, 13
real/substantive, 104–5
see also Support, building public and political
Public-sector programs aiding innovative efforts, 10–11, 183–84
Public service, collaborative relationships as a, 42–43

Quincy Library Group, 71–73, 117, 244

Recreation on public lands, 12, 28, 99
see also Alaska recreation plan; Coalition for Unified Recreation in the Eastern Sierra (CURES)
Regulatory standards and guidelines, 240–41
see also Legislation
Reinventing Government (Osborne & Gaebler), 17, 128, 237
Relationships, building and sustaining:
broadening traditional notion of collaborative relationships, xiii
communities and agencies, 42
established relationships, capitalizing on, 162–63
informal relationships, 92–93, 160–61
nurturing/honoring/respecting relationships, 166–67
organizational boundaries, building relationships across, 31
time and energy, it takes, 165–66
transitions in relationships, managing, 167–68
trust and respect, fostering, 163–65
Reporting requirements, 25
Research, managing uncertainty through, 29–30
Resource Conservation District, 199
Resource(s):
Advisory Councils, 95, 239
agencies developing capacity to deal with resource management challenges, 220–21
Bureau of Land Management, 239
community needs linked to, 206–7
constraints, 9, 36, 56–57
management, see Management practices/policies
mobilization, 39–41, 198–200
Responsibility/commitment, fostering a sense of:
accountability, 244–45
Applegate Partnership, 139–42
commitment, 63, 148–53, 225–28

Responsibility/commitment (*continued*)
  established relationships, capitalizing on,
    162–63
  fairness, 153–55
  mistrust and a declining sense of re-
    sponsibility, 7–9, 26
  ownership of the problem and the
    process, 146–48
  them to us, transforming, 142–46
Review, opportunity for appeal and independent scientific, 239–40
Rewarding and acknowledging efforts, 171
Rincon Institute, 97, 116
Risk, willing to take a, 182–83
Roan Mountains, 95–96, 136–37, 202–3
Rocking K Ranch, 97
Rocky Mountain National Park, 75, 94,
  167, 199–200
Russian River:
  cultural differences, 172
  fun as a motivator for involvement, 169
  outreach by individuals or groups, 90
  problem-focused approach, 145
  success begets success, 190
  trust, gaining, 164–65

Saguaro National Park, 116
Salamander, Red Hills, 135–36
Salt Lake County, see Mill Creek Canyon
  Management Partnership
San Bernardino National Forest, 28, 40–
  41, 171, 200, 207–8
San Diego (CA), 57, 112
San Gorgonio Volunteer Association, 28,
  40–41, 200
San Pedro River, 52
Science and management:
  acquiring scientific/technical expertise,
    201–2
  agencies losing control over decision
    making and direction, 13
  base of scientific information, 134–35
  independent science, 135–36
  review, opportunity for appeal and in-
    dependent scientific, 239–40
  understanding, building, 25
  videos used to convey images of success,
    215
Sediment runoff, 38
Self-determination, 181
Self-sustaining processes, 116–17
Sewage discharge, 38
Shared problems/fears/goals/interests,
  76–82
Shasta-Trinity National Forest, 44
Sierra, Eastern, 99, 143
  see also Coalition for Unified Recre-
    ation in the Eastern Sierra (CURES)
Sierra Club, 195
Silent Spring (Carson), 12
Siuslaw National Forest, 38, 178–79
Skills, process/people, 64–65, 218–19
Small, the value of starting, 187–89
Snake River, 92–93
Social capital, 16
Socializing informally, 160–61
Social networks, using community-based,
  185–86
Soil and water conservation districts
  (SWCDs), 39
Solution *vs.* problem oriented, 127
Sonoran Institute, 97
Southern Appalachian Man and the Bios-
  phere (SAMAB), 27
Spotted owl, xi, 60
Sprawl, suburban, 12
Staff, backing up field, 152–53
Staff capabilities, building, 43–44
Steering committees, 113
Stereotypes, 59–60, 160
Stormwater runoff, 38
Storytelling, xv, 216
Subcommittees, 113
Success, instilling hope by demonstrating,
  169–70, 186–91, 215, 247
Superordinate goals, 79–80
Support, building public and political:
  attitudes and perceptions, barriers due
    to, 62–63
  decision-making processes, 34–35
  elected officials, working with, 204–6
  media, working with interest groups
    and the, 204
  Oak Openings project, 203–4
  responsibility/commitment, fostering a
    sense of, 150–51
  see also Public involvement
Sustainability, 14
  see also Bridges to a sustainable future,
    building
Sustainable Agriculture Committee, 199

Targhee National Forest, 182–83
Taxes, 97
Team approach, problem-focused, 113–14

Technical advisory committees (TACs), 135
Technical planning process, 52
  see also Science and management
Tensas River, 75–76
Them to us, transforming:
  focusing on the problem vs. who to blame, 145–46
  interdependence, recognizing, 143–44
  leading by example, 144–45
  visions and goals, unifying, 142–43
Three-Quarter Circle Ranch CRM, 165–66
Time to develop understanding, taking the, 134, 165–66
Tongass National Forest:
  communication, working at outreach through, 91
  fairness, 154
  proactive, being, 180
  procedural constraints, rising above, 129
  public involvement, 28
  superordinate goals, 80
  support within agencies/constituencies, building, 151
  see also Alaska recreation plan
Top-down paternalistic process, 17, 52
Tortoise, desert, 102–3, 107
Training individuals and teams, 218–19
Transitions in relationships, managing, 167–68
Trinity Community GIS Center, 44, 97–98, 199
Trust in government and each other, 7–9, 12, 26, 58–59, 123, 163–65

Uncertainty, scientific, 29–30, 136
Understanding, building:
  communication with stakeholders/other individuals, 25
  educating the public, 28–29
  information explosion, 24–25
  information sharing, 26–27
  learning from the public, 27–28
  misperceptions and fostering understanding, shattering, 159–60, 162
  science and management, 25
  site level, critical at the, 26
  time to develop understanding, taking the, 134
  uncertainty managed through joint research and fact-finding, 29–30
Unfamiliarity with the collaborative process, 63–64

University of Arizona, 52
University of California, 199
University of Illinois, 82
Upper Klamath Basin Working Group, 8
Upper Stony Creek initiative, 186, 192, 202

Value-formation process, 30, 43
Videos used to convey images of success, 215
Virginia Coast Reserve, 125
Visioning process, 80–82, 142–43, 172, 222
Volunteers, partnerships involving, 40–41, 170

Wal-Mart, 90
Warbler, Kirtland's, 29, 39, 83, 125, 191, 241
Washtenaw County, 152–53
Water resources, management of:
  East Fork Quinn River, 195–97
  Florida, South, 53
  funding, 199
  Henry's Fork Watershed Council, 92–93
  Maryland's Save Our Shores, 202
  National Estuary Programs, 95, 183
  Natural Resource Conservation Service, 80
  soil and water conservation districts, 39
  Washtenaw County, 152–53
  wetlands, 35, 39, 40
  see also Anacostia River; Huron River; Russian River
Wenatchee National Forest, 129
West Elk Wilderness, 248
Wetlands, 35, 39, 40
Weyerhaeuser, 181–82
Wilderness Society, 12
Wisdom of public decision making process, 231
Wood-burning stoves, 30
Wood fiber, industrial-sized production of, 11–12
Wood for fires, U.S. Forest Service selling, 146
Workforce composition, enhance, 219–20
Wyoming Department of Game and Fish (WGF), 61

Yakima Valley, 129, 146

About the Authors

Julia M. Wondolleck is associate professor of environmental dispute resolution at the University of Michigan's School of Natural Resources and Environment. She teaches courses in conflict management and negotiation skills for resolving environmental disputes and has spent the past decade researching the use of collaboration and dispute resolution in resource management, particularly the management of national forests. She is the author of *Public Lands Conflict and Resolution: Managing National Forest Disputes* (New York: Plenum, 1988), and coauthor of *Environmental Disputes: Community Involvement in Conflict Resolution* (Washington, DC: Island Press, 1990). Dr. Wondolleck was a member of the Committee of Scientists convened by the secretary of agriculture to review the national forest planning and management process. She received her Ph.D. in environmental policy from the Massachusetts Institute of Technology in 1983 and has earlier degrees in economics from the University of California at Davis and environmental planning from MIT.

Steven L. Yaffee is professor of natural resource and environmental policy in the School of Natural Resources and Environment at the University of Michigan, where he teaches courses in natural resource policy and administration, negotiation skills, and biodiversity and public policy. Dr. Yaffee has worked for more than twenty years on federal endangered species, public lands, and ecosystem management policy and is the author of *Prohibitive Policy: Implementing the Federal Endangered Species Act* (Cambridge, MA: MIT Press, 1982) and *The Wisdom of the Spotted Owl: Policy Lessons for a New Century* (Washington, DC: Island Press, 1994). He is the senior author of *Ecosystem Management in the United States: An Assessment of Current Experience* (Washington, DC: Island Press, 1996). His most recent work explores multiparty, collaborative problem solving as a necessary element of an ecosystem-based approach to resource management. Dr. Yaffee received a Ph.D. in environmental policy and planning from the Massachusetts Institute of Technology in 1979. He holds earlier degrees in resource planning and conservation and natural resource policy from the University of Michigan. He has been a member of the faculty at the Kennedy School of Government at Harvard University and has been a researcher at the Oak Ridge National Laboratory and the Conservation Foundation/World Wildlife Fund.